UNDER SOMETHING OF A CLOUD

ALSO BY DOM MORAES

Green is the Grass: *Essays on Cricket* (1951)

A Beginning: *Poems* (1957)

Poems (1960)

Gone Away: An Indian Journey – A Memoir (1960)

John Nobody: *Poems* (1965)

My Son's Father: An Autobiography (1968)

Mrs Gandhi: A Biography (1980)

Absences: *Poems* (1983)

Collected Poems: 1957–1987 (1987)

Serendip (1990)

Never at Home: *A Memoir* (1992)

Out of God's Oven: Travels in a Fractured Land, co-authored with Sarayu Srivatsa (2002)

The Long Strider: How Thomas Coryate Walked from England to India in the Year 1613, co-authored with Sarayu Srivatsa (2003)

A Variety of Absences: Collected Memoirs (2003)

Selected Poems, Ed. Ranjit Hoskote (2012)

UNDER SOMETHING OF A CLOUD

DOM MORAES

SPEAKING TIGER

SPEAKING TIGER PUBLISHING PVT. LTD
4381/4, Ansari Road, Daryaganj
New Delhi 110002

First published in India by Speaking Tiger in hardback 2019

ISBN: 978-93-88326-65-0
eISBN: 978-93-88326-66-7

10 9 8 7 6 5 4 3 2 1

Typeset in Adobe Garamond by Jojy Philip, New Delhi
Printed at Nutech Print Services, India

Contents

Introduction

His mind bred words. He sat there, a stack of foolscap paper in front of him, sculpting out of nothingness, his right hand locked in a fist, index finger opening, closing, and opening again, until the words, as they though they had suggested themselves to him, unspooled out of his mind. He wrote down the keynote sentence on a blank page and held up the paper, measured the length of each word with his eyes and considered how the sentence sat on the page. Then he wrote the same sentence on a fresh page with a different selection of words. He did this repeatedly, the stack of rejected paper at his feet growing tall. Beads of sweat, sometimes of anger and frustration, and occasionally of trepidation and real fear, speckled his brow. He wrote with pure grit, stooped over paper, spectacles perched on the tip of his nose, as though he was working on an intricate tapestry: every stich in place, the sound and feel of them, and if they rose or fell, or paused or stalled, or lay deadly flat—all accounted for, and with them he embroidered the petit-point image in his mind. These images were embedded in real things: real people, places, events, and a real past, often juxtaposed, seen through a maze of amplifying lenses, or depending on the extent of his inebriations, through a misted cloud. He narrated them as he perceived them, not with his eyes, but from the inner reels of his mind. Then in the final years his shoulder bones were weary with cancerous ache; writing in longhand or on the typewriter was painful; he typed with one finger after all.

So he learnt the use of a computer. Computer terminology was alien to him: he would say 'wipe the word' instead of 'delete' and 'keep the page' instead of 'save'. He was most perplexed with the printer. He assumed that once the pages were printed they were 'taken away' from the computer by the printing machine. He was amazed that the computer had a 'memory', and could remember better, if not more, than he could. He had one complaint though: he couldn't hold up the page. Otherwise, all was the same. As the computer lit up with a tune he stared at his index finger, closing, opening and then closing again. Until they opened no more.

«

My first meeting with Dom Moraes was rather odd. I had finished the manuscript of my first book, *Where the Streets Lead.* It was originally meant to be a doctoral thesis on cities and their spaces, in particular the streets. However, a chance meeting with Mulk Raj Anand who advised me to write a book instead changed its destiny, and in many ways, mine.

When the manuscript was done Mulk Raj Anand suggested that I show it to Dom. I called him up on the telephone and he gave me a date and time. My father once told me that everyone's life is marked by an inevitable moment, a certain event, which channels and separates all that comes after from everything that came before. This was the moment. Only I didn't know. Neither did Dom.

'You are late,' Dom said when I arrived at his door a few days later. 'Did you not say 4.00 p.m.? I asked. 'It's not yet 4.' 'You are late,' Dom repeated. 'I think I have the date and time right,' I insisted, 'I can come another day if you are busy.' 'Don't argue with me,' he said tersely. 'You are twenty years late. Where the hell have you been?'

This was the beginning of a friendship, an unexpected partnership that was to last all of fourteen years. I still remember that day as though it was yesterday. His words still speak to me.

I was sitting across from him in the living-room as he flipped through the pages of the manuscript. 'How many words?' he asked. 'I don't know,' I answered. 'I haven't counted.' This was true. I couldn't hear clearly what he was saying. He spoke softly, and mumbled into his chin. 'You must have a structure before you start a book,' he said. 'The number of pages, sections, chapters, and each chapter should be more or less of the same length.' He smiled. I thought he looked charming when he smiled. But he was scowling a moment later as he started to read the first chapter. He read the last chapter, and another somewhere in the middle. Without looking up from the page, 'Who is going to read it?' he asked. 'Architects, students,' I said. He remarked sardonically, 'Do they read boring books?' He moved the manuscript towards me. 'Honestly, I can't read this,' he said, 'why don't you tell me about the book.' I explained at great length, excitedly, and a bit nervous. He smiled and said, 'Why don't you write the way you speak?'

I succumbed to rewrite the book, from memory instead of my notes, as an autobiographical account of my travels through twenty Indian cities. Strangely enough, the book, *Out of God's Oven,* that Dom and I were to co-author some years later had its origin in *Where the Streets Lead.* It happened this way: on the publication of my book on streets, Doordarshan commissioned me to write thirteen episodes for television. Dom suggested that I do this instead for Channel 4, the British public-service television broadcaster. Its commissioning agent in London stipulated that Dom collaborates with me; his work was known in England. The brief was to write about the architecture of the British Empire in four Indian cities. I was terribly excited to be writing with so known a writer as Dom. But he warned me that his name would overshadow me, and more, that he didn't know much about architecture. He preferred ruins. We wrote the script for four cities, not in the way I had intended, but in the way Dom thought fit. We talked to writers, poets and journalists in the cities we travelled to and documented their impressions of them. However, the project was shelved as the Channel 4 agent was replaced, and because the script didn't match the brief.

We had a considerable amount of material and I suggested to Dom that with additional travel and research we could write a book on India. Soon it would be the 50th anniversary year of the country's independence; this provided us with a clear reason to write this kind of book. Besides, as Dom and I were brought up differently, the book could describe the different ways in which we looked at the country—as an insider and an outsider. Dom resisted at first; it was a lot of travel, and immense hard work. Dom was concerned about his ability to do this, but mostly it was because of his addiction to alcohol. But in the end he agreed but never expected to finish. It was not easy.

When I was a little girl, my grandmother, a traditional Tamil Brahmin, told me a story. 'And then God decided to make a man,' she said. 'He made a clay image and put it into an oven. But He took it out too soon; it was pale and white. He made it the prototype for the white race. The second man God baked came out charred, and his descendants became the black people. The last one was perfect, evenly browned, and these became the Hindus.' This legend gave us the title of our book on India—*Out of God's Oven.*

Our travels over the country took us six years. On our road trips Dom noted down extensive details about the landscape that we passed. 'For the atmosphere,' he explained. When we interviewed people I resorted to the use of the tape recorder. But Dom took notes. I was surprised to see that they were not about what people said but about the setting: the room, the surroundings, how the person looked, sat, spoke and the little gesticulations they made. The smells, noises and sounds, he put them down too. 'We will talk to hundreds of people,' he said, 'we can't say he lit a cigarette if he didn't actually smoke, or that he had a handlebar moustache if he was clean-shaven. Opinions and views are easy to remember but not the situation or the specifics of personalities.'

Discernibly and inevitably, Dom was the advocate of the marginalized wherever we went—the castaways who, oppressed and exploited, had been subjected to relentless atrocities. A hardened form of Hinduism that led to rampant communal hatred had already started. Then in February 2002, in Godhra, a mob of Muslims attacked a train with firebombs. People were burnt alive. Many of them were Hindus. Over the next days Hindus fell upon the Muslims all over the state. Ahmedabad, in particular became the killing field.

Dom dashed to the city and returned a few days later totally broken. He told me about the five-year-old girl who had been raped. She had on a pretty yellow dress, he said. The girl didn't understand what had happened and her bewildered father's foremost worry was about her marriage. Dom was inconsolable and teary as he told me this. I saw in his tears not just his pain but also those of the girl and father, an entire population betrayed, and more, of a country gone terribly wrong. Dom wrote about the riots in the introduction to *Out of God's Oven.* It was beautifully written but the raw emotion he had shown was missing. He was absent, or at best, hidden behind unspoken words. Why couldn't he write the way he felt?

Dom introduced me to the works of many writers. Some of whom he knew, others whose works he liked, and even those whose writing he did not much care for. I mention two writers here not for any other reason except for their relevance. Ford Madox Ford wrote about images that yielded sensations. It was not sentimentalism, he wrote, so much as the putting of certain realities in certain aspects in juxtaposition with the other that suggested emotions. In his radical novel, *The Good Soldier* that epitomized the author's inventive view of literary impressionism, Ford employed the device of the fickle narrator. The main character revealed the story using a series of flashbacks in non-chronological order. By doing so, he compelled the reader to bridge the gaps, unravel ambiguity, and rebuild narrative events and their sequence.

Dom was hardly a fickle narrator. He was a deliberate crafter of information. He liked to talk to people; he was a good listener and he let them talk. From them he harvested facts, their experiences, their thoughts, their memories, and their past, which he frequently employed as flashbacks and not necessarily in the sequence they had happened, or who they had happened to. For him, the writing of a travelogue was not just of the physical and personal kind, but a travel through minds: his own and those of others.

For instance, I had told Dom about an interesting conversation I had with two Japanese businessmen. Indians were not Asians, they told me, and gave me reasons for their observation. I was surprised and tickled, therefore, to find this bit of information in Dom's introduction to *The Penguin Book of Indian Journeys.* I was glad; he had shared this in a better way than I could have:

> I once lunched in Mumbai with two businessmen. Like many other businessmen, not necessarily Japanese, they seemed cloned from a prototype, from what they thought, wore, and were, to what they ate: T-bone steaks and tiramisu. I've forgotten how I met them; but one unusual observation they made (jointly, so to speak) has stayed in my mind for years.
>
> At some point they said they found it difficult to understand the minds of Indian businessmen because Indians weren't Asians. I may have been surprised, for they explained the remark. Physically, they said, Indians were different from other Asians. In the north of the subcontinent, some true Asians lived, such as the people of Nepal, Sikkim, and Bhutan, and the Assamese. But the other Indians didn't look like Asians, or think like them.
>
> Semitic peoples who followed Islam lived west of India, and the 'true Asians', mostly Buddhists, lived east of it. The Hindus, according to the Japanese, were unique to the subcontinent, a separate race. They had persecuted the

Buddhists; only a few were left. The Muslims and Christians who lived in India were mostly converts from Hinduism. Therefore most of the Indian population was Hindu, or of Hindu descent, but not Asian.

Dom had the astounding ability to visualize and improvise. He created his own mythical world. Perhaps he did this even as a young boy. With poetic prose and vivid imagery, not just to be seen but felt, he fabricated a sense of atmosphere. In whole and in parts, his images might have seemed unreal, or appeared inconsistent, but their reality was enhanced by the manner in which they were made to fit into a factual situation. Very often he lent people, places and events the characteristics of being an illusion, or appearing fictitious, or fleeting—a craft he used to create a preconceived mood and effect that in some ways expressed the tensions and angsts of his own life and times, and the prejudices that grew out of them.

In *The Mirror of the Sea,* the sense of atmosphere that Joseph Conrad creates is tremendous. He uses symbolism and imagery to describe something as real and commonplace as the sea:

> Faithful to no race after the manner of the kindly earth, receiving no impress from valour and toil and self-sacrifice, recognising no finality of dominion, the sea has never adopted the cause of its masters like those lands where the victorious nations of mankind have taken root, rocking their cradles and setting up their gravestones.

Dom's words, in quite a similar manner, in his introduction to the book, *Voices for Life,* edited by him, suggest images that should be seen and ought to be felt.

> Today we have come to a new point in time, to a day of dilemma. This globe of metals and fire has whirled on its own axis, for millions of years, in a wilderness of space. It has survived the explosions of suns and swum away from the flying debris of

> the stars. Under its own private sun, over chasms of time we cannot start to fathom, the bacteria in its swampy seas turned into fish, the fish crept ashore and turned to carnivorous apes, and the carnivorous apes turned into men.

And further on he writes, nearly forty years ago, but still relevant today:

> The crisis of conscience we have suffered from since 1945 has now been doubled in intensity, for it seems that we may yet destroy the world as we know it even without the assistance of politicians and nuclear physicists, and that the earth may become once more what it was for our remote ancestors: an area of fear.

And in the prologue to *Out of God's Oven,* Dom writes about the communal riots in Ahmedabad:

> Flapping from a blackened wall, I see a poster for a circus. An image rises to my mind of Gujarat as a circus clown. Grotesque and tormented, staggering around a floodlit arena, it flails its arms for balance. A huge, astonished audience watches its agony. Its face is daubed with saffron, its body dyed red with blood.

Then in the following passage from *My Son's Father*, in which Dom's insane mother reached up to the tall plaster Christ in the niche and smashed it against the wall, Dom spins images of irony and torment:

> On the floor of the bedroom Christ lay broken. I had always thought he was plaster, and could break, but not that his intestines were straw, and bits of old newspaper. They spilled out through his breached belly, and his brain, a hard roll of paper, dropped from his fractured skull. I stared in wonder, as though at a real crucifixion. In some mysterious ways, this was the end of one part of my life.

The object of his craft was to weave imagery such as these into his otherwise lucid, tightly written travelogues and reportages to set a definite mood, scene and situation. However, his writing has been subjected to unfair criticism as being obscure and abstract, and often meandering, with far too much imagery. But, like Ford, Conrad and many other writers before him, he chose for it to be that way.

As a person, as a writer, Dom has been frequently misunderstood. The Navarasas in classical dance, as in art and aesthetics signify the mental state that evokes the essence of emotions—the primary feelings of love, mirth, sorrow, anger, energy, terror, disgust and astonishment. Dom's mental state, badly fractured as a child, contained in a child-like way mainly two of these: the need to love and be loved, and the irrepressible need to hate because of the lack of love. It isn't surprising therefore, that he chose to reject the country of his birth. Not so much the land as its people, their customs, and their conformed deviousness arising out of avarice and distrust, all of which perforated his fragile mind.

I must confess I can empathize with the way he had felt, though to a far lesser degree only because I am entrenched in my roots. I too had left the country for some years. I was in Japan, where honour and honesty is of utmost importance to its people. When I returned to India, I felt it had changed: it was no longer the country my father, who was with the Indian National Army in Japan, would have liked it to be. Or perhaps I felt this way because I had grown up and was on my own; I was no longer cloistered by my birth family. I was overwhelmed by the poverty I saw, and scarcity, corruption, fraudulence and dishonesty, the lack of consideration, and people's dire need to be egotistical and self-seeking. The country had transformed or had been bared.

'I have travelled far and wide,' Dom said to me, 'but I have never seen anything like this.' I didn't entirely agree. History bears witness to the fact that in this world, man is capable of ineradicable evil, brutality and fallacies. However, within his world, vast and small at the same time, Dom had set up the parameters and premise for everything based on his notion of 'himself and the 'others'—his 'private mind' against the 'public mind'. His deductions and bias arose from determining his relationship with the other. His idea of India was to a large extent based on the Manichean allegory: Western people are rational and intelligent possessing both order and integrity, and Orientals, whilst being overly emotional and sensuous, are primarily malevolent and disorderly. He had therefore set himself to testify in opposition of the violent and wretched acts of people against people, country against country, and India and its Hindu population became the focus of his antipathy. My roots: of old ethics and new money, terrified him most, Dom once told me.

Dom had travelled to Japan. I had lived there and so knew it more intimately. I told him about the unique phenomenon of *Honne* and *Tatemae*—the 'private mind' and the 'public mind'. This convention was a social necessity in order to keep united a large number of people on a small island. *Honne* represents the truth: person's real feelings and aspirations, and *Tatemae* stands for the facade, the masked authenticity: public behavior and shared opinion. As true feelings are hidden, *Tatemae* formally endorses the telling of lies and this might be construed as hypocrisy. But there is clear honesty in these lies; they adhere to the rule-book and its objective: to encourage cooperation and prevent conflict. Contrastingly, deceit and dishonesty in India, that Dom was so disturbed by, is of a deviant kind; it is entrenched in the furtherance of self rather than the community or the country.

It took me some time to understand that the hatred he felt and displayed was more a concept than a reality. He was surprised that he liked the people we met during our travels for books and was childishly chuffed when they liked him back. He was home, and had resigned himself to accept that he was, in Clark Blaise's phrase, a 'resident alien'. Blaise's following words, from his autobiography, *I Had a Father*, typify clearly what Dom, displaced and dislocated, could have felt:

> We are born to strangers we must learn to love, in a town or country we would not have chosen, into a tribe that defines and restricts our growth. We spend a lifetime overcoming the givens, only to turn back from the distant vantage point of fifty years when the parents are gone, to look back and say: this is what I am, something no larger, no freer, than they made me.

It is often said and believed that if one were to understand a writer, who he was or is, and who he had become, then it is possible to empathize with his writing. It is kinder, and simpler to understand Dom's writing if he was thought of as a very young writer, whose childhood was tragically aborted and therefore denied to him, than a man older, and possibly wiser. I have tried to do this, as in the last years of his life. When needed, I slipped on the make-believe guise of his mother. So deep, intense and hurtful where his feelings about the 'mothering' he had been starved of.

I could totally understand therefore, when he told me that the only passage, inarguably the most endearing part of the book, that ever made him shed tears was from John Steinbeck's novel about the dark realities of the Great Depression: *Grapes of Wrath.* Sheltering in a barn against the flooding rains, Rose of Sharon who, despite her many tragedies, commits an act of astonishing humanity. She has recently lost her baby, and she breast-feeds a starving man to keep him alive.

Dom's mother went mad when he was seven and he spent most of his adult life in England, a cold country that possessed him and yet marked him an immigrant. I remember the time in London, when we were getting out of a taxi and Dom fumbled in his pocket to get change for a tip. Another customer, a white man, was waiting on the curb for a ride. 'Get the fuck off, you Paki,' the driver roared at Dom unnecessarily. Dom got off and walked quickly ahead of me as though he didn't want me to see the hurt in his eyes. When I caught up with him he muttered, 'This is my problem. In my mind I am English, but regretfully in my skin I remain an Indian.' He mentions a similar situation in his autobiography *Never at Home*:

> One Sunday afternoon I was smoking and writing my book when I ran out of cigarettes. I pulled on a coat from an assortment in the hall, and set out for the tobacconist on the corner. The coat was suede and had once been very expensive, but was now torn down one side. I hadn't shaved that Sunday. Halfway down the street a policeman stopped me. I knew most of the policemen in the area, but this one was new. He barked, 'Here, you! Stand against the wall. Let me see your papers.' I was startled, and stood against the wall, and he moved forward to frisk me. As he did this, I found that I was angry. 'What the hell is this?' I asked. At the sound of my accent, he stopped and looked at me hard. Then he said, 'I'm sorry, sir, I'm really very sorry.' He then stepped out of my way and saluted.
>
> After this I felt even more furious. England was my home. Was I to be treated like an immigrant? Then it occurred to me that I was an immigrant.

In the end he was a stranger wherever he was, and perhaps even to himself—'They by their treasons made me whatever I am'—he writes, assigning blame for who he had become. Bereft of his roots—his mother, his birth-country that he despised because of his mother, and orphaned and forgotten by an insular Britain, he faced the world a bit lonely, but more lost.

That afternoon when I first met Dom, he said, 'I feel the deep loneliness in you. I know this because there is a similar loneliness deep within me.' Before I left he gave me a copy of *My Son's Father*. 'So that you can know me better,' he said. Reading the book I sensed his loneliness concealed behind the arabesque of words. Words comforted him, kept him sheltered and together, distant and remote from people and events that confronted and confused him.

I have read most of his books that I could find. It was not easy to select passages from them for this anthology. Should it include those that are popular and most admired? Or those that are relevant to our times? Or those that reveal the sort of writer he was—his views, thoughts and predilections. I don't wish to inflict a form and contour on his life and writing, nor censor or distort all that I know personally of him. In the tradition of the Haiku form that selects a simple moment and illuminates the minute in it rather than the overall, I am trying to find a simple way of seeing the infinitesimal relationships of things in the world he inhabited.

The selection, therefore, is steered by something hidden in them: of the sense of loss and losing, of loneliness, and the consequent pain, his and those of others, those of the world's tragedies. Essentially, this collection is an attempt to share his way of seeing the world—with the eyes of a bewildered boy and the mind of a man who saw too much too soon.

Dom wrote the preface to my book, *Where the Streets Lead.* Now with this introduction to a collection of his travel writing, the circle is complete. The introduction is not an academic, literary analysis of his writing, for who am I to do this. I have neither the adequate faculty nor the distance. It is therefore a mere sense of him and his work, and a glimpse of his eventual journey that didn't last very long.

~

On a wintry morning in October 2006 I found myself in the churchyard of Odcombe, a quaint little village in Somerset, holding a bunch of wild flowers that I had picked on my way up the hill. An old woman who was tidying a flowerbed looked up at me. She hurried over to the edge of the lawn, and pulling off her plastic gloves, she wiped away bits of grass and dust from the gravestone. I stood beside it, read the inscription on the slab of yellow stone: 'Dom Moraes who followed Thomas Coryate's footsteps and returned home. July 1938–June 2004'.

In April 2002 Dom noticed a lump on his neck. It was malignant and the doctors said he had about three months to live. It was not entirely because of a desire to live longer that Dom didn't believe them; he wished to be able to live long enough to complete the book he had wanted to write for forty years. This book was about Thomas Coryate, an eccentric Englishman who in the 17th century decided to walk from his village of Odcombe to the court of the Great Mogul, Jahangir.

Dom refused to undergo chemotherapy or radiation. 'It's essential I keep an account of time,' he said. 'I don't have enough of it.' The doctor had prescribed a strict regime for better health. No cigarettes, or alcohol. No pork sausages or chocolates—all of them Dom's favourites. I read up on the deviant ways of cancer cells and learnt that they depended on healthy cells for their nutrition. 'Let's keep you unhealthy then,' I told Dom.

One evening I found him crouched in the corner of his bedroom, weeping. He was smashed. I pulled him up by his arms and held him. His tears did not dry quickly. 'Let me go, Mummy,' he cried. It was a cry of private, individual desperation. He didn't remember much of this the next morning. All he said was, 'You can never imagine how my memories haunt me.'

Two years later the Coryate book was launched in the Odcombe Village Hall, which was filled with people who had driven from nearby villages. The vicar, then ninety-eight, launched the book. The older people of the village had tremendous pride in their hero. In the front row four old women aged between 101-103 years wiped away the tears from their eyes. People lived to be very old here. Only Coryate died young in India. And thankfully Dom survived.

One evening he said, 'A mobile phone's some good use sometime. You have to let me go now. I will send you an SMS from wherever I am. If you can, bury me in Odcombe. I would really like that.' It was the start of June, and I said, 'Let's go in July and celebrate your birthday there.' Next morning Dom was full of the imminent trip to Odcombe. 'I couldn't sleep too well last night. Think I will lie down for a bit,' he said. He then slumbered in a sleep that knew no margins of time.

The last image that I remember of Dom is of his hands crossed over his body, glowing, as though the moon had touched them. He lay in a coffin, too small, not for his body, as it had shrunk, but for the writer he was. His face had acquired a surreal sort of quietness that comes with the absence of pain or memory, and perhaps gratitude for the final rest. Then they shut the coffin cover.

Dom was buried in an old cemetery in Sewri. I wrote to the vicar of Odcombe and asked if he would bury the earth from Dom's grave in the cemetery at the back of the old church. It was an unusual request but he agreed. I smuggled fistfuls of earth from his grave in the casing of a Cadbury's chocolate box. On July 19th 2004, many friends drove down from London to celebrate Dom's birthday in Mason's Arms, the only pub in Odcombe. Dom had drunk here the last time in memory of Thomas. With wine glasses raised we drank now in Dom's memory.

The memorial service was held in the church. The ancient organ had been dusted and an old organist played Dom's favorite pieces of music. The vicar performed the service interspersed with psalms that we sang. In the front lawn just outside the main door to the church, Dom's only son Francis Moraes sprinkled the earth from Dom's grave. Not surprisingly it smelled of chocolates, all together fitting since Dom couldn't ever resist them. On top of the earth I placed the Jaisalmer memorial stone that I had brought with me from Mumbai.

It was a good birthday party. I wished he had been there.

Sarayu Srivatsa
Mumbai
2018

His Father's Son (1945)

A Lame Monkey in Ceylon

'How would you like to go to Ceylon?' my father asked me. 'The *Times of Ceylon* want me to be Editor. We'd have to live in Colombo.'

'I don't mind,' I said.

'I'll have to tell your mother,' said my father a little wearily. Apparently, that evening, he did. The first I knew about it was an explosive crash which brought me flying into the drawing-room. My mother had just smashed a decanter on the wall. She emitted a curious bat-like shriek and rushed past me into the hall, where she smashed a picture. My father and I followed her into the bedroom in time to see her reach up to the tall plaster Christ in his niche on the wall. He had not moved from there within my memory, but now my mother lifted him down and with a careful and deliberate sweep of the arm smashed him against the wall. I was dumb-struck. At this moment the phone went. My mother rushed to it. My father obviously thought she was about to break that as well, and went after her, but she picked it up quite decorously and said calmly into it, 'Hullo. Oh, it's Gladys.' (Her sister.) 'Darling, how are you. I've got a wonderful bit of news. Frank's just told me we're going to live in Ceylon.'

On the floor of the bedroom Christ lay broken. I had always known he was plaster, and could break, but not that his intestines were straw, and bits of old newspaper. They spilled out through his breached belly, as his brain, a hard roll of paper, dropped from his fractured skull. I stared in wonder, as though at a real crucifixion. In some mysterious way, this was the end of one part of my life.

The weeks before we left for Colombo were a confusion of parties. At the office party my father was presented with a silver salver: I touched its smooth surface, bemused by the unfamiliar. So much was unfamiliar: daily my home melted away where I stood. Chairs, tables, cupboards, that had stood in their places, gentle and solid, since I had been born, were lifted from around me by strangers, and bedded in straw in huge plywood cases. Lids came down on the cases, in a thunder of hammers, a strange wood smell filled the flat. On the fitted carpets where our furniture had stood, there were paler patches rimmed with dust: and eventually the carpets rose like spectres, revealing stone floors I had never known were there, floors with the odour of absence.

We left one evening, the servants bowing and weeping on the pavement as we climbed into the car and were driven to the station. None of them had wanted to come with us to Ceylon, so my father had employed two men who did: a bearer, Vincent, and a driver, Kutthalingam. They were with us in the car, Kutthalingam driving. I had not met them before, and their presence underlined the strangeness of departure that I felt. The night smelt as always, of talcum powder and the sea.

In the station there was a noise and smell of people, and of trains. The trains shrieked wildly and rushed into darkness: a spatter of sparks, receding like an alley of stars. Numbers of people had come to see us off: they all shook hands with me, the women in sudden downpours of scent stooped to kiss me: they talked incessantly: hours seemed to pass like this. Then we climbed into a small compartment filled with the sullen buzz of air conditioners, like climbing into a cold bath from the moist heat of the platform. The train snorted, shook, plunged forward, shaking off the station and the cloudy waving hands and smiling faces, and the night started to pass the window. Soon we clattered over a bridge, a glycerine sea gleaming below us. My father said, 'We're leaving Bombay.'

After this I settled back in my seat and started to read my comic books. My parents sat opposite, talking in low voices. Presently the steward came in with dinner, shepherded by Vincent. Vincent was a skinny smiling young man with black hair that smelt of brilliantine, and a small moustache. 'The arrangements in this train aren't very good,' he told my father. 'They only had mutton curry in the restaurant car. It was bad curry, sir, so I myself with my own hands made three omelettes in the kitchen.' I decided I didn't like him, but the omelettes were delicious and runny.

Later Vincent came in once more, and made the bunks up. I slept up on top, the sway of the train rolling me gently from one side to another, like being suspended in a cloud. The lights blinked off, and in the smell and sway of the train I eventually fell asleep.

Vincent awoke me with a tray. He placed it neatly across my knees, and said, 'Nice breakfast, baba. Rissoles, I made them myself, with my own hands.' I did not reply. When I had finished the rissoles, which were excellent, I climbed down to find my father reading the papers and my mother varnishing her nails. Except that this was in a train, not in their bedroom in Bombay, and that the plaster Christ I knew was irretrievably broken, it was like earlier days. I looked out of the window at a curious new world.

To get to Ceylon from Bombay by train, at least then, one had to travel down to Dhanushkodi, at the extreme southern tip of India, before crossing the short sea. The landscape grew progressively drier: it stretched vastly out as the train rippled by, but that first morning the earth was black, with patches of lustrous bushes and trees, and fields where peasants worked, clad in bright colours: and by evening the earth was red, with an occasional stunted tree; black, loin-clothed men, skimpy as ants, pecked at it with sad scythes. As the train roared south, too, the heat increased: to step from our compartment into the corridor was scalding, incendiary. Windows notwithstanding, all day first black dust, then red, covered the seats of the compartment, making my fingers and eyes gritty and uncomfortable. From time to time curious faces were pressed to our window, as the train rumbled and hammered dustily south: my parents appeared to ignore them, and I had a feeling that I was dreaming these brown, inquisitive faces, covered in black and red dust like the faces of clowns. Only when I climbed out to stretch my legs with my father at some wayside halt did I discover that the entire external length of the train, like a dead snake infested by ants, was swarmed over by people who stood on the foot-boards as it moved, clinging to any appreciable protuberance, or to each other. At the halts occasional railway officials would brush a few of them off: but they only climbed on again further down the train. 'They can't afford to buy tickets,' my father said.

The wayside halts were usually small, dusty stations lonely in a waste of fields, or adjacent to some decrepit village: the third-class travellers and those who clung ant-like to the train-skin would rush across the platform to the solitary water tap: dirty trickles coiled through the dust. One palm tree standing, dishevelled, with open wings, against a dying red sky: and like the harsh voices of birds, the voices of the passengers calling.

In the large stations, there was always turmoil: great masses of people ran aimlessly first one way, then another, carrying bundles and tin trunks: they cried out constantly, as though in pain, and the faces of the women clutching children showed an imbecile terror. At these stations Vincent and Kutthalingam stood guard at the compartment door, preventing anyone from entering. On all sides whiteclad, hysterical people pressed against them, shrieking their need for space: but 'This is a reserved compartment,' said Vincent in the black earth area of the north, in Hindi, and Kutthalingam in the red earth area of the south in Tamil. At one point I asked my father why we couldn't let some of these people in: he replied, with one of his stern looks, 'Don't be silly.'

Vincent was always there: with meals, with iced water, with fruit, with beer for my father. He was wearing a suit of some sort: 'Excuse me, sir and madam,' he would say at every entry, 'that I am not in my proper uniform.' Kutthalingam, less decorous, had donned the costume of the south, his own territory, a vest and sarong, and instead of perching in one of the wicker chairs that Vincent had set up in the servant's alcove by the compartment, sat phlegmatically and comfortably, cross-legged in a heap of his bedding.

Dust, and bottles of iced water, and as the train pounded further and further south, bottles of warm water: Vincent in his suit fetching meals, Kutthalingam fat and happy in his accustomed clothes: the little spaniel puppy I had recently acquired whining and nosing my hand: then at last the sea, vividly blue, under the bullnose of a ship, and gulls racing like scraps of blown paper over green palm-spiked headlands and white beaches spread out like drying washing. It was the end of the first of my journeys. We had come to Colombo…

My father was trying to find a house: meanwhile we were staying in an expensive and ugly red brick hotel by the sea. A long sweep of polished turf ran down from the hotel to the ugly House of Parliament, also in red brick, opposite. On this flourish of turf, on morning walks, we usually encountered the Prime Minister, Mr Senanayake, thudding along on a huge, sweaty horse. The Prime Minister had a walrus moustache, and was rather stout: he greeted us always with a beam and a bow, and I thought of him as the White Knight in *Alice in Wonderland.* Some years later he was shot dead by a Buddhist monk.

Things were splendid when we first arrived. Green Colombo was spread out for our inspection, under a hot and clammy blue sky: the sea beat its drums beside the hotel, brilliant birds spired out of violently coloured trees. My spaniel, Kumar, had to be boarded out with friends, and the servants were living in a hostel nearby. These were minor sorrows, for a week.

During this time my mother was gay, witty, her old self: swathed in peacock saris of shot silk, she departed with my father to parties in the evening: in the morning she put on slacks, and we all walked by the sea. One day, however, as we started on our walk, one of the hotel servants came up and advised us to take an umbrella. 'Monsoon he break very sudden in Colombo, master,' he said. 'He break today, I can smell him.' My father looked up at the sky, and laughed.

But by the time we had reached the far end of the green, quite a considerable distance, little rags of wind were shipping up from the sea: large grey waves raised hostile heads over the seawall, and dark clouds obscured the sky. 'Let's turn back,' said my father. As he spoke, a gun of thunder thumped dully overhead, and the rain swept in from the sea, a loud barbarous rain, so thick in its fall as to obscure vision. We stumbled through it towards the hotel. Somewhere on the way my mother lost a sandal. When we got back all three of us were like waterfalls walking. My father and I laughed when we looked at ourselves in the mirror.

Then we discovered my mother was in tears, and nothing we could do could stop these tears. They rippled on like the rain. Finally, through them, she said dully to us, 'You've humiliated me in a strange country.' Then she went on crying. From time to time, in the same leaden, uninterested way, she would repeat her remark.

We found a house. It was a whitewashed modern house in a fairly fashionable part of town: in the garden the grass was as fat as butter, and sunbursts of flowers made the air heavy. Ceylon is almost on the equator, and the garden soil was so rich, so blackly fertile, that if one dropped a seed, a shoot would rise within hours. Rather inappropriately in these green ferocious environs, the house was called 'Salcombe'.

Here the huge plywood cases that had followed us from India found :heir last home: they were split open, and books, furniture, crockery lifted out, only distantly familiar now, and found new positions. The servants were installed, Kumar was reclaimed, and we moved in.

My mother took no interest in the house, or indeed in anything else. She stayed in her room and cried impossible reservoirs of tears. Streams of doctors appeared once more. They recommended that my mother return to India. This seemed rather foolish: my father summoned some of her relatives, and they strove without success to penetrate her veils of tears and silence. To me she was now an utter stranger: I breakfasted and dined with my father, but while he was at the office, lunched alone, ministered to by Vincent. To him and Kutthalingam I turned increasingly in the time when my father was at work.

Kutthalingam sometimes, when his duties permitted, took me for drives around Colombo. He was a plump, kindly man, very black, with a pug face and a little grey moustache, and had seven children of his own in India. He told me about them. 'The eldest be damn rascals, baba. But the young-young ones, they be good. When you be old, be good to your Daddy and Mummy. Very bad otherwise.' He was proud of his knowledge of Colombo, he had driven for a planter in Ceylon for twenty years before the war. He took me to the parks and the zoo, and showed me the big shops. Once he drove me to Negombo, a beach outside Colombo, and watched with pleasure as I lunched off what I still think were the best crabs I have ever eaten. He himself wouldn't have any. 'Master not liking if I eat at same-same table as baba,' he said undemocratically. 'Also,' he added, 'I not liking crabs.'

He was puzzled by my mother, and worried by her. 'Why she no take some air?' he demanded of me. 'No good for health, if you taking no air.' One day, to my dismay, as we were about to drive off on an excursion to Mount Lavinia, another nearby beach, he switched the engine off and said with determination, 'I going ask your Mummy to come.' I tried to dissuade him, but he marched upstairs and tapped my mother's door. Very gently, he began to wheedle her out. 'It be fine place, memsaheb,' he said. 'Lovely beach there, hotel, everything…you come take one look, if you not liking I bringing you straight home.'

To my amazement, my mother consented. Pallid, dishevelled, her eyes red with weeping, her hair straggling and lank, she came stiffly downstairs and got in the car. We drove off. All the way to Mount Lavinia Kutthalingam pointed out places of interest, and my mother listened, and even asked questions.

The beach at Mount Lavinia twined like a white ribbon through explosively vivid trees: a dazzling blue sea shone and lifted beside it. My mother and I walked rather desultorily down the beach, Kutthalingam following at a respectful distance, then we went back to the smart tourist hotel on the headland for a lemonade. The lounge of the hotel was full of Americans who looked as if they had just climbed off Rockefeller's yacht. My mother wisped through them like a ghost, and reluctantly I followed her. I knew I was ashamed to be seen with her, and did not want to be ashamed. However, at eight years old, my mother's pallid unkemptness seemed to me a deliberate attempt to embarrass my father and me, which I hated and did not understand. To make matters worse, it transpired that she had not brought out any money, so Kutthalingam had to pay for us. But he was obviously delighted by the fact that my mother had come with us, and 'taken some air'. He beamed as he opened the car door for us, but his smile faded as my mother, having got in, began to weep.

We belted back on the open road to Colombo. Kutthalingam still made attempts to point out beauty spots, but my mother wept on in silence. Then, suddenly, as we swept round a curve above the sea, she lurched forward, grabbed the door handle, and wrenched it open. A great fist of wind reached into the car, and seemed to draw her with it. She made to jump out.

Kutthalingam, while I sat paralyzed, slammed the brakes on. With his right hand he reached over and pulled my mother back, with his left he dragged the car out of a swirling spin that took it to the edge of the cliff. I came out of my paralysis and shut the door.

'Memsabeb, whyfore you do that?' Kutthalingam cried. He was still grasping her arm. My mother did not reply for a second. Then she raked his hand with her nails, and an absurd tremulous scream burst from her.

'Take your hands off me, you black swine.'

Kutthalingam took his hand off her arm very quickly, and put it back on the wheel. We drove home very slowly and in utter silence.

A few days later Kutthalingam took me back to Mount Lavinia. We walked on the beach, and in the deep azure pools amidst the rocks I discovered an immense number of small, incredibly beautiful fish. They were all in gay paintbox colours, almost unnaturally brilliant: and wove in and out of the wreathed weed, flickers of peacock blue, turquoise, vermilion, rose madder. I was enchanted. Kutthalingam fetched me a bottle, and very carefully I scooped a few fish into the bottle, put some weed in the water, and returned to the car.

But as we drove home, and I peered at the bottle and cradled it in my hands, one by one the beautiful fish, milling in the water, lost their brilliance. The colours died like sunset on their scales, and then they died floating belly upward to the surface, ugly, whitish little corpses. Only one remained alive when we reached home, and within a few minutes that too was dead.

My mother was not silent and tearful any more. She had suddenly started to have astonishing fits of fury. They exploded at any time, and for no reason: I would hear that terrible banshee-like scream, and the crash of thrown objects. Vincent, the driver, the other servants, and most of all my father, suffered these furies, but I was immune. For some reason, however, she decided that I should witness it all: wherever I was, she would at some point rush in, shrieking, breaking china, her hair standing up around her head like a fright wig, her eyes rolling. Visitors no longer came to the house, the servants lived in terror, and I myself became so nervous that any noise made me jump. The doctors prescribed sedatives for my mother but they appeared to have no effect.

My father, meanwhile, was in a quandary. For some reason I cannot remember, there was no place for me in a day school, and he didn't want me to be a boarder. But he didn't want to leave me with my mother. What he did, therefore, was to take me with him to his office, in order to keep me out of my mother's way.

This involved a great deal of planning. My mother had become inordinately possessive towards me, and when not throwing fits was constantly (to my dismay) with me. She objected violently if I went for a walk with Kumar: I must stay indoors, she said, there were people who wanted to kidnap me. When, therefore, my father first tried to take me to the office with him, my mother produced so violent a scene as to decide him that my removal could only be effected if she didn't know.

This meant that every morning Vincent had to keep watch on my mother, while my father sat outside in the car. As soon as the coast was clear, Vincent sent me rapidly downstairs and out, Kutthalingam started the car, and we shot off. We later had to change this plan, because my mother started to watch until my father had actually left. What then happened was that Kutthalingam parked a little way up the road, and at a favourable moment I slipped out of the house and joined them.

I must have been a considerable embarrassment to my father. I sat in his office all day reading, while his staff, his contributors, and his proprietors came in and out. Eventually, I suppose, people found out the reason why I was always there, but I am told it caused a great deal of comment, not unnaturally, at the time.

I didn't worry. I loved to read, I loved to be with my father, now the only parent I could trust, and after home the busy office seemed like a rest camp. Moreover, I particularly liked lunchtime. We lunched always in one of the large hotels, and my father always allowed me to choose what I wanted. I discovered that restaurant food tasted better than food at home, and, chomping some leathery chop, would exult in the knowledge that the idea of it had originated in my mind, been transmitted by me through the waiter to the chef, and by the chef through the waiter back to me.

My days with my father, however, produced an unfortunate effect on my mother. She had previously believed that she was protecting herself and me against a world that sought to entrap us both. Since I obviously accompanied my father from choice, she had apparently started to believe that the other side had corrupted me. Her tirades now included me.

One morning my mother discovered me getting into the car with my father. A hysterical scene followed, at the end of which I stayed, nervous and sulky, at home. My mother was in a very excitable mood. I locked myself in my room and listened as she rushed about the rest of the house, screaming at the servants. Then she started to throw things. I had, even then, a great respect for objects. A glass, an ash-tray, any shaped object, seemed to me intact, like a person, and inviolate. To see or hear them hurled about, abused, angered me. I unlocked my door and went down, discovered my mother about to throw a small bronze statue through a window and caught her arm.

Her reaction was very rapid. She wrenched free, then deliberately threw the bronze through the window, in a crash and tinkle of glass, then rushed out of the room. A moment later she reappeared, with a large kitchen knife in her hand. She came at me with it, like something out of a nightmare. I dodged rapidly round her, raced upstairs to my room, and locked the door. A moment later my mother started to hammer at it, ordering me, in a hoarse shout, to open it. I wouldn't. Meanwhile Vincent ran upstairs, and I heard a scuffle outside the door, then silence.

Vincent had tried to take the knife away from my mother, received a cut on the hand, and gone to telephone my father. My mother had retired to her room and locked herself in. In my own locked room I sat in the vast silence, trying with shaking hands to read a book. Finally I heard my father's voice at my door, and opened it. He stood there, very grave, and put his arm round me. The staircase was crowded with people in white coats.

'Come on,' my father said quietly with his arm round me, my head pressed with comforting discomfort against the buttons of his suit, 'let's go to the office.'

We went downstairs. As we reached the front door, there was an outcry, and my mother came rushing after us, hair and eyes wild. 'You're not to go out,' she shrieked at me, 'you're not to go out.'

The doctor, with two women in white, was behind her. He gave a resigned little shrug, and nodded to the women. They moved efficiently forward and pinioned my mother's arms. My father swept me out into the car.

As Kutthalingam was about to start it, my mother appeared at the front door. Both her arms were held, and she was struggling violently, so that she appeared to be on a cross. In her eyes was terror and a sort of sanity. Her eyes met my father's, and she called in a voice like her old loved voice, 'Help me, Frank, help me.'

My father's face went grey. He leant forward and said to Kutthalingam, in almost a shout, 'Drive to the office.'

The house was now full of nurses. They stood like police-women outside the door of my mother's room, where she lay under heavy sedation. The doctors made daily visits. They recommended that my father authorize electric shock treatment. At this time the treatment was very new, at least in Asia: my father telephoned my mother's relatives in Bombay, and presently they flew in to Colombo, and made the house even more crowded than it already was. There were long family conferences as to whether or not my mother should be given the treatment, but it was eventually decided that she should.

During all this, I spent a great deal of time in Vincent's pantry. Like Kutthalingam, he had children in India, and he knew how to entertain them. He told me folktales from Mangalore, his birthplace, and sang me small birdlike songs. We frequently groomed Kumar, Vincent whistled between his teeth as he brushed the thick golden coat, and once remarked, 'He'll be a champion if we put him in the dog show.' I inquired if he really thought so. 'Oh, yes,' said Vincent. 'When your Mummy's better, we'll put him in for it, and you'll see.'

As a result of this, the dog show was much more on my mind than my mother, whom in any case I scarcely saw nowadays, when one day my father told me that she was to receive her treatment that evening. 'I want you,' he said, 'to go and spend the evening at Negombo with Kutthalingam and Vincent.' In the monstrous way of children, I was delighted. That evening my aunts and uncles arrived; the doctors came, and brought complicated boxes of apparatus with them: for some reason, the treatment was to be done at home. The doctors set up a long trestle, like a coffin, in the study, next to the drawing-room: cobwebs of wires filled every corner.

I was ready to leave for Negombo when my father, looking very worried, came up and told me that my mother refused to have any treatment unless I was there. 'I'm sorry, son,' he said, 'I don't want you to stay, but I'm afraid you'll have to.' This upset me considerably. However, I sat down with an uncle and aunt and began to tell him about my hopes for the dog show. He listened inattentively, and presently started up: the nurses had led my mother, pallid and wild-eyed, into the room.

I was terrified of my mother, and I resented her: she had stopped my evening out. To the natural cruelty of a child I had added in adult sophistication, through being so much with adults. As my mother started across the room towards me, I turned to the aunt on my far side and continued my disquisition on the dog show. She said indignantly, 'How can you talk about dogs when your mother's ill?' and in an odd hysterical jerk, not even knowing I knew the words, I said, 'Because my mother's a poisonous bitch.' There was a frozen silence, and when I looked up I saw the doctors leading my mother away, to the coffin-like trestle in the study.

There was a lot of rustling and whispering, flexing of wires, creaking, as, unseen, they laid my mother on the trestle. Eventually, all the lights went out. The creaking and rustling went on in the darkness. Then a loud lilting Ceylonese voice said, 'Are you ready, Doctor?' and another voice said, 'Yes, ready.'

Then came an extraordinary crashing whistle, and with it, raised jerkily in ululation, a voice I knew must be my mother's. Without any pause for breath, this ululation went on. It went on and on, then stopped, and the lights went up.

Everyone was very breathless and shaky. Later I was allowed into the room where my mother lay wanly amongst pillows. She looked very small. She blinked up at me, then said in a whispery but natural voice, 'Oh, darling, how nice to see you,' and I wept.

Of course, it didn't work. My mother became less violent, but she also became more hazy. The consultants consulted, not for the first time, and recommended that my father try insulin treatment. This could only be obtained in Bombay. So my father sent my mother back to Bombay...

~

Now that the house was at peace, I did what I had always done, read all day. I read children's books, by Arthur Ransome and Hugh Lofting, and even by Enid Blyton, but I also read adult novels, memoirs, and political books from my father's library. In his library I also came upon Swinburne, and those thunderous rocking-horse lines intoxicated me. Sometimes I tried to write poems like this, but could never make the words fit into the lines, though I rhymed in a fairly facile way. However, I wrote a biography, six pages long, misleadingly titled 'The Epic of Gandhi', and in a hideously twee way wrote and edited a weekly magazine on the affairs of the household, which I presented to my father every Friday morning.

Vincent did not approve of all this. 'You,' he said sagely, 'are a boy. Boys should play games. I shall buy you a football.'

He bought me a football, but his efforts to instruct me proved wholly abortive. He therefore made me a fishing rod. 'Go and fish,' he said.

'But where?'

'Kutthalingam will drive you to Mount Lavinia. Fish in the rock pools.'

'But the fish in the rock pools die if you take them out.'

'They are supposed to die,' said Vincent, exasperated.

'Well, I don't want them to.'

'Toba, toba! O my Lord Jesus!' said Christian Vincent, and made me a fishing net.

On my walks with Kumar, I discovered what, since like most small children I lived in a small area of contact, I had not previously known: that near the house was the race-course, and that on Saturdays there was racing there. Just behind the course was a field full of rough shrubbery. I took to walking Kumar through this field on Saturdays. When we reached the white painted rails, I lay down, with Kumar palpitating impatiently in my arms, and looked towards the grandstand, where the horses tittuped, straddled by jockeys in silks as varicoloured and beautiful as the fish in the rock pool. Presently when the race started, I clutched close into the earth. The tall centaurs came hammering round the curve, and were suddenly upon me: the great hooves, as they struck, raising clouds with a cluck of sound, glossy vast flanks matted with sweat, the whips flying with a mosquito noise as they passed. I lay out of harm's way with my dog, but in that second of passage I had the illusion of becoming them, twenty tall centaurs, their horse, leather, and sweat smell, their eighty hooves. For a sedentary boy, it was a curious pleasure.

Rooting round the tussocky field one day when there were no races, I came upon a stream, hidden in the bushes. It was about three feet wide, and perhaps a foot deep, and ran from a drain to a drain, but the water was clear, and tiny fish and weeds wavered together in the water. The fish were silvery brown, with red and yellow dots on their sides. I hung, absorbed, by the edge of this shallow trickle, my Amazon, watching this sealed, frozen other life for hours. Presently I remembered my fishing net. With great labour and wetness, I captured some of the fish. Vincent found me a capacious glass jar, which I filled with mud, weeds, and water, and I kept the fish in that. They weren't very beautiful, but I liked to watch them.

Later, burrowing in the drain, I saw what I had taken to be a round stone move, and poke out a slowly weaving, wrinkled, yellow head. I scooped it up. It was a mud turtle, with a smooth yellowish carapace to which moss and slime adhered in copious quantities. I took it home in triumph. There was a water-tank in the yard, about sixteen square feet. I filled this with mud and water, dropped in some weeds, and erected a pyramid of stones so that the turtle could sun itself if it so wished. Then I introduced it to its new home.

At first it behaved very well, coming up from the bottom with a slow flail of blunt limbs to peck up breadcrumbs which I dropped in. Kutthalingam, however, didn't like it. For one thing, the tank it occupied was the tank from which he washed the car. For another, it was just under the window of his quarters, and as time passed and the sun blazed, a greenish slime formed on the surface of the tank, and a stench of turtle rose from it. 'Baba,' he said despairingly, 'throw it away.' Being a spoilt little boy, I utterly refused. Then came the monsoon. On the first morning after the rain, I went out to see to the turtle. It wasn't there; Kutthalingam emerged from the garage, looking very pleased with life. 'Baba,' he said, 'last night it raining, tank overflowing, and turtle going away.' I pointed out that the tank was only half full. 'Baba, what anyone can doing?' he said piously. 'These things God's animals, they going back to God.'

We had now been in Ceylon for some while, but I didn't really know anything about the country, beyond Colombo. I could see how the Sinhalese were different from the people in India: they had gold skins and small bones: the men had lilting feminine voices, but the women's voices were rather more husky. The servants called their employers Master instead of Saheb, and the food was different from Indian food: our cook, for example, despite Vincent's imprecations, almost daily produced a rice pancake called a hopper, and a mush of rice and salt fish, wrapped and baked in leaves, called a lumfry. I rather liked the food, despite Vincent, and the people, despite Kutthalingam, whose countrymen, the Tamils from south India who came to Ceylon as labourers, have always suffered oppression from the Sinhalese.

But my father, anxious because I wasn't at school, had determined to educate me. When his yearly leave came round, he told me, very gravely, that he had plans for us. Was I aware that Ceylon was littered with interesting ruins? It was time I learnt something about Ceylonese history. We would drive round the island, looking at ruins. Some of them, he added, were deep in the jungle.

This fired my enthusiasm. I had carried my ichthyological research a step further, had filled the house, to Vincent's annoyance, with bottles full of earth and ants, and now subscribed to the magazine published by the Ceylon Natural History Society. In this I had discovered with joy that Ceylon was populated, apart from humans, by elephants, leopards, antelope, wild boar, buffalo, and monkeys. I yearned to see them outside the zoo. Moreover, Ceylon had a Missing Link: a legendary man-monkey that walked and talked, but was elusive and ferocious. It was called the Nittaewo, and no authoritative naturalist had ever seen it. I determined to be the first one.

The house was shut up, the servants sent on leave, and Kumar lodged with the same family that had had him before. Early one morning my father, Kutthalingam, and I drove off round the coast, past Mount Lavinia, down a road filled with traffic, to Galle, a seaport town that had once been the capital. Here my father led me, disinterested, round the old Portuguese fort, and other antiquities.

Next day, however, beyond Galle, we came to the jungle. The road narrowed, and arrowed down between aisles of trees whose heavy green crowns were alive with blackfaced, greycoated langur monkeys. It was dusky between the trees, and into this dusk I peered intently as we sped by, looking for the Nittaewo. I did not see him, but was pleased enough to see a few jackals, dusty scuttlers, and on a turn of the road a tame elephant, a garland of red flowers round its head, rather pointlessly pulling along a small log. My excitement increased when that night at Hambantota, where we slept, I heard during dinner a sputtering cough like a motorcycle exhaust, and was informed by an impressively casual hotel keeper that it was a leopard hung round the hotel in order to dine out of the dustbins when everyone was asleep.

We progressed along the coast, through jungle and towns, till we reached Batticaloa, where we had an introduction to a local naturalist. He was a tall, white-haired Sinhalese with magnificent whiskers, and immensely gratified me by presenting me with the tusks of a wild boar he had recently shot. He also offered to take us out into the bay to listen to the fish singing. These musical fish constitute Batticaloa's main claim to fame.

So in the night full of crickets, we paddled out into the bay. The rowboat moved in a chain of splashes through a sea so dark and shiny it seemed pliable, under a vast constellation of glittering stars. Behind us, like fallen stars, the kerosene lamps of Batticaloa glittered in the arm of the bay. In the cool still air the plangent music of a radio set floated to us over the water. The tall naturalist let a metal pole down into the sea, and we applied our ears to the top end, and presently heard, spiralled up from the warm undersea of coral and ocean flowers, a sequence of thin, splintery chirps. Over us hung a very yellow sickle moon. 'They sing best at the full moon,' said the naturalist in a low voice, and we rowed slowly back. Between the sea and the stars we were alone and I realized for the first time the otherness of nature.

In the morning we breakfasted at the naturalist's house. His wife, a fat, graying woman like a badger, with curious patches of whiskers on her cheeks, which seemed a blurred mirror image of his, fed us egg hoppers, salt fish, and sweets, frequently patted me on the head, and chuckled at every remark anyone made. The naturalist uttered measured words on the probable existence of the Nittaewo. As we were about to leave, however, a young man bicycled up to the sunny verandah where we sat, and announced in a dramatic voice, 'Ponniah has passed away!'

'That is very sad,' said the naturalist. His wife's reaction was more violent. She flung her sari over her head in a gesture of mourning, and began to rock to and fro, wailing 'Aiyo! Aiyo! Ponniah has passed away.'

'Do not be so distressed, my dear,' said the naturalist. 'We were not well acquainted with the good fellow. But how did he die?'

'He was struck by a bullock cart yesterday,' said the young man, 'and being very aged, could not sustain the shock, and passed away this morning.'

The naturalist began to express his sympathy in a measured Victorian way, but his wife rocked to and fro with increasing violence. Tears poured down her cheeks and dripped from her whiskers, her massive body shook with sobs, and in a loud bleating voice she cried, 'Aiyo! Aiyo! Ponniah has passed away. It will come to us all. Aiyo! Aiyo! Why? Why?'

My father and I said hasty goodbyes and departed. Once in the car, we were convulsed with shared laughter. The comedy of it was obvious: but years later, the scene, forgotten all that while, returned to me, and without mirth I remembered the fat whiskery woman crying and rocking on the verandah in Batticaloa, demanding why anyone had to die.

After Batticaloa we swung inland, and drove into the true jungle, the heartland of Ceylon. Kutthalingam plotted our daily course. In the early morning, with multicoloured birds whistling wetly in the trees, we would leave the resthouse where we had spent the night. The laden branches shook down langur monkeys which bounded like kangaroos across the road, or, playfully, alongside the car. They hooted like owls as they went. The morning earth smelt herbal and moist, before the great sun had swelled to full power. We passed occasional forest villagers, skittering like mice down the road, with poles across their shoulders on which dead birds hung suspended.

Early day was the best time to see the larger animals. A leopard stood frozen, once, in a dry watercourse, one paw raised like a tabby. Another time a large brown beast scooted out of the forest, crashed into the bumper of the car, ricocheted, and was gone. 'That be wild pig,' Kutthalingam explained dispassionately. I looked desperately for the Nittaewo, but didn't find him.

Later in the day, the gonged sun almost audibly roared as it poured down heat. The jungle, so rich a few hours before, became motionless and ashen. The animals slept, except for the monkeys. In dry watercourses I saw crocodiles, squatting on ridiculous bowed legs, that yawned like antique colonels in the sun. As afternoon passed, the shadows lay down quietly in the forest. At evening a small wind moved the trees, they grew green, and rustled, and the animals began to appear.

In the midst of this twined, entrenched woodland, with its separate life of animals, birds, reptiles, insects, plants, rocks, we came to the abandoned kingdoms of Anuradhapura and Polonnaruwa, capitals of the first Sinhalese kings. Their temples had been burst open by vines, trees grew through their thick stone walls. Hidden in a clearing, with langurs whooping round, an immense fractured Buddha lay on his side, sealed eyes calm. At this time the ruins were not as well cared for as they are now: at Sigiriya, a great forested rock on whose summit was a cave full of decayed frescoes, immense brown beehives, like enlarged pine cones, hung by the spiral iron stairway to the top, and the air was full of a sound like the thunder of a distant war.

Yet to see these fallen monuments, invaded by the jungle, inhabited by beasts, made me aware of history. They were more alive to me because though the human life in them was dead, another, prehistoric life had taken over. History to me was the way a spindly shoot sprouted through Buddha's stone eye.

In a reserved area of the forest, a Government man introduced us to some Veddahs. They are the original inhabitants of Ceylon, a stone-age people, who fled to the depths of the forest when the Sinhalese first came. They still live there. The Government man brought half a dozen men up to the verandah of the resthouse where we were staying. They were ugly: diminutive, very dark, and scruffily bearded. Their thin, naked bodies were smeared with ash. From them had come the Sinhalese legends of gnomes and elves, but they were unaware of it: they stood shifting their splayed toes uncomfortably in the courtyard dust. They offered my father birds' eggs and a dead pheasant. My father explained through the Government man that he didn't want them, but gave the Veddahs some money. They seemed puzzled, kept offering the eggs and the bird to my father, but he wouldn't accept them and eventually the Veddahs disappeared. They left behind them an acrid smell of ash, leaves, and bark. Later that evening the resthouse keeper brought my father the pheasant and the eggs. They had been left on the steps of the resthouse. Later the memory of these people invaded some of my poetry.

We drove on as far as the arid yellow sands of Jaffna on the northern tip of the island, then swivelled down the west coast back to Colombo. Just after we passed Mihintale, where hundreds of steps led up to a rather scruffy temple, my long search for the Nittaewo was rewarded. At a curious lopsided run, an animal moved through the undergrowth at the side of the road. It was reddish in colour, and as it moved it kept lifting its head and emitting a plaintive human cry. I made Kutthalingam stop the car, but by the time I had walked back to where I had seen it, the Nittaewo had disappeared.

When we returned to Colombo, I wrote a very graphic account and sent it to the editor of the natural history magazine. In due course I received a kind letter back from him. 'What you saw may of course have been a Nittaewo,' he wrote, 'but I do not myself think so. However, yours is the most vivid description I have ever read of a lame monkey.'

A Cricketer in Brisbane, a Spy in Bangkok

I was on a ship, with my parents. We were going to Australia. It was my father's first leave since he had started to edit the *Times of India,* and, since he had never been to Australia, he had chosen it for our holiday. I knew nothing about Australia except that from it came cricketers, kangaroos, and the duck-billed platypus, but the idea of travel pleased me. The great liner pleased me, an organized complex city borne on dark waters: mealtimes, when in the huge chandeliered saloon I looked through the long menu, and, deliberately chose: bedtime, in an austere but comfortable bunk cleated to the wall. The motion pleased me: the thunderous run of the engine, the slow surge forward, the ploughed white field of the wake, with flying fishes flittering like daytime bats over the waves. The only thing I disliked was that there were so many other children aboard, but once it was established that I was not expected to play with them, that was a fact I could disregard.

We stopped at Colombo, where old friends came to see us: then came the long landless plod south, and the ship became an isolated community. Because of my mother, it was difficult to meet people: but they gravitated to my father nonetheless, and our table in the bar was always crowded. I sipped lemonade and prayed that my mother, sitting waxen amidst the talking faces, would not start a scene. She never did, but whenever we were with someone else my nerves fluttered like butterflies.

We started off under bald blue skies: but after Colombo grey squalls raked down across the sea, spattering the decks and portholes, and the ship rolled wildly, so that at meals the stewards had to cleat the plates down. One morning, with garish violets and reds in the thick clouds, and rain and wind flying over the decks, the engines slowed. From deck we were able to see a clump of islands, very green, but hazed in cloud and mist, rainbeaten, remote: these were the Cocos Islands, and the ship was to deliver and collect the mail.

Presently two small boats put out from the nearest island, and hesitated towards us over the heaving sea. The waves lifted high over them, then burst down on them in spray: they disappeared repeatedly, then reappeared, streaming with water, but determined. As they neared the ship the sailors tilted black oil into the sea: it stippled the grey viscous water, slipping from the crests to the troughs of the waves. The little boats edged over it, but when they were nearly alongside, the sea lifted suddenly in a huge wave, and both boats floated belly up in the oil and water, with heads bobbing all round. The sailors dropped rope ladders: one by one the heads materialized as dripping Englishmen, helped on deck by vicariously excited passengers.

Later the dripping men materialized as dry men, bronzed, with ragged beards and hair, drinking beer in the bar. A tornado was blowing up, which meant that they would have to come to Australia with us. I eyed them with awe. I had read my Robinson Crusoe. My awe increased when I was told that one of them, the only clean-shaven one, was the King of the Cocos Islands. When, once, he spoke to me (making some such observation as 'Hullo, son') I was so overcome that I could not reply. As the voyage continued, however, the glamour started to fade. One of the shipwrecked islanders had a drink at our table, a speechless, bearded young man, who seemed not to understand a word anyone said. Though silent, he was obviously not strong, in fact he was positively weedy. I tried to imagine him killing tigers, snakes, sharks, and hostile natives, which was what I thought the King and his lieutenants probably did daily, but even my imagination was incapable of the effort. I was bitterly disappointed. People, I decided wisely, were never what they seemed to be.

We were supposed to disembark at Melbourne, but before that the ship stopped at Perth and Adelaide, where we wandered around. A nervous child, I hated to be conspicuous, and I had been terrified that my brown skin, in a country of red ones, would make me so, but I needn't have worried. Everyone was tremendously friendly. I was puzzled when taxi drivers called my father 'mate', told him all about their lives, and invited him into bars for 'a brace of ice colds', but it was obviously well meant, though I myself objected to being called 'nipper'.

I didn't like Melbourne quite so much. A hot, very dusty wind seemed always to be working down the grey, towering streets, blowing people before it. Sydney was better, with the sea, filled with swimmers and sharks, a blue field dotted with foam-flowers, and the green arms of the land reaching into the bay, where the bridge like an eloquent bow tied in steel pronounced its epiphanies of traffic. The rush and racket of the city was more intense than that of Melbourne, and therefore more sympathetic: and in Romano's I ate my first oysters.

Canberra was even better. At that time it was a prefabricated kind of city, full of temporary-looking red brick bungalows. But the India High Commissioner there was K.S. Duleepsinhji, the cricketer, a plump, gentle man, with a pleasantly cracked, husky, whispery voice. He showed me how to bowl, persuaded me to bowl him a few deliveries on the lawn of his house, allowed me to bowl him, and in token of my triumph, presented me with his Cambridge Blue scarf, which I cherished for years.

From Canberra we went north. I was trying to keep a journal of our trip, and worked at it every night, while my parents were at dinner. Into this journal came bits of verse which I seemed to produce without much effort, and which read like it. I did not really know why I wrote these verses, except that I had a vague yearning to shape and say my experiences in a more complete way than I could do in prose. I cannot remember now what they were about. We were mainly in cities, and the people I met with my father were generally politicians…

Eventually we drove into the Blue Mountains (which produced a spate of verse) and then went further north, to the Queensland cane country around Mackay and Toowoomba. It was very hot here, with a sticky quality in the air, like the thick warm ooze of the canes. At one plantation, as we were inspecting a dully rustling canefield, a small black man in dungarees shuffled up and asked my father for a cigarette. The overseer waved him impatiently away. 'Don't take any notice of him,' he advised my father. 'He's one of the abos, Abo Charlie, scrounges all he can get.'

But the small man shuffled closer, and said to my father, 'You from India, eh? I too. I from Jhelum side, bloody fine country that. You gotta cigarette?'

My father said in incredulous tones, 'He's an Indian.'

'Is he, by Christ,' said the overseer. 'Never knew that.'

It turned out that Charlie (his real name was Chauhan) had come to Australia before the Great War as a camel driver. When the utility of camels in the Australian desert ended, he hadn't enough money to return home. He had made a living through casual labour for thirty years, had married an Australian wife, and had several children. His one regret was that he could not get his wife to cook Punjabi food.

He was terrible: he begged my father for cigarettes, for whisky, for money to buy them with. The overseer looked disapprovingly on, but eventually my father presented Charlie with a pound. He took it with a lifting of his clasped hands to his forehead in thanks, which after forty years in Australia was still purely Indian.

He was the first expatriate I had ever met, and I eyed him with a waxy kind of scorn, not knowing that in a few years I should be one myself, in a country that didn't want me.

In Brisbane, a town of shanty houses and palm-trees, rusted by the sun, I was introduced to an old man named Roger Hartigan, who forty years before had made a hundred runs against England. This was his only claim to fame as a cricketer, though, he had since become a prosperous businessman. He had very white hair and very pink skin: a kind, rather equine face with bright blue eyes. In spite of the dust and heat, he was always immaculately clad in a suit, and he moved his highly polished shoes with precision, keeping them exactly parallel as he walked. Whenever he came to our hotel, he brought my mother a bunch of flowers or a box of chocolates.

The Press officer who was arranging my father's interviews had produced him when I asked if I could meet some cricketers. Mr Hartigan was apparently the only cricketer left in Brisbane: all the others were away. It was true, said the Press officer apologetically, that he wasn't a very famous cricketer: but he was a cricketer.

It made no odds to me whether the Press officer thought Mr Hartigan famous or not. He had played in a Test match and made a hundred, and anyone who had done that was famous so far as I was concerned. My awed silence when I met him obviously puzzled Mr Hartigan, for it must have been some decades since schoolboys sought his autograph. Equally obvious, it must have pleased him. He paid us a daily call, arriving punctiliously at ten every morning. He would hand my mother her flowers and chocolates, stand my father a drink, and then take me on a slow, processional walk round the dusty pavements of Brisbane, talking about all the people he had played cricket with. At first I drank it all in, but later it started to bore me a little. The attention that had been riveted to him during our first walks began to wander to people, to houses, to trees and the sky. Mr Hartigan eventually noticed this. As we walked along one day, he said, in his courteous and elaborate way, 'I hope I am not boring you?'

I liked Mr Hartigan very much, but I wanted to be truthful. 'No, not exactly,' I said, 'but I was thinking of something else.'

'Ah,' said Mr Hartigan. He escorted me back to the hotel, bowed to my mother, bought my father a drink, patted me on the head, and walked off, keeping his highly polished shoes precisely parallel. That was the last time I saw him.

In New Zealand I remember the boiling mudholes at Rotorua, the shiny brown mud turning itself over and over in its bestial trench, bubbling and rumbling, sometimes with a suck drawing its own viscous self down into itself: the gulping power of the earth, greedy for us all. It seemed a mysterious country: behind trees and rocks, in a mountain shadow, I glimpsed shapes that weren't there, speaking or moving shapes. I became aware in New Zealand of being in some sense separate from my body. Looking at the mud boiling, or at a lake shivered by fish, in which I glimpsed indeterminate shadows under the skin of the water, I seemed to look down at myself looking down, from a long way away. I would repeat my name, and it meant nothing, it had no connection with what I was. In certain types of landscape, these symptoms have recurred in me ever since.

Perhaps it was because I was now aware of my parents as separate people, no longer flesh of my flesh. I had become more and more abstracted, and sought my loneliness deliberately, speaking less, and at the same time writing more. My journal had spread into several volumes, and the passages of verse had become very frequent now. I knew that I wanted to be a writer, and like an athlete, but quite unconsciously, I was going into training.

When we flew back to Sydney from New Zealand (in a seaplane, landing in a bounce and flurry of spray which, as it flew, rainbowed in the sun, so that it was as though slow constellations of meteors fell past my window) a message was waiting for my father. The Indian Government wanted him to tour South-East Asia and prepare a confidential report about the Press relations in the various countries. My father drew up a list of places: Djakarta, Singapore, Saigon, Bangkok, Rangoon: the names delighted me, and I made a sort of litany of them, which I chanted softly to myself.

My mother was less pleased. She wanted to go home, she had had enough of travel. Throughout the trip she had been subdued, though not unhappy, but now the excitable hysterical mood which signalled one of her storms was on her. Surprisingly, it was Duleepsinhji who calmed her: he flew to Sydney, and told her it was a Government mission that took us through Asia, important to the country: memories of her nationalist youth stirred in my mother, and she agreed to come.

We flew from Sydney to Darwin, landing at midnight on a barren airstrip loud with mosquitoes. Skeleton shapes showed in the bush beyond. It was suffocatingly hot, and in small cubicles, with fans siphoning humid air over us, we slept uneasily till dawn. Then we headed northward. Below us Australia petered out in a morass of khaki headlands and creeks, and the aeroplane lumbered steadily over a powdery blue sea towards Djakarta. The hostess brought round the morning papers, coffee, and biscuits. We were on our way.

Eventually the sea faded into land, sprawling away in forest and hill below. We landed at Djakarta at dusk. The Indian Ambassador, an affable old man from the south, was there to meet us. We drove to his house through the warm and redolent night, down roads lined with shacks, past glistening canals. His wife welcomed us, and I was sent to bed, where I lay awake wondering what it was like outside.

Next day the Ambassador's wife took my mother and me for a drive. Djakarta was beautiful in the strong whitish sunshine, with broad avenues lined with trees, the trees all in extraordinary, explosive flower, and canals in which, to my great interest, women were bathing, their fig-like, dark-nippled breasts bare. We drove to a beach where a white clubhouse, formerly reserved for the Dutch, stood, and ate rijstaffel, and drove back at evening, with the Javanese in bright colours fluttering among many kindled lamps.

To my surprise, my mother made friends with the Ambassador's wife. She was a small, very neat old lady, with silver hair and spectacles, and had had several children. Her gentleness was visible in all her movements, even in the movements of her hands when she sewed, which was all the time. I was surprised because my mother seemed neither to expect nor require friends: she had dropped all her old friends in Bombay, and in Australia had withdrawn so completely as to make friendship with her impossible.

She took to the Ambassador's wife completely, however, and since I think the Ambassador's wife was herself rather lonely, they tended to spend the whole day together, talking. This meant I was free to move about as I pleased. I accompanied my father on several of his interviews, listening to fat, dejected Dutchmen who talked about the extortionist policies of Sukarno's Government, and bespectacled Javanese, until recently terrorists, who talked of Sukarno as though he were the risen Christ. In consequence, I saw quite a lot of Djakarta.

My father obtained an interview with Sukarno. I went with him in the car to the President's palace, and then the chauffeur drove me around the city for an hour. My eyes drank it in, the flowers in the trees and the hair of the people, the ramshackle bungalows of the old colonists, the spruce white houses of the modern Dutch, many of them now requisitioned by Sukarno. The small-boned, golden, cat-faced Javanese struck me as the most beautiful nation I had seen.

We returned to the palace and waited for a while, and eventually my father and Sukarno, followed by two bodyguards came down the steps. Sukarno was short and fanatically neat, in white ducks with a Moslem fez. As my father limbed into the Car he leant forward, shot out his arm in a Hitler salute, and shouted, 'Jai Hind!'* My father looked baffled for a moment, then responded, 'Merdeka'† I echoed him feebly, Sukarno once more shot out his arm and shouted, 'Jai Hind!' We again murmured, 'Merdeka!' Fortunately the chauffeur started the car at this point, thus obviating the necessity for any further exchanges.

On the day before we left, the Ambassador's wife called me into her reception room. She was sitting on the sofa, sewing. She patted the sofa beside her and I sat down. She blinked at me over her spectacles like a kind little owl.

'I have been talking a lot to your mother,' she said. 'You're a big boy, so you know that she has been ill. She is still very troubled in her mind, and it is mostly about you. She feels that you are not in contact with her. She is afraid she will lose you. You know, you must be very patient with her.'

'She hasn't been very patient with me.'

'But she loves you very much,' said the Ambassador's wife. 'You must know that.'

'Well, I don't love her.'

'You may not think you do,' said the Ambassador's wife, 'but some time, perhaps very soon, perhaps in many years' time, you will find that you are wrong.'

Singapore was hot, teeming, and filled with muddled rumours of terrorist activity. We stayed in the Raffles Hotel, under mosquito nets and fans. At night, while a Eurasian dance band blared, the local magnates, English, Chinese, and Indian, moved round the

---

* Long live India—Indian nationalist slogan.

† Freedom—Indonesian nationalist slogan.

ballroom in slow, inelegant rhythms. The blotchy shoulders of the planters' wives, revealed by their ill-chosen décolletages, and their raucous and confident voices, revolted me. I refused to go down to dinner, and had it sent up instead.

A Chinese millionaire friend of my father's invited us to his house. His garden was full of plastic deer, emblems of the salve from which he had made his money. In his drawing-room two obscenely fat Cupids pissed whisky and soda respectively at the turn of a tap. Puritanically I decided that Singapore was an entirely vulgar place, and not to be borne.

As usual, however, I accompanied my father on his interviews, which included one with Malcolm Macdonald, whom I was to meet years later under different circumstances. In this way I heard a lot about the terrorists who were then busy on the mainland, and about Malayan independence. I had an excellent memory, and could remember a poem by heart, for instance, as soon as I had written or read it, so I remembered most of what I heard.

My parents were asked to an evening party, and the host said I could come too. So we went. It was in a pretty house, shadowed with bougainvillaea, by the sea, with enormous gardens which were soon alive with adulterous couples. I wandered about for a while, and presently, in a corner of the garden, came on an Indian police officer smoking a cigar. He said hullo, we introduced ourselves, and after a few remarks about the night's beauty, I started to ask him questions about the terrorists. He had just returned from the mainland, and knew quite a lot about them, and I was delighted at the thought that I would be able to retail some first-hand information to my father. So I went on asking, he went on replying, we strolled across the garden, and presently reached my father, surrounded by a group of people.

'I say, Mr Moraes,' said my friend the police officer, 'I must congratulate you upon your son. How intelligent are the questions he has asked me about the terrorists! How profound is his knowledge of the situation! A remarkable boy altogether!'

My father smiled, and I saw that he was pleased. Flushed with triumph, and by the proximity of an audience, I promptly started to ask more questions. They were mostly rather pointless, and the policeman, now surrounded by adults, was soon visibly bored.

On the way home my father said grimly, 'There's a lesson you must learn, and that is, not to show off. If you'd left well alone when you should have, you'd have made a wonderful impression. But by asking all those other silly questions, you simply made a fool of yourself. That tends to happen when you show off. D'you understand?'

'Yes,' I said meekly, but looking out of the car window at the crowded and noisy streets, felt more than ever confirmed in my belief that Singapore was a nasty and vulgar place.

The day before we arrived in Saigon someone had thrown a bomb at a café in the Rue Catinat. From the high window of our room in the Metropole Hotel, I could see the scorched pavement, and the splintered glass of the café window. Nobody seemed to care. The other cafés on the boulevard were doing a roaring trade: sitting under gaily striped umbrellas, ex-S.S. men from the Legion were drinking pastis and making passes at every woman who went by. It was their night off. 'It would be better not to go out,' said a harassed-looking First Secretary from the Indian Embassy, 'till the Legionnaires have gone.'

They went about an hour later, cuffed and kicked into a lorry by a roaring bull of a sergeant. When we ventured out a smell of cordite still hung in the air round the bombed café. We dined in a place full of French officers and Vietnamese whisperers. 'Full of spies,' said the First Secretary. 'It's a curious place, Saigon.' He was loose with wine and murmured, 'A very curious place. Either you get a nervous breakdown if you live here, or you come to treat explosions like the chimes of a clock.' All this talk excited me: I longed for an explosion like a sunburst in the window, or for rifles to spit in the street. I thought of them purely as themselves—not as the causes of death.

We drove about the city for the next few days, while my father interviewed people, but I heard no explosions, saw no shots fired, only the spruce French officers and the small, cool Vietnamese, drinking, buying and selling in the shadows of the street. Then one night we went to a cabaret, where a troupe from, of all places, England, was dancing the can-can. My heart pounded wildly at every kick, every flurry of lace, as stout pink legs flew into the air, and turned into the flashing spokes of a wheel. By now I knew exactly what my emotions in this matter were about, and was in process of selecting the prettiest dancer, to dream of, when abruptly the lights went out. There was a loud stuttering noise outside, and several sharper sounds, like sticks snapping. My father pushed my mother and me under the table. I crouched there, my head pressed uncomfortably against my father's knee, till a shout from the door brought the lights up once more.

'Just a small incident up the road,' said the First Secretary affably. 'A patrol must have run into some Viet Minh.' I was deeply disappointed. I had missed the firing, and now I missed the dancers as well, for they didn't reappear.

After a week in Saigon we flew to Dalat, where my father was to interview Bao Dai, the puppet ruler set up by the French. Dalat was in the mountains, with thick forest all round: I saw three naked, dwarfish Sakai aborigines, with bows and arrows, flit away from the kitchens of the luxurious hotel where we stayed. A waiter told me they had come to sell game. The hotel stood by a lake, blue as an eye, on the far side of which Bao Dai's palace stood.

At this hotel I ate snails for the first time. It was my sole cause for excitement. My father refused to let me come to see Bao Dai, since he had been threatened with assassination a few days back, and the attempt was likely to take place at any minute. In point of fact the attempt, which failed, was made the day after we left Dalat, which seemed to be a shame.

After Dalat we travelled north to Hanoi. It was a ramshackle, far-flung town, and across the Red River, a brown snake that lay still in the grassflats on the outskirts, we heard, like a large door slammed with monotonous regularity, the reverberations of French howitzers. The house of the Indian Consul vibrated gently at each reverberation, but he seemed unmoved. Attended by a pretty Vietnamese maidservant, he sat on a chair, his bare feet tucked unaffectedly under him, complaining of the shortage of whisky in Hanoi. 'Tomorrow,' he told my father, 'you and I will drive to a French post. It is forty kilometres. But today we shall drink, and what is there to drink? Pah, only rice wine.'

'Can't I come, too?' I asked.

'Bah, it is no place for a boy,' Kutty said. 'There may be shooting on the road.'

'I'd like to come,' I said, glad that we had left my mother, who wanted to shop, in Saigon.

'If you want to come,' said my father gravely, 'come.'

Kutty shrugged his shoulders. 'It is your responsibility. Now, since there is only rice wine, let us drink rice wine.' So they did.

Next day a jeep with a Vietnamese driver stood at the door. Kutty climbed into the front, and my father and I into the back. Then we rattled out of Hanoi. Outside the town inundated paddy fields lay on either side, an endless vista of muddy water, with occasional green shoots poking through, till a faint blue haze of hills broke the horizon. Along the road, at regular intervals, were French sentry posts, concrete pillboxes with slots for windows.

'Sometimes,' said Kutty, 'the Viet Minh lie down in the fields, under water, and breathe through straws, till a French convoy passes. Then—zzt! no convoy.' He laughed heartily. 'They may be there now.' We passed a ditched truck, its bullnose twisted hopelessly to one side. Some of the pillboxes, I noticed, had caved in at the side. 'Grenades,' said the all-explanatory Kutty. He began to talk about the French casualties. I no longer felt the zest with which I had started the day. The casualties Kutty enumerated had made a leap from statistics into actuality.

The landscape stayed the same, flat fields flooded with muddy water, across which in wind a slow ripple occasionally passed. In the distance the blue haze of mountains and along the road the pillboxes, so often violated and sad, their slotted eyes staring vacantly. So we came to the French post. It was an assembly of prefab huts and tents thrown roughly together on high ground, and surrounded by thick tangles of barbed wire. Sentries demanded our passes. One of them chucked me under the chin. We squelched through a hundred yards of mud to the Commandant's hut, where Kutty introduced us. The Commandant, who had a blue chin but friendly eyes, handed me a bon-bon. Though I felt rather too old for it, I accepted it with thanks.

The interview started. My father's French was limited, so Kutty acted as interpreter. The Commandant put his muddy boots on the table, tilted back his chair, and emitted guttural replies to the questions. They had had an engagement with infiltrators, he said, two nights before, and had driven them back. All the while that he spoke he appeared to be listening to something outside the hut.

Eventually he offered to take us round the post. We squelched round with him, staring in an embarrassed way at the soldiers, who, stripped to the waist, many with crucifixes round their necks, whistled, played cards, and stared back. I noticed with a strange sick feeling two crosses in the field behind the post. In the hospital tent several men were lying, bandaged and worn-looking. One of them had rusty stains of blood on his bandage, but they all seemed quite cheerful.

The Commandant asked if we would like to see the prisoners taken in the skirmish two days before. They were brought out by two tough-looking Germans with sten guns tucked under their arms: half a dozen tiny young men, skinny, clad in dark brown tunics and trousers. I never discovered whether this was the Viet Minh uniform or the uniform for prisoners. They were lined up, and my father, through Kutty, asked one a question. The Vietnamese looked back with the rolling eyes of a frightened pony. His upper lip was shaking uncontrollably, and soon his thin shoulders also began to shake. He didn't answer. At this the Commandant, with a smiling, rather complacent look, slapped him three or four times across the face. They were not very hard slaps, lazy almost, the slaps a cat might give a kitten, but the Vietnamese staggered and nearly fell. At this my father hastily said that he thought he had asked enough questions, and we squelched back to the jeep.

As we started off, I said to my father, 'Why didn't you stop him hitting that man?'

'How could I have stopped him?' inquired my father, and Kutty chuckled. 'The Commandant may be having some friends who were killed by that fellow's friends also. What you can do? War is war.'

That evening we went to visit a Vietnamese professor who was a Viet Minh sympathizer. He had been educated at the Sorbonne, and had married a French wife. They made a very handsome couple, in a large drawing-room looking over a garden from which the scent of magnolia floated. From an inner room came the sound of a violin. Presently this ceased, and a girl came in. She was about fifteen, two or three years older than I, slim, and very beautiful, with a soft face in which the almond eyes of her father and the rather full, smiling lips of her mother blended. 'This is my daughter Jacqueline,' said the Professor. 'Jacqueline, show this young man the garden. You can practise your English at the same time.'

The girl and I went into the garden. The rustle of her dress sent a hundred tiny needles through me, and we stopped under the magnolia tree, still pouring its heavy odour into the air. It was dark now, till the southern sky lit up with the crump of an explosion.

I asked her about her school and her future plans, and she answered in a quiet, husky voice, which seemed to me doomed and therefore beautiful. After a while I ran out of conversation. We stood under the magnolia tree. She leant on it, crumbling the waxy white petals between her fingers, and letting them fall. Her thick dark hair framed her face which was waxy and white, like the petals that she crumbled. I could not speak, yet the silence in which we stood became as intense as though I spoke and she listened. Then lights shone in the doorway to the garden, and our parents came through.

Bangkok is mad and lovely: I thought so even as a child, walking amidst its pagodas in the rain, or boating on the muddy Chao Phya, which runs through the city, cluttered with houseboats and floating shops. The golden, dotty people, with their insipid, delicious-looking food, their hours-long dances to a thin inaudible music, appealed to me then, and still do. One of them, who during the war had been imprisoned and tortured by the Japanese, and, chained food-less in a dungeon, made a diet of cockroaches, offered to take us to the best restaurant in town, run by a Chinaman. We took a taxi through a filthy cobweb of streets near the river, then walked for some distance. Finally we reached a bolted door. 'This restaurant,' said our Thai friend, 'is known only to a favoured few. It seems to be closed, but so'—he disappeared into an alleyway, and emerged with an ill-favoured Chinese who had been sleeping there—'so we will gain entry.'

The Chinese, who seemed by no means pleased at being awakened, unbolted the door and we entered a very small room which contained a kerosene lamp, a deal table, and some chairs. Our friend and the Chinese whispered together, and the Chinese disappeared into the shadows. 'Now,' said our friend, 'we will have a meal fit for some kings. When I was a Japanese prisoner I used to dream of meals such as this.'

We sat in the flickering and odorous light of the lamp till the Chinese reappeared with a dish which contained our first course. The Thai told us what it was.

'Fried rice?' said my father dubiously, peering into the dish.

'No, no,' said our friend, indignant. 'I told you this place was special. Fried mice.'

Several years later, in a hotel bar in Bangkok, a Thai girl on the next stool asked me to buy her a drink, and since she was very pretty I agreed. We went on to dinner, and presently she asked me what I did. 'I'm a writer,' I said, 'what do you do?' She leaned towards me and whispered, 'Don't tell anyone. I'm a spy.'

Figures in the Landscape (1955)

I reached Paris at twilight. At twilight London was shabby and furtive, but Paris wasn't. The bars and cafés were brilliantly lit, and the people in the streets seemed in less of a hurry than Londoners, and also more pleased about their destinations. The city smelt interesting too, especially round the Sorbonne, where, on Oliver's advice, I sought an hotel. When eventually I found one, I was thrilled by its large, comfortable bed and strange lavatory arrangements. Most of that first evening I walked round the quais, dropping into the odd bar, goggling touristically at tarts, gendarmes, and sullen slinky Algerians. From then on, every day, I set off on foot early, and within a fortnight had more or less traversed the city.

After that I developed a working schedule. I awoke at eight, and worked till ten. Then I went to the nearest café and sat there amidst the strong coffee smells and the posters about alcoholism, drinking first coffee then pastis, and continuing to work. What I produced wasn't particularly brilliant, but at least I had the sensation of pursuing my vocation, which I had lost in London.

I didn't talk to many people, though I developed friendships with the concierge at my hotel and the waiter at the café. Through them I developed a knowledge of Parisian argot, which later stood me in good stead. My command of English argot was, I realized, more limited. One night I was in a St Germain café, when a young American at the next table started to stare at me intently.

Rather crossly I stared back. He rose, came over, and demanded in a husky whisper, 'Are you gay?'

I had no wish to be thought depressed, an object for pity. 'Oh, yes,' I said, with a broad smile, 'very gay,' and was much surprised to be invited back to his room. It took me a long while to extricate myself. Many people thought I was homosexual at seventeen. I suppose it was a combination of shyness, large sad eyes, and longish hair. I resented it deeply.

In my last days in Paris I plucked up the courage to telephone David Gascoyne. I had always admired his poetry and I had introductions to him from Stephen* and Oliver†. I was also very interested in him because Stephen never ceased to say how much I reminded him of Gascoyne.

We arranged to meet in the Deux Magots. I arrived, eager, an hour early. He arrived an hour late. I was not at all annoyed: why, after all, should he be in a hurry to meet me? When he eventually appeared, I sat and looked at him in respectful silence. He was tall, angular, with a beautiful twitchy face, masked in spectacles, and long hands which he plaited together incessantly. In fact his entire aura was one of such nervousness and sensitivity that, respect apart, I felt almost afraid to speak: it was as though I might upset him if I spoke. This was a pity, because Gascoyne himself seemed neither to intend to speak nor to be able to speak. From time to time he pursed his sensitive mouth, as though about to utter, but no words were ever audible, and I soon realized this was a nervous mannerism.

After about twenty minutes of this, he heaved himself forward in his chair, and with an apparent effort, said, 'This is rather a treat for me. I haven't been out of the house for three weeks.' I inquired

---

* Stephen Spender, English essayist, novelist and poet, who was at the time the editor of the literary magazine, *Encounter*.

† Oliver Bernard, poet and memoirist, best known for his translations of Arthur Rimbaud and Apollinaire.

if he had been ill. 'No,' he said, and relapsed into silence. At last even I became desperate. I reached into my pocket, fished out some poems, and asked if he would read them. An expression of dismay flickered over his face. 'I don't,' he said, 'read poetry at all now.' Crushed, I put my poems away. After another twenty minutes or so he suddenly rose. 'Goodbye,' he said. He turned away, leaving me feeling dejected and inadequate. I ordered another drink, and was sipping it when Gascoyne suddenly reappeared by my side, as though by some feat of levitation. 'Er, perhaps,' he said, 'you'd like a drink at the flat tomorrow. Six o'clock. Er, goodbye.' He vanished once more, but left me much more cheerful.

At this time Gascoyne had lived in Paris for several years. He had recently written a radio play, *Night Thoughts*, which had been his first work for some time. I resolved to ask him whether he had written anything more since. I arrived at his flat to find him very carefully mixing vodka martinis. Several platefuls of canapés stood on a table. He gravely handed me a martini and inquired if it was too dry. I said it was delicious, it was, and then blurted out my question. Gascoyne looked stricken, and said, 'I can't write poetry any more.' Like most of his statements, it was final: he didn't bother to elaborate, but left it to stand like a No Trespassing sign. He continued to look extremely displeased for some time, but then sat down, and asked me if I knew various friends of his in London. Unfortunately, I didn't, at that time, so the conversation once more came to a halt. I nibbled at the canapés, which were excellent, and finally I said they were. To my amazement, Gascoyne's eyes lit up. He proceeded to explain, in a lively and even witty way, how they were made. This took him a long while, but afterwards he seemed to unbend, and even talked about contemporary English poetry, little of which he seemed to like.

My admiration and affection for Gascoyne have always remained absolute, and for years now I have been trying to discover whether or not he has in fact written new verse. Once, when he was staying with me in London, years after our first meeting, I thought I was on to something. In his luggage was an enormous notebook, of which he took the greatest care, reassuring himself every so often that it was intact and safe. I felt that it must be filled with new poems, and one day I asked him boldly if I could look at it. To my surprise, he consented at once, and with an air of pride. The book was full of recipes for dishes, carefully cut out of French and English magazines, with notes in Gascoyne's own tall poet's hand. 'It's taken me twenty years to collect all those,' Gascoyne said.

In Rome I found a small hotel near the station, devoted a fortnight to exploring the city on foot, as in Paris, and then evolved a new working schedule. It was February, and occasional flutters of snow fell from a dirty sky. This excited me because though I had seen snow lying still on mountains, I had never before actually seen it fall. I started to walk in the snow, working poems out in my head, and I was pleased with the results. The feathery sting of the flakes aroused something rich and bitter in me, which I was able to transmit to paper, to my own satisfaction at least. I was happy in Rome, I was working well, and also I liked the people very much, the elaborate courtesy and occasional vivacity. Armed with a phrase book and a sharp ear, I was able in a short while to pick up enough Italian to get around with.

Stephen had given me an introduction to Marguerite Caetani, who published the massive quarterly, *Botteghe Oscure.* Princess Caetani was an American, who had married into an aristocratic Italian family, and she had been associated with literary magazines for years: in the '20s she had worked with T.S. Eliot, and most writers of reputation had appeared in *Botteghe Oscure.* A lot of awful writers had too, but Princess Caetani's taste was very catholic.

I sent her some poems, with Stephen's note, and a few days later received a letter in large scrawly handwriting, inviting me to tea. I put on my best suit, and arrived at the palazzo, in the street from which her magazine took its name, exactly on time. The gatekeeper put me into a creaky lift, and I rose slowly through several floors. When the lift stopped, an old lady in a drab dress opened the door. Beyond stood a svelte elderly woman, I stepped up to her, murmured, 'How do you do?' and made to shake her hand. She refused to take it, and waved towards the old lady. 'That is the Principessa,' she said, 'I am the maid.'

To my relief, when I turned back, the Princess was laughing. She was, I now saw, a very beautiful old lady. There was a girl's laugh inside her laugh. She took my arm and led me firmly into a large room, filled with manuscripts—'before you make any more mistakes'—and there she sat me down on a sofa and sat herself down by me. In the next half hour she took my shyness in her hand and calmly threw it away. She appeared so interested in me, and so enthusiastic about my work, that I started to talk. I talked so much, in fact, that she asked me to stay to dinner. Here I met her husband. The Princess was then about eighty, and her husband was some years older. He was grave and courteous, but did not speak much, except to say that he had been in India, for the Durbar in 1902, and to inquire whether I numbered any of the Indian princes he had met then among my friends.

After that I called at the palazzo a good deal. The Princess mothered me in a brusque, unfussy way. 'You aren't used to the cold,' she said. 'You must wear a thick sweater,' in that soft voice that had not quite lost its American accent, and next time I arrived she handed me two sweaters which she had bought, and insisted I put one on. She had decided to print a substantial number of my poems, and paid me far more than the normal rate for them. In some curious way she filled me with confidence, and, unfailingly, made me talk as much as any unshy person.

Several young Americans resident in Rome whirred round the palazzo like a circus of tiger moths. They were all writers, who assisted the Princess in the production of the magazine. One of them, Eugene Walter, the novelist, infuriated me by always calling me 'Dear Plum-coloured Creature'. But they were all very friendly, and after leaving the palazzo, we tended to drink together through the afternoon. Through the Princess I also met Giorgio Bassani, so handsome and polished I could scarcely believe he was real, Moravia, pale and austere, with an impressive limp, and Pier Paolo Pasolini, who, scowling in Italian under a dockworker's cap, deliberately untidy in blue denim, I liked the best of the three.

Through her I met also another American poet on a fleeting visit to Rome. He had taken a flat in the Lungo Tevere, and invited me there for a drink. I arrived to find him already very drunk. He was slumped in a chair, his large, hairy hands hanging slack, his mouth working and producing muffled sounds. One of his friends, a young Italian, shrugged his shoulders expressively. 'What the hell? He's often like this in the evening. Have a drink anyway.' Presently the American lurched slowly to his feet, stared blindly at us, and stumbled off down the passage. 'The trouble is,' said the young Italian, 'he can't write poems any more. What the hell, I say, what is it so marvellous, to write—you have *soldi,* anything you want you can have, me, too, what the hell—but no, no, he can't write, so he drinks like pigs. *Allora...*' and he wrung his slim shoulders out like towels, and flashed his teeth. We had a few more drinks, and he became very comradely. 'Those pigs in there has passed out, what the hell, we go out and find some womans now.' He waved ample curves into the air. 'I like womans better,' he explained.

I asked, at this point, where I could pee. He pointed down the passage. 'At the ends there, I will telephone some womans meanwhile.' I went down the passage, opened the bathroom door and discovered the American seated, naked, on the lavatory seat. He opened his mouth and bubbled at me. I was about to withdraw when I saw that he was holding his hands out towards me, and on each wrist was a sickle-shaped cut, from which blood dripped to the floor. The stippled red and white arms, sliced like pomegranates, waved slowly in the air, as though in appeal. I shouted for the Italian. He arrived and surveyed the scene with a certain disgusted calm. 'This is not the first time, what the hell. You better leave now, I take care of him. No womans tonight,' he said, wrinkling his lips furiously, and took a first-aid kit out of the bathroom cupboard.

I had always known that my vocation was ferocious, but not that it was as ferocious as this. It terrified me when I thought of the years ahead. The wrestle with words was difficult enough, but when that wrestle stopped, the horror happened. Eliot had remarked that anyone once visited by the muse was thereafter haunted by her. What appalling ghost had caused Gascoyne's silence and the dripping wrists of the American poet? I took my problem to the Princess, who shook her wise beautiful head. 'Dear boy,' she said, 'you poets are temperamental people.' I loved the Princess, but her answer disappointed me. Perhaps nobody who wasn't a poet could understand.

Rome, full of beautiful women, filled me with frustration. So aware of their bodies under their clothes, so aware that the men around were aware of their bodies, the young actresses primping their way down the Via Veneto were the incessant objects of my lust. I actually met some of them, on the occasions when I drank with Italian writers, but their presence paralysed me: scented, stroked, no hair out of place. A flutter of Italian came from their petalled lips, only ceasing when they threw back their heads to display round white throats and send deliberately projected laughter towards the café awning.

I had become a great deal more confident. Travel had done it for me, probably, and the Princess: I was still quiet, but I could now take part in a conversation without strain. However, towards women my attitude remained the same: I was too terrified of making a fool of myself to ask a girl out. I therefore adopted a cool, disdainful attitude towards the young women I met, to conceal my desire and fear, and thereby confirmed everyone's opinion that I was homosexual.

After some weeks in Rome, I decided to try somewhere else. The idea of islands appealed to me: Sardinia and Sicily were my chosen destination. With considerable difficulty, I packed my case myself, and departed for Sardinia.

I landed in Sassari, in the north of the island, a tilted town that climbed the side of a hill. I had booked, through an agency, into the biggest hotel, and into it, unshaven and tired, I wandered one crisp clear day. An effusive manager welcomed me (I appeared to be the only guest), consigned my case to a porter, and informed me that the receptionist would collect my passport. The receptionist took some time to appear, but when she did she turned out to be a pretty young blonde. Her breasts...swelled out her pink sweater, and as usual I concealed my little leap of desire with a cold and disdainful expression, which she answered in kind.

I went up to my room, had a bath, changed, and explored Sassari. Everywhere I went in the tilted streets I was followed by long trains of intent children. They had obviously never seen anyone my colour before, and were anxious to drink me in. After a day of this, I returned to the hotel anxious for a drink myself. I had just ordered one in the bar when I found the receptionist at my elbow. To my surprise, she smiled a very sweet smile, and then raised her arms to arrange her hair in a way that ensured a certain effusion of bosom under the pink sweater.

'I speak French,' she said in French. 'My name is Raffaela.'

'Oh yes?' I murmured.

'I come from Milano, and I am here to study hotel management. But Sassari is very boring. There is no culture here. In Milano we have all the arts. Here there are none. However, there is a cinema. There is a performance tonight. Would you like to come? I feel it is our duty to care for our visitors.'

She hadn't told me that the hotel manager was coming too.

Winter or not, the night was dry, hot and dusty. The manager drove us to a plaster-walled hall, whose tin roof confronted the galaxies afloat above. A large and noisy crowd sat on wooden chairs inside. We sat down too, Raffaela in the middle. A Disney film, dubbed into Italian, started. As it started, I had the peculiar, detached, weightless feeling I had so often experienced before, of being separated from my body, and as though from a long way off I felt the weight of Raffaela's hand in my hand. This warm and solid object was something I did not know what to do with: I turned it about helplessly in my fingers, and, still as though from a distance, noticed that Raffaela's other hand was entwined with one of the manager's hands. After the film Raffaela smiled a flushed happy smile and said, 'I hope you liked it.' I said I did.

Thereafter, throughout my fortnight in Sassari, I seated myself, every night, in the bar. The manager usually served, and a crowd of friendly Sardinians milled around, buying me drinks, and trying to explain dirty jokes to me in Italian. But at a certain time Raffaela floated in, blonde, pretty, bosomy, and there was a silence. The crowd rifted. She sat down beside me, and started demurely to sew. The crowd went to the bar, and appeared to chaff the manager, whose face at these moments became unhappy and sweaty.

Raffaela told me how miserable she was in Sassari, and how she had loved to play the violin. I told her I was a poet. 'Ah, when I saw your beautiful eyes,' she said tenderly, 'I knew you were like me.' Though unused to this sort of conversation, I retorted gallantly that her eyes were beautiful too. Sometimes she bent towards me, and her hair brushed my face. I tried not to look down her blouse. She was unhappy, I remembered, and I felt compelled to play the role of *preux chevalier.*

The night before I left, Raffaela whispered, 'You haven't shown me your poems.' I suggested that I bring them down to the bar. 'Oh, not here,' she said. 'There are too many people. I'll come to your room later, but we must be very quick. You see, I sleep quite close to the manager's room. He,' she explained, 'is my uncle, and he swore to my parents that he would look after me.'

I retired to bed in a state of nerves. Eventually, there was a knock at the door. Raffaela floated in. 'Oh,' she whispered, 'I'm so tired. May I lie down?' She lay down on my bed, and smiled a gentle, absorbed smile. 'It's very hot,' she said, and undid the top button of her blouse. I averted my eyes chivalrously, produced some poems, and began, laboriously, to translate them into French.

'Oh, how beautiful they are,' Raffaela murmured. 'How beautiful.' She rubbed her nyloned feet slowly together, with a noise like that of Eve's serpent. 'I haven't much time,' she added, rather briskly. I wavered above her. I knew precisely what I wanted to do, but it seemed to me it would be awful to betray the trust of someone who had actually ventured to come to my bedroom, starved of culture, to listen to my poems. 'There are,' I said, 'a lot more,' and started once more on my translations.

I kept my eyes carefully averted from Raffaela, so that she could rest assured of my trustworthiness, and after a while was surprised to hear her sigh deeply and rise. 'I must go,' she said rather coldly, 'it's late.' I said, 'There are still quite a lot.' She said it didn't matter, and departed.

All next day, on the bus to Cagliari, the capital of the south, I wondered.

I was in Mycenae. I had arrived hot and dusty on the local bus from Corinth, my stomach in disorder after being loaded with bread, cheese and retzina by the other passengers. I booked into the Belle Helene at the foot of the valley. Agamemnon, the proprietor, beckoned me into his office after lunch. 'Antichi,' he said, putting his fingers to his lips, 'very old, very valuable,' and produced a few bits of broken pottery. 'I sell,' said Agamemnon hopefully. I shook my head. He frowned. 'You American?' he inquired in a strong Bronx accent. I denied this. He beamed.

'Aha. You no American, I no sell. Drink wine now,' and he stood several drinks. He was a square-set, pleasantly shabby man with a grey military moustache. Outside his valley shook out its humped dramatic hills in the cold sunshine.

I had rummaged round Sardinia and Sicily for a few weeks, and then returned to Rome, where the Princess showed me the proofs of my poems, the first I had ever corrected. I told her I was leaving for Athens. 'Well, dear boy,' she murmured, 'I'll send you some money there.' I protested that I had already been paid. She raised her beautiful eyebrows. 'But you're *bound* to need money in Athens. I'll send it to the American Express.' I sailed next day from Brindisi, and presently, across the short sea, a white headland rose into the dawn, bathed in the strange iridescent sunshine which is a property of Greece. As the ship chugged down past the broad white face of the headland, I leant on the rails and, looking up, imagined that the ridges and fissures in the rock detached themselves into the flesh of statuary, so that gods and dead Greeks floated in the substance of the cliff. This illusion of the past and present intermixed persisted in me wherever I went in Greece.

Except Athens. On later visits I knew in which cafés I should find the poets, Odysseus Elytis, Nikos Gatsos, or Nanos Valaoritis, and sought them out always. In this first visit I didn't, and patrolled the white city alone. I was disappointed because Athens was like any other city. But once, in Constitution Square, I was astonished to see hundreds of leaflets, like gulls, fly from a window and float upon the wind, while a hoarse voice thundered like the voice of Zeus, and the people turned wild dark faces upward to the falling and fluttering scraps of white. It was only part of an election campaign, but for one sculptural moment it was like a frieze out of history.

From Athens I visited all the usual places, but because the gold masks, lions, and beehive tombs of Mycenae fascinated me, I left it to the last. Now, under the patriarchal eye of Agamemnon, I started to walk the shaly road up the valley. The afternoon sun burned and stood still overhead. There was nobody about and no sound apart from the scrape and swish of my steps. I passed a couple of beehive tombs slotted into the hillside: it looked dark and cool inside, but I did not enter. I climbed the fortress hill to the Lion Gate. The massed, hewn stone, in the hot silence, hung like a promise or threat. Beyond, the burial pits, with grass and spring flowers shrouding them, absorbed me, and I passed, as had passed at Kanheri, into a concentrated fixity, studying an ant, a grass-blade, the porous skin on my hand. Nothing moved except the sun: the only sound was the boom of the wind as it slapped at hollows in the rock. For a century I stood on the hill, with time below me.

Afterwards I remember descending endless slippery steps into the belly of the fortress, and emerging at last at an embrasure that stared from darkness down a sunlit thicketed hillside to the valley. When I came up once more, the sun was dying: the wind had turned cold, and hooted like an owl: the fortress hooded itself in shadow. Prescience of blood filled me with a static sort of fear, and I scrambled down the hillside and walked fast all the way back to the hotel.

This first visit to Mycenae later influenced much of my work, poems in which images of kings, hills, and burial recur. I did not know this then, but was very elated, and consumed a quantity of alcohol before, during, and after dinner. Then I decided to walk to the hill tombs. Agamemnon, clearly acclimatized to the oddities of his visitors, furnished me with a torch and a bottle of ouzo. It was very dark outside, the wind had picked up density and volume, and made a rustling, crashing, and roaring noise all round me as I leant into it. I fought it all the way up the road to the nearest tomb. The entrance was closed, but I scrambled up on the hill above, lay down, sipped my ouzo, and looked at a vast yellow moon dragging clouds across the sky. After a while, above the roaring of the wind, I imagined that I heard a deep, vibrant humming, as though the former occupant of the tomb below me was singing in his sleep. I listened, entranced, for some time before I stumbled back to the Belle Helene. All night the walls of the hotel creaked and swayed in the wind as though they were planks of a ship built perhaps by Ulysses.

On my first day in Iraklion, the capital of Crete, I was puzzling over the cauldrons in a taverna kitchen, trying to work out what to eat, when a stocky man with a moustache approached me, and said, 'Allow me to suggest another place. This place is very bad.' As usual, I allowed myself to be led, and followed him out, pursued by the imprecations of the proprietor. 'I am Carrousis,' said my new friend, once outside, 'here is my card.' His card, a very grubby one, said he was a guide. I eyed him warily, but he made no approaches. He led me to another taverna in silence. Then he said, 'Permit me to order. I can recommend the kirios to try the cheese pie.' He ordered, and vanished. Later, mellowed by an excellent lunch, I ambled out into Venizelos Square, and suddenly observed Carrousis at my elbow. 'I hope,' he said, 'that the kirios enjoyed his lunch. Permit me to buy him a drink.' Half-an-hour later, full of raki and goodwill, I employed him to charter a car and show me round the island.

Carrousis had worked under Pendlebury, the archaeologist who was killed in Crete during the war, and he knew his profession. He was, I think, the only good guide I have ever met. He had no patter: he only explained what I asked him to explain, and he explained laconically and without fuss. He took me all over the island: he even, though plump and elderly, scrambled with me up the slopes of Mount Ida to the rocky Khameres cave, one of the holy places of the Minoans. At first, however, he was a little aloof: he had the withdrawn pensive appearance of a seal, with his whiskers and mournful eyes. He was, in fact, a proud man, and had perhaps suffered too many rebuffs from tourists to attempt friendship with one. When we lunched in some village taverna, therefore, he sat apart with the driver, leaving me alone with the excellent lunch he had ordered. He always addressed me in the third person, as 'the kirios'. It got on my nerves.

Eventually, one day, as we were prospecting the ruins of Gortyna, a shepherd rose out of a wilderness of thistles and inquired where I came from. He spoke a kind of Italian, and informed me that he had been a guerrilla, with Pendlebury, during the war. Once reassured that I was not German, he elaborated on this.

'Italiani bad soldier. Fire rifle, Italiani run, Italiani kaput. Tedeschi good soldier, Tedeschi brave, no run. But Italiani very good man, like children, kind. Tedeschi bad man, shoot children. Bad soldier, good man. Good soldier, bad man.'

This piece of philosophy i6+mpressed me. Apparently it also impressed Carrousis. As we ate a picnic lunch in the shade, he unbent. He talked about the occupation of Crete, and his friendship with Pendlebury. That night, in another village taverna, the driver and he both sat at my table. We started to buy each other drinks, and to converse on subjects other than archaeology. Carrousis's wife had died in the war, leaving him with several children to rear. He had developed arthritis in his hands, which prevented him from doing archaeological work. So he had become a guide. But he was perpetually short of money, because tourists preferred guides with a patter, and perhaps a line in local humour.

He started to adopt a very fatherly attitude towards me. He introduced me to his unmarried daughter, a considerable act of friendship on the part of a Greek, and particularly a Cretan. He gave me advice on life, most of which was sensible, but all of which I have forgotten. We had a marvellous time. In those blue brilliant days, climbing against the senile white-haired mountains, with the glittering sea spread out beyond the vineyards and groves of olives: or driving through the hot plains, occasionally stopping at a poor, dusty village with beautifully carved lintels above the doors, to drink coffee with a brigand-like headman, we became friends. There was no part of Crete he did not show me, and explain to me. We called each other by our first names.

But at last, the day before I left, he brought me his bill. I was appalled. It was three times the price he had quoted at the start. It meant that I would have just enough left to pay the hotel, and would have to return to London at once. Friendship and treachery, someone had told me, were closely allied in some Greeks, but I could not believe it of Carrousis. Because we were supposed to be friends, I didn't want to haggle with him. I paid him, but I was full of hurt and fury. When he invited me to have a farewell drink with him at his house, I coldly declined. He was obviously hurt too, but I didn't care, in fact I was pleased. He went off quietly and proudly. His last words were, 'I hope the kirios has a pleasant voyage.'

Next day, smouldering still, I went down to the harbour. Carrousis was on the quay. He came up rather awkwardly and said, 'I have arranged for the kirios to have a single cabin, and I have ordered his meals from the steward.'

'What do you charge for that?' I inquired, and was instantly ashamed of myself.

Carrousis flushed deeply. He said, 'I'm sorry that my charges were more than you expected. Here is half the money back.'

He pushed it into my hand. I was pleased and repentant all at once. 'Don't be silly, Theodosius,' I said. 'I had a wonderful time, and it was worth much more.'

He smiled, but continued to press the money on me. I continued to refuse it. Eventually he laughed and said he would buy me a drink instead. So we had one, quickly because the boat was due to leave, and he waved goodbye as it surged away from the Cretan coast. We had parted friends, but not quite the same friends as before. For the first time I thought about money as something in itself, an entity which affected relationships between people, and decided that money was a terrible thing.

The Princess saved me. When I returned to Athens £100 was waiting at the American Express. More scrupulous then than now, I wondered if I should accept it, then decided I could pay it back in kind, with the poems I had written in Greece. I bought Frank Harris's autobiography in the five-volume Olympia Press edition, and took the Orient Express to Belgrade.*

Just before the Yugoslav frontier, sudden doubts overcame me. I knew that Harris's book was banned in England. I wondered if it was also banned in Yugoslavia. There was no logical reason why it should be, but I wondered. I was not yet eighteen, so it seemed to me highly likely that if it was banned, I should spend some considerable time inside a Communist prison. I seized a moment when the compartment was empty to stuff the five volumes into the ventilator. The result of this was that for the next five hours the temperature in the compartment rose steadily, till it resembled an oven. Streaming with sweat, I climbed out of the Orient Express into a wilderness of Belgrade snow. Thickly it carpeted the ground, and thickly it fell from the sky, which was pitch dark, since it was two in the morning.

I shivered my way down the platform till I found a decrepit and toothless porter, who spoke a mixture of German and English. I demanded a hotel. There were no taxis. He heaved my case and typewriter to his shoulders, and plodded ahead of me through the arctic weather. We traversed numerous deserted, snow-covered streets, till we came to the Moskva. It was full. The porter, a phlegmatic man, led me to two more hotels. Both were full. He then conducted me to the tourist office. Despite the hour, it was open. As we entered, like two travelling snowmen, an elderly official from behind the information desk bounded forward, kissed me loudly on both cheeks, and exclaimed in English. 'Ah! My African brother!' For some reason I was infuriated, but my supposed nationality seemed to work wonders. Within minutes he had found me a room in somebody's house. I paid my rent to the official. Then the porter, who was nauseatingly cheerful, and I set off on another terrible trek through wind and snow.

---

* *My Life and Loves*, privately printed.

After about half an hour, I began to feel like an icicle. Doubts assailed me as whether I would ever thaw out. Suddenly the porter dumped my luggage in the snow. 'Is it here?' I chattered, relieved. 'Ja, ja,' said the porter. He took me by the arm and led me for some distance past faceless houses, till we arrived at the foot of a large statue entirely covered in snow. The porter pointed at this. 'Tito,' he said. 'Ist gut.' I restrained an impulse to hit him. 'How far are we,' I asked carefully, 'from das Haus?' 'Ja, ja,' he said. We plodded back to my luggage and the journey continued.

We reached the house at last. A cheerful Serbian maid opened the door, and whisked us into a warm kitchen, where an enormous wood stove crackled and spat. I paid the porter, and, dripping with melted snow, followed the maid to a large and handsome bedroom. Into the snowdrift of an immense bed I sank, wet, cold, and miserable, and slept heavily.

When I awoke next morning I felt very ill, but felt also that I must bestir myself. So I rose and dressed. I noted, while I was doing so, that this was obviously a woman's room. There was a dressing table littered with cosmetics, and on the bedside table stood the photograph of a very beautiful, dark-haired young woman with a child.

The originals of these photographs were seated in the kitchen. The woman was even more beautiful than in the photograph. She had very vivid violet eyes which contrasted with her raven hair, and a pearl-pale Slavonic face. Her daughter, who was about six, looked very much like her. Also in the kitchen was the maid, and to my dismay, the porter. He looked more decrepit and toothless than ever in the day.

'How do you do,' said the beautiful brunette, in French. 'This is my house. You are very welcome. Please have some coffee.' I drank some coffee, while the porter nodded and winked conspiratorially at me. Presently I inquired what he wanted. 'He says,' translated the lady, 'that he will show you round Belgrade.' Though I could not imagine a more undesirable guide, it struck me that, since I didn't know where I was, and spoke no Serbian, he might be useful. So we departed together.

I had no idea where we were bound for, but the porter did. Half-way down the snowy street, he stopped, pointed to a bar, made repulsive drinking noises, and said, 'Schnapps.' I replied, 'New.' '*Ja, ja,*' he said. '*Ist gut*' Inside the bar he smacked down three rapid tumblerfuls of *slivovitz,* for which I paid. We then continued. But the porter's broken boots only seemed capable of leading him to bars. Utterly helpless, since I would have been lost without him, I followed him through about six. Meanwhile I began to shiver, not only because of the cold. I could feel my cheeks burning with fever, and an iron vice seemed to have fastened round my chest. Frank Harris had bequeathed me a very bad chill. Finally I said to the porter, '*Das Haus.*' '*Nein,*' he replied defiantly, 'schnapps.' I didn't even know the address of the house, and was starting to feel as though I would collapse. In the next bar I waved a fistful of dinars in the porter's face. He put down his *slivovitz* and squinted at them. '*Raus,*' I said. '*Das Hause.* Then *sie baben* this.' He appeared to understand, and we crunched back through the snow. The house, to my surprise, was only five minutes' walk away. Once there, I did collapse, and was put efficiently to bed by my hostess and the maid.

They didn't report my illness to the tourist office, which they were supposed to do, so that I could be removed to hospital. Instead, they nursed me, fed me broth, herb tea, and medicine, and supplied endless hot bricks for my feet. My hostess went into town and found some English magazines. She would sit and talk to me in a soothing husky voice. Her name was Dragika, and she had been a widow for three years. Her husband, an engineer, had been killed in an accident, and since then she had let rooms to guests to supplement her income. The room I slept in was in fact her bedroom.

Dragika's brilliant violet eyes brightened and darkened like a cat's, under her long dark lashes. One day, when they were dark, she told me that she had been raped, when she was twelve, by a dozen German soldiers. I felt sorrow and pity: her gentleness when she described the incident touched me terrifyingly. She was now about twenty-five. I fell, naturally, madly in love with her.

Winnowing the Wind (1959)

The Rana's Palace

Ved* had decided to come to Nepal with me. My father arranged that we should stay with a Nepalese general of his acquaintance. He armed me with introductions to the general and to Mr Gupta, his correspondent there, and the day after I had seen the Dalai Lama, Ved and I left for Patna en route to Kathmandu.

From Patna we flew for an hour across the yellow flood-smudged plains of Bihar. Ved slept phlegmatically at my side, and I took surreptitious pulls at my hip-flask, avoiding the cold eye of the air-hostess. Then the Heron began to flounder among clouds, and knobbly forested hills appeared below. The hills matured and became mountains: the Heron mountain-hopped, sailing between two scarred peaks, rising to miss a third, dropping between two more, and Ved awoke amidst the bounces. 'What in hell is happening now, Dominie?'

'Mountains,' I said. 'We must be nearly there.'

We were, for the Heron skipped neatly over a final peak, and slanted down to the Kathmandu Valley.

We landed on a narrow brown airstrip, with slate-coloured

---

* Ved Mehta, journalist, traveller and memoirist, who has written twenty-seven books of fiction and non-fiction. He has been completely blind since the age of three.

buffaloes scattering along the runway as the Heron came down. When we climbed out the sun hit us: a gross sun looking from the exact centre of the sky, frizzling the grass.

'For a seasoned traveller,' Ved said, 'your information is a bit unreliable. I thought you said it would be freezing in Nepal.'

'I thought it might be,' I said humbly, and we walked to the Customs building.

We were clearing our luggage when Mr Gupta came up. He was small and plump, in a brown suit, and he said, 'Mr Mehta and Mr Moraes?'

'Yes.'

'Your plane is very late. The General Sahib came yesterday, he came today, but you did not come. Now he has gone to Parliament, but he has left you his car.'

We cleared our luggage, and Mr Gupta showed us to the General's car.

'I will see you later,' Mr Gupta said. 'You will be very comfortable in the palace.'

As we drove away, Ved said, 'What did he mean, the palace? We're not staying with the King, are we?'

'Well,' I said, 'this general probably lives in a palace.'

'This,' said Ved, 'is going to be quite something, Dommie.'

The Kathmandu valley is very flat, but it is ringed round by mountains. It was these mountains, enormous and thickly forested, their shadows slanting into the lowlands, that were the first things one noticed, and we never got away from them. Wherever you go in Nepal the mountains come with you, in shadow or in substance: the eastern Himalayas; and away to the north, Everest.

The valley is cultivated, mostly: the peasants grow rice, maize, and beans, buffaloes pull the carved wooden ploughs in the narrow acres, and everywhere the bearded speargrass waves in wind, and red hibiscus coils suddenly out of the trees. We passed through three or four villages on the way into Kathmandu: Nepalese women, full-breasted and brown, dressed in tunics and skirts, pounded maize before every door, and the doors were as beautiful as they: very old, wooden, carved intricately, rather meaninglessly, but intricately; now and then they leant open and children fell squalling into each dirty street.

It took us about half an hour to reach the palace.

We reached it by turning off the main road and scrambling a hundred yards up a dirt track. People sat on each side of the track, mostly women, with cloths spread before them on the ground, covered with red peppers and speargrass drying in the sun. As we passed, they rose, making deep obeisance, unsmilingly respectful. I told Ved.

'They must be very polite people in Nepal,' Ved said.

'It's probably only that we are in the General's car.'

We drove through wrought-iron gates, shushed over a gravel drive winding through ornamental gardens, and arrived at the palace. It was a huge, ugly building, four storeys high, uncompromising in the green September, the Himalayas behind it.

The driver turned to us. 'The palace of the Rana,' he said.

Two servants met us in the high entrance-hall of the palace. They took our bags, and led us through a courtyard to a flight of stairs. Then we climbed four floors, through winding corridors and anterooms, to a long gallery with rooms leading off it. All the corridors were hung with framed illustrations from *Picture Post*, *Titbits*, and so on, alternating with the heads of assassinated tigers, glaring soulfully through glass eyes, and photographs of dead Ranas, tiger-whiskered, soulful-eyed, clutching their jewelled swords. The servants showed us into a sitting-room off the gallery. The gallery was obviously part of the General's own quarters; the sitting-room was festooned in the same way as the corridors had been, and furnished with huge overstuffed chairs, elephant's-foot ashtrays, and beautifully carved Nepalese tables. Presents from Clacton stood on the tables. The tigers leered inexhaustibly from the walls. We sank into a sofa and the servants disappeared. We heard voices in the distance.

'I expect someone will come for us,' I said.

'Coo, Dommie!' Ved said, 'this really is a palace.'

At this point I became aware of an enormous Himalayan bear crouched next to the sofa. It glowered at me. I gasped.

'Now what is it?'

'There is a bear next to us. It must,' I added, groping for commonsense, 'be stuffed.'

'Honestly, Dommie, I know you have a fantasy-life, but what do you think? Have you ever known anybody who kept a live bear in their drawing-room?'

'I only wondered,' I was beginning lamely, when the bear rose, snarled at us, and shambled loosely out through the farther door.

I was saved from the necessity of comment by the appearance of a plump, handsome lady in a sari. She floated toward us, smiling and making the namaskar. We introduced ourselves and she sat by us, smiling still. She was the General's wife, and she spoke only Hindi. In fact she was Indian, from the Kangra Valley, for the Ranas from time immemorial have married in India in order to keep the Rana blood uncontaminated.

I had picked up a little Hindi, by now, and was not as embarrassed as I might have been. Ved filled in my gaps.

'You look very much like your father,' said the Rani; she had a very soft, calming, dreaming voice, and I even forgot the bear for a few minutes. Then I felt I should mention it.

'There was a bear here a few minutes ago,' I said, feeling idiotic.

'Ah yes,' said the Rani dreamily. 'Which bear?'

'You have several?'

'Oh yes. That is one thing you must be careful about: don't go out at night; they don't see very well in the dark, and they might not know you were guests.'

And then, smiling, 'Would you like some tea? And then a bath? I know what boys are.'

It was very soothing. 'I will send my son in to see you,' she said. 'He is your age.'

The son came in a few minutes later. He was thin, pale and bespectacled; he wore jodhpurs and a long coat, and on his head a bucket-shaped cloth hat.

'You are poets,' he said.

'Mr Moraes is,' said Ved. 'So he frequently tells me.'

'That is good, I too am a poet.' He paused and beamed.

We remained silent, so he went on, 'The best in Nepal, except for Devkota of course.' After another short silence, he continued, 'That is because I am the only poet of high birth: I am the only poet who is a Rana.'

'What are your poems about?' Ved asked.

'They are about the struggles of the poor. I am very liberal-minded, you see.'

The Rani brought in the tea. We drank it in silence.

Finally the poet said: 'You are here for long?'

'Oh, fairly long,' I replied.

'Excellent! I shall read my poems to you frequently in the evenings. It will help to pass your time.'

We finished our tea. 'Poor boys,' the Rani said, 'you must be tired. Your servant will take you to your room. Pannalal!' she called. A lean sulky Nepalese appeared and the Rani handed us over to him.

Our room was one floor up, at the top. It was a sort of hall, furnished with two vast mosquito-curtained beds. The walls were entirely covered with photographs of dead whiskery Ranas. Pannalal stood by the door, hands folded.

'The dining-room is next door,' he said. 'You will take your breakfast there.'

'All right,' I said.

He remained where he was.

'It's all right,' I said. 'We don't need you.'

'I am your servant,' he said. 'I will stay here. You may need me suddenly.'

Suddenly there were footsteps on the stairs. The poet appeared.

'Is everything all right?' he said. 'If this dog here does not serve you properly, beat him. My father will see you for dinner at seven-thirty.' He nodded, and went away. A minute later he came back.

'I have written four new poems today. I am very prolific. I have nothing to do all day, and I find poetry a good pastime. Shall I come before dinner and read them to you?'

'That would be a great pleasure,' Ved said limply.

The poet departed. Pannalal remained.

I fished the whisky out of my suitcase. 'I think we need a drink.'

'Yes,' Ved said.

We drank in silence, under Pannalal's eye. Then Ved said, 'It's an odd prospect.'

'Yes,' I said.

They were the last feudal overlords that the world has seen, these Ranas. Originally Indian princelings, they crossed the high passes into Nepal hundreds of years ago, and established themselves as the ruling class. The King still sat in Kathmandu, but the Ranas pulled the strings, and he danced for them. All over Kathmandu they built their fantastic palaces, where they lived, bearded pard-men in jewelled robes, surrounded by the women they had abducted from their families, with the power of life and death over any Nepalese who was not a Rana. When one of them passed, any ordinary citizen who failed to do obeisance till he was out of sight was thrown into gaol. As late as 1942 the chief Rana used to ride an elephant through the streets of Kathmandu every month. The women of the town were required to stand outside their houses, and whichever took the Rana's fancy were immediately seized by his soldiers and taken to his harem. If husbands or fathers bothered the Rana thereafter they were gaoled. One village, Halembu, in the mountains, renowned for its beautiful women, was raided and the entire female population taken off to the harems.

One reason for this abounding appetite was probably that the Ranas were bored: they had nothing to do but copulate. One result of it was that over the years three distinct grades of Rana emerged: first-class Ranas, born of a legal wife, second-class Ranas, the sons of established mistresses, and third-class Ranas, the unfortunate result of slips that passed in the night. Every Rana, however, whatever class he belongs to, is born with the rank of general. He is also born with a name: Shumshere Jung Bahadur Rana.

Nepal is an independent state. It has been invaded, but not often. For one thing, it was always difficult to get to the Kathmandu Valley, which is sealed in by mountains: Tibet to the north, Sikkim to the east, Bengal to the south, and Kumaon westward. The Gurkhas were the most successful of the invaders: they conquered and occupied the country in 1768, but in due course eddied away into the stream of Nepalese life and became one of the races of the country. Later the Nepalese signed treaties with the British, and helped them during the Indian Mutiny and the First World War, supplying them with men, and, rather inexplicably, cardamoms.

Contact with the West had a strange effect on the Ranas. The British officers who visited Kathmandu brought whisky and soda in their mule-trains, and apparently offered it to the Ranas, who drank it, but seem to have felt a little irked at having been outdone. Accordingly they sent emissaries over the mountains to India; and next time the British came, they were offered a drink that put their plebeian beverage to shame. It was whisky and champagne. Excessive consumption of this elixir may explain why most of the Ranas in the nineteenth century died before forty.

The Ranas did everything in a big way. One of the sons of the house where we stayed told me of the time when his father wanted to send him to Eton. To finance the trip they had to approach the head of the family, the grandfather, a Rana of the Ranas. On being told of the project, he flew into a rage.

'No grandson of mine will be permitted to defile himself by

crossing the black waters to England,' he said furiously. 'But I will be reasonable. If you like, you may hire all the masters from Eton and bring them here.'

Later, the grandfather fell ill. A British surgeon was fetched from India. When he arrived, he discovered that the old man's palace was on top an unroaded hill; he could not imagine how he was to get his equipment up. He went to bed that night, still in a quandary, in a tent at the foot of the hill. He awoke next morning to find a road leading from the door of his tent up to the gate of the palace. It had been built in six hours by relays of slave-gangs working through the night.

So the Ranas lived on in their mad palaces, drinking their invented drink, begetting hundreds of children, taxing the men of Nepal and kidnapping the women, until 1951. In that year the Nepalese rose. The Ranas tried to seize the King, who fled to Delhi. They were overthrown. Most of them left the country and settled in Bangalore, a kind of Indian Cheltenham. There they still moulder, seedy old generals planning revolution over glasses of orange juice. The Nepalese Congress took over government and drafted a constitution. Elections were held in 1958, and the Congress, under the youthful B.P. Koirala, came in again with a crushing majority. It is a Socialist party, and such Ranas as remain in Kathmandu are now taxed for the first time in recorded history.

They were also required, in 1951, to cut down on their concubines (some houses had as many as seven hundred) and ordered to reduce this number by two-thirds. As a natural result, on the day when the order was executed, the streets of Kathmandu were filled by hundreds of loudly lamenting women with nowhere to go. Koirala solved the problem very resourcefully by marrying them off to the Assam Riflemen who had come in from India to help him keep the peace.

We were drinking rather gloomily when a plump young man in spectacles, with a round smooth smiling face, bounced in.

Pannalal promptly fell to the floor, kissing his feet. The young man looked embarrassed.

'Get up, get up,' he said, and to us, 'I'm the General's second son, his engineer son. I came to see how you were getting on.'

'Oh, fine,' we said, and he laughed.

'You mean you're bored? Me too. Can I have a drink?'

'Do,' I said, and poured one.

'I thought,' said the engineer son, rapidly draining his glass, 'that you might like to have a peep round the palace.'

'We would indeed,' I said.

'It's very large,' said Ved doubtfully.

'Five hundred rooms. Don't worry, we won't go round them all. They're mostly full of pictures of my ancestors. We could have a look at the courtyard and the grounds.'

'Good,' I said, 'but have another drink.'

We had finished the bottle by the time we rose, and the engineer son was more expansive than ever. He led us down to the ground floor. It was a long way.

'Who lives in these five hundred rooms?'

'Well, my father has five of us, you know. Five sons. We each have quarters for ourselves and our families. Then lots of the rooms are guestrooms, drawing-rooms, that kind of thing. And of course the maidservants have one wing.'

'Maidservants?' inquired Ved. The engineer son laughed and inserted an elbow into Ved's ribs. 'We had more of them before 1951, of course. About two hundred and fifty. Now I think the actual number is about a hundred and fifty. Useful girls, they do everything, ha, ha!' The elbow drove into my ribs this time.

We went out through a carved wooden porch into the main courtyard. The palace was rectangular and the courtyard a rectangle within a rectangle. It was very busy: men and women in loose tunics and felt shoes moved ceaselessly through it—the servants: the women almost all young and pretty. And on three sides of the courtyard there were shops. There were a blacksmith and a goldsmith, a cobbler, a tailor, a barber, a dispensary, and, in one corner, an anonymous doorway to which the engineer son pointed.

'That's the most important of all. The bank.'

He nudged Ved again, laughing.

'Who uses these shops?'

He looked at me, surprised. 'Why, we do. The family. We pay all these people, and they serve us.'

'What's the idea?' Ved said.

'When these palaces were built the Ranas had the idea of setting up autonomous communities in each one. All these people live in our house, and we take care of them. We feed and clothe them, and they serve us. It is like a little city. We even have a school in the grounds, for their children.'

'And are all the Rana's palaces like this?'

'They were,' said the engineer son. 'This is one of the last ones left. Things are changing. It was all very well, but the kind of life we led couldn't have gone on much longer: after all, not so long ago, I would have had the power of life and death over most of these people. It's a good thing,' he added surprisingly, 'that that's all over.'

We moved back through the house into the gardens outside. It was getting dark, and mist came bubbling gently in from the mountains. The engineer son shrugged.

'We'll have to see the grounds some other time. But I'll point a few things out. The stables and the dairies are over there. And the vegetable gardens. The fruit gardens are on the other side of the house. We keep the livestock beyond the stables: they have their paddocks there. Sometime I must show you our pigs; they are the best in Nepal.'

He said, 'We'll have to give it all up in a few years. The taxation is going up under Koirala.'

'Don't you regret it?' Ved said.

'No. I was a boy when the whole thing changed. I've grown up with it. It's the older people who find it difficult. You'll meet some this evening. Meanwhile, why not come up to my sitting-room and have a drink?'

'A pleasure,' we said.

We dined with the General. He was a youngish fifty, and looked very much like his engineer son, except that he wore delicate gold-rimmed pince-nez. He made us a small effusive speech of welcome, but then said nothing: it was obvious that he didn't quite know what to do with us. In the uncomfortable hour after dinner he kept plunging across to one or the other of us, fetching a drink, a cigarette, or an ashtray: he would give it to one, stare searchingly into one's face, his lips rounding as if in surprise, and then plunge back across the room. The poet son sat sulkily quiet, annoyed because we hadn't been there to listen to his poems; the engineer son maintained a discreet silence; there was a third son, who had been at Sandhurst, who talked about shooting, and he was the only one who did talk. The Rani fussed over Ved and me, murmuring like a dove: now and then she asked us if we had any brothers or sisters. That was all, except for a very old Rana, a Field-marshal who sat hunched in a chair all through the evening. He was small, with a round starch-coloured face, the lips puckered in with age; he kept his tiny slippered feet together; his hands, dry leaves, lay together in his lap. He ate and drank with an almost inconspicuous flutter of hand to mouth, a sudden ingestion of the lips: after dinner he smoked, delicately, a cigar. He did not speak at all, except once. Ved was trying to draw the General out on some question of Nepalese politics, the General being a Member of Parliament, and Ved was not succeeding. Finally with a courteous little Oxford swivel of attention, he turned to the Field-marshal.

'What do *you* think, sir?'

The Field-marshal said in a high crackling voice: 'I wish the days were back when we chased the peasants through the streets with *whips*!' Then his face became once more starched and impassive, only he kept sucking in his lips after his remark, as though it had made him thirsty.

It was not a very successful dinner.

When we said goodnight, the General drew himself up, looked over our heads, and said rapidly, 'I hope I have not forgotten anything that would make you comfortable.'

'Oh no, sir,' we said.

The engineer son winked at us and said softly, 'One for the road.'

'What a good idea,' Ved said, and we followed the drink-giver.

When, at about midnight, we stumbled back to our room, we found Pannalal asleep across the doorway. We stepped over him.

'Do you want the light, Dommie?'

'No,' I said.

We undressed in the dark. Ved was quicker than I was. He moved over to his bed while I was still fastening my pyjama trousers. I heard him struggling through the mosquito-curtain, and then came a yell of horror.

My first thought was of stray bears. I rushed to the light-switch and turned it on. Ved was scrambling out of his bed, which now contained a very pretty Nepalese girl. She didn't have any clothes on. When I turned to my bed, there was one there too. She laughed and made an unmistakable gesture.

Pannalal had now woken up. He stood doomfully in the door, wiping the sleep out of his eyes. `What are these girls doing here?' I said.

'The General Sahib sent them to entertain you. If they are not pretty enough I will fetch two others.

'No, no,' I said, and cravenly retired into the dining-room, leaving Ved to cope with the situation.

When I returned the girls had gone, Pannalal, looking very indignant, was going back to sleep. `How did you get rid of them?' I asked admiringly.

'I said we both had a contagious disease.'

'Genius,' I said.

'Just a knack, just a knack, nothing at all,' Ved said, crawling back through the mosquito curtain. 'Poof, they use very strong scent.'

He added, 'Apart from our other responsibilities, Dommikins, there are two of us in this damned room, after all.'

'Not to mention Pannalal.'

'Not to mention Pannalal. I don't think they believed me, you know. They'll probably think we are queer, and send us two menservants tomorrow.'

A Village with No Walls

A flute playing in the garden dragged us out of bed next morning. Pannalal was clattering in the bathroom with buckets of hot water for our baths. It was very blue crisp weather outside, so I tried to whistle 'Greensleeves' till Ved, whose colic was unabated, implored me not to.

I went down instead, after my bath, and stood benevolently in the sunshine till Professor Gupta arrived in a jeep.

'What do you wish to do today?' he asked.

I looked up to where the Himalayas stood, green shadows against the sky. 'Go to the mountains,' I said.

'Why not? While it is good weather you should go. Otherwise in rain it will be difficult. But you will have to spend the night there.'

So I went and told Ved, who continued to mourn over his stomach. We packed a toothbrush and a razor, and we left the palace at nine.

There were no clouds in the sky. The driver sang happily, and Gupta beamed at us. 'We will get horses at the foot of the mountains. We will visit Thoka, perhaps. Typical mountain village of Nepal. On the way we will see Patan and Bhatgaon.'

Patan is a little way up the valley from Kathmandu. It lies amid paddy-fields, not a town really, a patch of town, starting suddenly and tailing away into huts to the east. There was a market on, when we arrived: wooden stalls had been put up, cluttered with fruit and vegetables: people bargained shrilly, but nothing ever seemed to be bought. We pulled into the centre of Patan, around a small temple-filled courtyard, which included a squat and celebrated Hindu shrine carved out of a single rock. The gateway to the courtyard was lined with the shoes of devotees. I had decided that I did not like temples, and the shoes were off-putting; it was almost as if they might get bored and come flip-flopping out while their owners were still prostrate before the god. One of the priests emerged, coughing and blowing his nose with his fingers. The smears of ochre on his face were roughed with sweat.

Gupta, who is a Hindu, advanced and made the namaskar. The priest replied. He was like a Catholic priest in some backward Italian town, planted like a fat persimmon in the sun, strong in parochialism, with bored eyes. His first words were even more reminiscent.

'The people do not make offerings at the temple as they used to. They are swollen up with selfishness and wickedness. I will teach them, I will teach the godless ones: no more blessings shall I give till there are offerings at the shrine again.'

He said this not so much in conversation as in proclamation, and the bystanders stirred uneasily and flickered an eye at each other. I cut in:

'How long have you been at this temple?'

'Twenty years. These rapers of their sisters have felt my wrath before now. If they are not respectful to the servant of the gods, he will blast their crops on the day of the harvest!'

'What is the history of this temple?' Ved queried. The priest looked at him with a severely practical glint in his eyes.

'Give me money and I will tell you.'

'Go to hell,' said Ved in English, and turned away.

But the priest raised one arm in the air, flapping and croaking.

'I know what it is that you say! Evil one! Have you no respect for the servant of the gods?'

The bystanders began to mutter ominously, obviously seeing an opportunity to reinstate themselves in the priest's favour without spending more than a little energy.

'We have annoyed him,' Gupta said. 'I think we should go.'

So we left Patan under something of a cloud.

Bhatgaon was much the same, only wilder, more straggling, with the same mud houses, and we hesitated in the main square, and finally Gupta said, 'Shall we continue?' and we said 'Yes, rather,' and so went on.

The mountains were closer, they rose towards us, always larger, and the track climbed through, foothills, and eventually we had to get out and push, there was so much mud. Then we lumbered like a military tank to a village in the shadow of the Himalayas, and there stopped. Gupta climbed out.

'We will get horses here.'

The villagers gathered round us. They talked all together, quickly, and their hands slewed up and down. Gupta ignored them.

'They are not the owners of the horses. Keep close to me and do not enter into negotiations with elsewise persons.'

So Ved and I got out, and stood silent in a storm of voices, till Gupta, who had nipped up the street, returned.

'The horses are ready. Let us go.'

There was a short pause, while we instructed the jeep to come back the next day. Then, trailed by our adherents, we moved farther up the street to the headman's house, before which three sidling ponies stood, saddled, but rolling crimson nostrils, and gently and angrily flattening their ears.

In the midst of their pirouettes, we seized them, I feeling piratical, and came aboard. The saddles were wooden and horned, and hurt as soon as one sat on them. A trail of villagers clung to us, shouting, as we wheeled the ponies around and trotted out of the village.

It was midday.

For the only time in my life, I felt slightly anxious about Ved. As I bounced on the wooden saddle, I decided I must keep an eye on him. I was much aggrieved when he came cantering back down the bridle-path.

'Are you okay, Dommie? Do you want a hand?'

'No,' I said sourly, and followed the other two thereafter.

The road was steep, rock-strewn, and occasionally flooded. Progress was slow. Every now and then the ponies had to tiptoe along the edge of a precipice. At first it was all right: the precipice was low to the ground, and a fall would have meant a cut elbow, perhaps, and reminded one happily of one's childhood. Later it grew higher; a fall would have meant a broken neck. My pony insisted on the edge, and I kicked it despairingly. Occasionally, squinting down, I would see clods disintegrate from its hoof, and its previous foothold rain down crumbwise into the valley beneath.

All round the mountains got bigger, hairier, more menacing, and the valley dwindled to small Chinese roofs and rivers like saliva-threads from the sudden lips of the hills. I held the reins, pressed my knees tight into the pony's sparse ribs, and hoped. Finally we emerged from the edge into an area of trotted-up slopes, the trees steaming mist on either side. I had to lean forward on the pony to keep in sight of the others, and also, with the mist steaming in through my shirt, it became exceedingly cold.

'Are you all right?' Gupta shouted back through the mist, and I replied haughtily, 'Excellent.'

Then more climbing. The pony stuttered his feet every so often, and yawed his head back, and squiggled his behind, and riding became agony. The mist had fortunately blotted out any prospects of a fall, and my entire consciousness was concentrated on avoiding the next bump. Eventually we climbed to a village, where people came out and stared amazedly.

'Is this Thoka?'

'A few miles yet,' Gupta shouted back. 'Do you wish to dismount?'

'Yes,' I said, and slipped off into a dung-smeared street.

A girl came to my side, like Florence Nightingale, and said, 'Do you want a drink?'

'Yes,' I said again, and she brought me some Nepalese beer in a copper bowl.

I drank it and felt slightly better.

'Come on, Dommie,' said Ved enthusiastically, still from the saddle. 'We must go.'

We did, then, scrambling up a steep track dissolving now in the faint mountain rain, always higher; the wooden saddle unbearable each time the pony trotted: but luckily that wasn't often.

Finally, in the mist, the ponies clinging with slithery hooves to the edge, lights glimmered in the stew ahead, and Gupta called 'Thoka' back to Ved, and Ved called it back to me. So I stuck my heels into the pony's side again, and managed to arrive, at a species of canter, in a village of nervous mud huts sticking to the mountain. People came out to stare. We dismounted and looked around.

There were about twenty huts in the village, mud and thatch; a single narrow street; goats; a pig. The headman came out and showed us to his hut. We had been riding for five hours. Women brought us tea and a kind of pop-corn. The doorway of the hut was filled with the rolling pony-eyes of villagers, darting away when we returned their look.

The hut itself was a low two-roomed building, with blackened beams across the ceiling, from which brass and copper utensils and ladles dangled. The only furnishing was a rope bed, on which we sat, and in the corner a broken-legged chair. The headman squatted on the floor in front of us. He was a wiry middle-aged man with quick eyes and bristly cheeks, over which he kept rubbing his hand.

'Where have you come from?' he asked, and when we told him nodded, impressed. 'You come from the capital. I welcome you. My name is Thapa.'

We exchanged namaskars and he said, 'How long will you honour us with your presence?'

'May we stay for the night?' Gupta asked, and Thapa spread his hands wide.

'It will be a privilege for us. We will give you a feast.'

And he clapped his hands and summoned his wife, and said to us, 'Do you drink spirits?'

'Some of us more than others,' said Ved, and the headman turned to his wife and said, 'bring the drink of three waters.'

The wife returned in a few minutes with four copper bowls and a copper jug. She filled the bowls with a transparent liquid that had a curious smell of dry grass. Then she brought a copper dish with bits of pickled lime in it, and went away.

'Drink,' Thapa said; so I lifted the bowl and drank deeply.

It was as if the top of my head had been blown off. I closed my eyes and blew my nose. After some critical moments I felt a little better. I even laughed a little at Ved, who had just taken his first swallow.

'You don't like it?' asked Thapa, disappointed.

'It's remarkable,' I said. 'What is it?'

'We brew a liquor of one, two, and three waters. The difference is in the length of time it ferments. This is of three waters, the best and the oldest.'

'It's very good,' I said, and drank the rest. It got better, like most things, the more you drank. Also if you kept a bit of pickled lime in your mouth when you drank, as Thapa did, it went quite smoothly. One bowl of it, however, was enough. I staggered slightly when I rose.

The mist had lifted, and outside a damp world waited. The air was cold and good. We walked through the village. People came out of their huts to watch. Some of the young men joined us. They were small and sturdy, their cheekbones higher and their skins fairer than those of the people in Kathmandu, and were very friendly.

'It is time for the singing,' one of them said. 'Come and listen.'

'A concert?' I asked.

'No, no,' said the young man, laughing. 'You will see.'

A pale distinctive twilight; we walked to the edge of the village, where it abutted on the forest path. Scarlet hibiscus made wreaths among the trees. Thapa pointed.

'It is the guras,' he said, 'the flower of the mountains.'

The path came down from the mountain, lined on either side by enormous shadowy oaks. It ran parallel with the village for fifty yards then curled down the mountain again. The young men—there were about a dozen by now—lined up by the curve, some sitting on boulders, some standing. Gupta explained to me.

'The girls from the next village have gone up the mountain to cut firewood. Soon they will pass by, and the young men will sing.'

And while we waited in a twilight full of expectant whispers, other voices came from farther up the path, the bird-clear voices of girls, and seven or eight came into sight, each carrying a sort of wicker pannier full of firewood, walking with a swinging mountain gait towards us. The flowers of the hibiscus were twined in their black hair.

One of the young men stepped forward into the path, spreading his arms like wings to block their passage; a little self-consciously, swaggering a little, thrusting his chest out, he began to sing. It was a high wavering tune, with dying falls, as if a flute should have a voice and sing words. As he sang, he made cajoling gestures with his hand, looking uneasily every now and then at the other young men, to see if he was doing well. But the others looked embarrassed, and turned their heads away for the most part: a few laughed in the twilight, slapping their thighs. The girls had gathered into a little knot vividly miming first surprise, then anger, then indifference; but all of them cocked their dark eyes at the young men, and occasionally they giggled. At last, when the first singer had done, another took his place, and later another. The young voices piloted the high tune into the twilight gathering now to night, till it was lost; and at last the young men stood forlornly in the silence, looking at the girls.

Then one of the girls stepped forward. She gestured the young men out of her way, she stamped her foot, she mimed anger. Then she sang. Her voice was a soaring treble that broke on the high notes, but as she sang some of the other girls joined in, till it sounded like a little choir. The young men laughed again, freshly, and slapped their thighs: then the girls laughed too and moved forward, and the young men gave way. And the girls went on down the long path, still singing; and even when they had turned the bend and were out of sight the clear pure singing came back through the cold air. The singers stood staring after them long after they had disappeared, with their faces pleased and longing at the same time, like puppies after their feed. Mist came again, and we walked back into the village.

The young men cheered up on the way, laughing loudly and slapping each other's backs. I walked with Ved.

'What do you think of that?'

'It was very strange, Dommie. They were like little Nepalese angels.' I walked ahead and caught up with the first singer.

'That song you were singing, it's very beautiful. What is it?'

'You like it?' he said, pleased and flushed, and the others laughed, slapping his back harder. 'It is an old tune of our people.'

'What are the words?'

'Oh, those we make up as we sing.'

'You improvise them?' I asked, genuinely surprised.

'Oh, yes. Each of us sings what he wants to say.'

'Can you remember what you said?' I asked.

'I can try.'

So I asked him back to the headman's hut. The other young men came too. We were all given copper bowls full of the liquor of three waters, and slices of pickled lime. Ved and Gupta talked to Thapa and the young men in one corner, all rapidly getting very drunk, and the first singer and I sat in another. Charcoal braziers were brought in by the women, for outside night had fallen in a final mist.

I got an old envelope and jotted down a translation of what had been sung to the girls:

> Since your childhood you have picked the red flowers from
> the hibiscus tree.
> Sixteen summers I have watched those flowers fall,
> But as yet I have not climbed to the summit of Dhaulagiri,*
> As yet I have not understood the hearts of the people of Nepal.
> Queen of the mountains, hibiscus-fountain, goddess of
> Dhaulagiri,
> Come quickly, be gentle: the old men say time flies:
> Come quickly to the forest, where your father will not see us.
> Show me the hibiscus flower between your thighs.

'What did the girls answer?' I asked the young man.

'I do not recall: they improvise their words too.'

'But did they say yes or no?'

'They said, "Not today",' replied the young man, and laughed immoderately. 'That is what they always say.'

'But do you do this every day? Is it a custom?'

'No, not a custom,' said the young man. 'We do it because we like to do it. Who does not like to sing?'

Later, when we were all very drunk, the women brought in spiced buffalo meat and flat wheat pancakes, boiled eggs and curds. Thapa tasted the food first, then the rest of us served ourselves. We each had a dish of beaten copper to eat off, and one of the women produced a teaspoon, but nobody used it. After supper

---

* A Himalayan peak.

bowls of warm water were fetched, for us to wash our hands in. Then we sat on the floor and smoked.

'How long have you been headman?' I asked Thapa.

'Fifteen years now, ever since my father died. I am fifty years old.'

'You were a headman under the Ranas, then?'

'Yes,' Thapa said.

'Did you have much trouble under them? Taxation, things like that?'

'We were too far up in the mountains for them to bother us,' Thapa said. 'Sometimes, yes, sometimes they came, they, took a pretty girl now and then. But even then, unless she was married, nobody objected. It was good for the girl; the Ranas fed and clothed her better than we could do in the village: what more could she desire?'

'Happiness?'

'My friend, you are sentimental. Happiness is to be fed well and clothed well. Even Devkota says that in his poetry.'

'Who is Devkota?'

'He is our great poet,' Thapa said with pride. 'He is the poet of the people of Nepal.'

'He is dying,' Gupta put in. 'He has cancer of the intestines and he is dying in Kathmandu.'

'Dying? Hai mai! What misfortune have the gods brought to Nepal?' There were tears in Thapa's eyes. 'It is hard that a poet should have to die.' He clutched his drinking-bowl, lifted it, and said, 'Let us drink to Devkota.'

So we all joined in the toast. Afterwards I said, 'Do you get books of poetry here?'

'Not books, my friend. I cannot read. But the poems of Devkota are repeated among us Nepalese. If my brother were here, he would recite some, but he has gone to Bhatgaon. Devkota was a sensible man, you see, for a poet. We can understand what he means, and it is always good sense.'

After a while Ved asked, 'What is life like in this village?'

'It is our life. It is as it has always been. The families who live in this village have known one another for two hundred years.'

'You live off the land?'

'Yes,' Thapa said. 'We grow the things we eat.'

'What happens if there is a bad season?'

'If one family's crops fail, the other families help it. After all, if the entire harvest fails, we would all starve together; so if one field does not bear, we all eat together. There are no walls in our village.'

It was past midnight. Thapa said, 'I have prepared a hut for you. Do you wish for women? My youngest daughter is a virgin.'

We said no. Thapa laughed.

'Too tired? That's right, it's no good when you're tired. But if there is anything else you desire, tell us and we will bring it.'

The hut had three rope beds in it, each with a straw quilt. It was cold; we were all tired and full of alcohol; we slept. I awoke sharply in the small hours to hear a deep creaky roaring outside. It died away into a muttered snarl, and then began again.

Ved was awake too. 'What's that?'

'Tiger, I think,' I said.

We listened, but there was no further sound. So we fell asleep again. Thapa's wife awoke us, bringing buckwheat cakes and raw onions for our breakfast. We washed at the well. Most of the villagers were standing round, including some of the young men from yesterday.

'Was that a tiger in the night? We heard something—'

'Yes, a tiger,' one of the young men said. 'He came quite close. The fires he did not like, therefore he roared. But he went away.'

'Do you have many round here?' I asked.

'No; it is too high for tigers. A few come, not many.'

He added, 'It is clear weather.'

'Yes.'

'If you climb a little higher,' the young man said, 'you will see Dhaulagiri and Everest. I'll come with you.'

We left Gupta in the village talking to Thapa, and climbed the slope. We took the path down which the girls had come the previous day. The guras bled through green leaves everywhere. As we climbed, the forest grew thicker, and the path little more than a furrow through the undergrowth. Brilliantly coloured birds flew away at our approach. There was no sign of human habitation anywhere, except here and there a felled tree. Presently we turned off the path, struggled through the forest for a hundred yards, and came abruptly into the open. We stood on the rocky lip of a precipice, moustached all over with smooth green turf. Purple and yellow poppies grew in the grass.

Our guide advanced to the edge of the precipice, and waved his hand outward.

'That way is Tibet, and there are the mother-mountains.'

I looked out from the precipice. In the brilliant sword-bright air one was able to see for miles, like an eagle. Ranges of small mountains, rocky or forested, stretched away before me; and at the very farthest point to which the eye could reach, beyond the hacked and rivered flesh of the smaller ranges, projected a line of snow mountains, like a row of teeth. 'Everest,' the young man said, 'Everest is one of those. Also Jalpaiguri and Dhaulagiri.' He paused, smiling back at us, lowering his pointing arm. 'Is that not beautiful?'

'Have you ever been that far?'

'Only with my eyes,' said the young man, smiling. 'Come, we must go back.' On the way down he plucked some guras flowers. 'If you have girls whom you love in Kathmandu, give it to them, that they may put it in their hair.'

'It's a very kind thought,' Ved said, 'but they are a long way farther than that.'

'Never mind. Keep it for them. The guras is red for many days.'

When we left the village Thapa and some of the young men walked with us a little way. None of us said very much, but smoked and spoke of the weather. The neck of my pony was hung with red flowers. Finally, where the track tilted steeply back toward the valley, Thapa stopped.

'We will go now,' he said, and smiled. 'Come back soon.' 'Come back soon,' the young men said, and we rode on toward Kathmandu, and I was sorry, because I did not think I would ever be able to come back.

The Dying Poet

It was our last morning in Nepal.

Peculiar, to leave a place. 'When I return,' I thought, 'if I return, I shall be older, stiffer, less drunk, more settled: I shall stay in a hotel and have breakfast in bed. For by the time I return there will be a Hilton Hotel, and there will be a motor-road to Thoka, and we shall drive there to take photographs of Everest. And the same for Ved.'

But meanwhile Pannalal was sneezing his way out of sleep, and Ved was climbing through the mosquito-curtains and looking for his dressing- gown. 'Hallo, Vedkins,' I said.

'Hallo, Dommie. Where the hell did I put my dressing-gown?'

'Foot of your bed. I say, do you realize we're leaving today?'

'Yes. We shall have to send some telegrams.'

'Let's not,' I said. 'Far nicer to arrive in Calcutta with nothing fixed.'

'You old romantic,' Ved said, laughing.

'That's one of the things about leaving a place, one always has to send these damned telegrams. If we don't, we'll be able to breathe our way out of Kathmandu, not just leave, destination Calcutta.'

'Okay,' said Ved tractably. 'But I must send one to my father.'

'Come to think of it,' I said, 'I must, too.'

Pannalal fetched the hot water. We shaved and washed, and in the middle of it Gupta arrived.

'Suman says you want to pay your respects to Devkota. I will take you.'*

'Is he in hospital still?'

'They have carried him to Pashupatinath today. He may die at any moment.'

'Oh, I say,' I protested, a little absurdly, 'one doesn't want to disturb him at this time.'

'No, that is all right. He will be glad to see anybody, especially two writers. He is alone, you see.'

We dressed, and went down to the jeep-taxi. 'Drive,' said Gupta to the taxi-man, 'to the ghats of the dead.'

It was a long drive, through the valley lying green and brilliant all round, before we bumped down a slope into a dusty village. The usual children surrounded us, asking for alms. Gupta waved them away like a cloud of gnats.

'The jeep can go no farther. The temple premises are down there, and the Basumati beyond.'

We walked down from the village to where a wooden gateway let us through to an unpaved courtyard. Women were drying red peppers in the sun, and the overflow of children and dogs from the village harried our ankles. Little heaps of dung, from different sources, lay about.

'This is the temple.'

At the other end of the courtyard was another wooden gateway, and through this we saw the river, the Basumati, a brown languid grease scumbling over stones between two wide banks. There was an extraordinary smell hanging over it, an unmoving, pervasive smell: a smell partly of burning, partly of excrement, and partly of death.

---

* Dr Suman was a leading Hindi poet and the Indian Cultural Attaché to Nepal at the time.

We walked down a flagstoned pathway, the river at our right. On our left a line of one-storeyed buildings, with stone floors and pillars, and wooden roofs, ran down to the long stairway leading into the temple. Two wooden rafts floated on the scummy surface of the Basumati. Gupta pointed to these.

'There must be two people near to death. They will be cremated on those.'

A few steps farther there was a concrete projection into the river. 'That is where the King is cremated, and the Ranas.'

And then, pointing to one of the buildings on our left: 'The house of the dying. There we will find Devkota.'

This building consisted of a stone-pillared veranda, on which wooden trestles were laid, about ten feet apart. On most of these trestles lay undistinguishable figures, swaddled in sheets, most of them attended by one or two bored relatives, some unattended. The relatives hummed, in appropriately sepulchral voices, the final hymns, but there was an undersong, a deep tortuous humming, and as we came nearer we saw what hummed it: the veranda was black with flies; great clusters buzzed along the floor, and around the heads of the dying. A priest lolled on the steps, fanning himself to keep the flies off. He glanced up as we came.

'Where is Devkota?'

'The poet? I think he is dead.' He rose, yawning, and glanced leisurely along the line of trestles. 'No, not yet. There he is.'

He pointed, and we edged past the foot of deathbed after deathbed, till Gupta stopped, bowing deeply, and making the namaskar.

On the trestle before us a man lay on his left side with a dirty white sheet drawn up over him, so that only the top of his head showed. A woman with her sari over her face, in token of mourning, squatted by his side, fanning the flies away. Gupta said softly, 'Devkota sahib. Devkota sahib,' and the woman drew the sheet away from Devkota's face.

We moved to the side of his bed, and the woman signalled

that we should sit down. One hand never ceased moving the fan over Devkota, so that the flies could not settle. We squatted on the floor.

The face that we saw was a mask, with thick dark hair drooping dryly above. Beneath the hair was a fine forehead, with large eyes that opened a little to look at us. Below the eyes the face had fallen in: the cheeks like craters, the lips sunken and wrinkled like a very old man's. But from under the dirty sheet two long hands projected from stalk-like, sand-coloured arms, crept slowly together, and made the namaskar.

Then again the beautiful eyes closed, and he lay still on his side, his hands fallen. He breathed in deep painful sighs, and between each breath give a faint moan. We sat in silence. Phlegmatically the woman moved her fan.

After a long pause, Gupta introduced us. The eyes fluttered open. They were brown eyes, inanimate as lakes, so far had they gone into death. But when something struck them they reflected it: in flashes and for seconds. They were naked eyes.

One thin hand groped painfully over the mattress toward us.

I grasped the hand in both of mine and squeezed it. It was very cold and dry. There was a long pause. Then the mouth unpuckered from its creases of pain. Very slowly, groping and whistling, it said: 'Cosmic conflagration....'

The woman, with the same complete resignation as had marked all her other movements, produced a chipped green thermos flask from the head of the bed. She opened it and took a lump of ice out. This she fitted between the poet's lips.

He sucked it for a while, still looking at us. Then he whispered again, 'I am in a cosmic conflagration...'

None of us said anything. The mask twitched in a summoning of strength.

'I am burning. This is like hellfire. Nothing...man has not invented a torture that can equal cancer.'

We were still silent. He whispered at me, 'I have read your

work.... I know your friend's name also.... It is a miracle to find you here as I am dying.'

'We wanted very much to see you, sir,' I said.

'Cancer...it burns me, I am dying. If I was alive I would show you my poems. Have you seen my poems? Tell Sama,' he whispered to Gupta, 'to give him my poems.'*

Then to me: 'Some of my poems I tried.... I tried to translate. Translation is a very difficult work...but I did my best....'

His eyes closed, he had gone away from us, and again came that faint regular moaning. The woman put another bit of ice into his mouth. After a while he looked at us again.

'I have so few words left to say.... I want each one to mean something...but now there is nothing I can say. They gave me blood transfusions: they said they would keep me alive a few days longer. But I grew tired of drinking human blood. So I have come here to die...

'My poems were too materialistic...they were too much of the world...but I will not renounce them. I am here in the temple of Pashupati, I am dying. But somewhere there is one inch of me left...one atom of me left, that will not allow me to let go. I pray that I may let go...if the God Pashupati were to come, I would beg him to crack my skull....

He looked at us again, striving to say something with his eyes, but could not, and wearily they fluttered shut, and wearily opened again.

'You see before you the carcass...of a man who once weighed 175 pounds. Now it weighs fifty-two...it is a carcass...there is one inch of Devkota left...one atom...that too will die. What is the use of lingering here, in this misery? Pray for me...pray that soon I may die....

'They called me a Communist, because I went to Russia....

---

* Balkrishna Sama was a poet and dramatist, and one of the leading progressive intellectuals of Nepal at the time.

I was only a poet...pray for me...pray for Devkota, that he may die...

'Even if I go into hellfire, it would be better than this...pray that I may go quickly...for me...I am the most unfortunate of the writers of Nepal...

And suddenly the mask tried to cry. The sunken lips twitched, but could not sob: they were too far divorced from human function: only tears slipped down from his eyes, to make lakes in the deep crater of his cheek. I clasped his hand in my hands, and at last he looked at me again.

'Recite some of your poems...let me taste a little peace.'

I came closer to him, so that he could hear properly, and began to recite.

I had just begun, when from one of the other beds came a wail of women, high and monotonous; the priest came rushing from the steps, officiously; somebody had died.

Devkota paid no attention; he fixed his eyes on mine and whispered, 'Recite.'

I went on. When I had finished, Devkota sighed. Behind me the relatives were carrying the dead man out to the burning-ghat. Devkota whispered one of the lines.

'"Earlier in Time I prayed to be forgiven..."'

And then, strengthening, 'Recite another.'

And when I had finished: 'You are a much more natural poet than I was.... I was always more mechanical...too professional... there was so little time.' And for the only time he tried to smile. 'You will forgive me for that?'

I squeezed his hand again, and he whispered, 'Recite some more.'

'I'll recite somebody else's,' I said, and thought of Edna St. Vincent Millay's 'For Any Dying Poet':

> Time cannot pluck the bird's wing from the bird.
> Bird and wing together

Go down, one feather.
No thing that ever flew,
Not the lark, not you,
Can die as others do.

Devkota said, 'Yes, that is beautiful.... The image in the first three lines is bad...but I understand...it is true, perhaps....'

Gupta touched my arm and said, 'Your plane. You have only just time.'

He said to Devkota, 'They must go. Today they are flying to Calcutta.'

Devkota whispered, 'Will you not stay...two writers...will you not stay till I die?'

And I said, helplessly, 'I suppose we must go.'

Again the mask trembled, trying to weep. Then the lips quivered together. 'Give me your blessing on my road,' Devkota said. 'You both have mine on yours.... Go then.'

Ved and I both bent and kissed his forehead. It was like his hand, already cold. With a great effort he lifted his hand in the sign of benediction.

'Pray for me.'

So we walked away from that place. We stumbled through the dusty courtyard back to the jeep. My eyes did not seem to focus on anything properly. From the Basumati a plume of evil-smelling smoke rose, gently tickling the nostril, from the pyre of the man who had died.

The Chinese at the Doorstep (1959)

One recalled the oddest things: I remembered a toy-shop in a Knightsbridge arcade where I used to go when very unhappy, during my first days in London, in order to buy small delicate glass toys which I later smashed, one by one, in the fireplace of my flat, with a malediction against anything beautiful. Also an evening on the hillside above Agamemnon's tomb in Mycenae, when I pressed my ear to the grass and thought that I heard the old king humming to himself in the beehive cavern beneath. There was a moon above the hill, and I had a bottle of ouzo.

Calcutta seemed conducive to this: in the sweats of daytime and the nostalgia of the night, one fed on memories, drying them up quickly by sucking at them too hard. Also, of course, I was worried, because I didn't know where I was going to go next. All my life since I was fifteen I have travelled light, always thrown things away because I wasn't sure where I would be next day, and cherished a romantic ideal of myself as wanderer. This ideal became a little ridiculous when one was stuck in a large expensive hotel with the minimum of necessities in one's suitcase, and a typewriter that had jammed through being dropped into a cold bath. The people with whom I had been going to stay in Assam were not available: I bit my nails and wondered.

From all this I was saved by a good angel in a brown suit. He came bouncing into my room early one morning, while I was swearing at the typewriter.

'Hah! You are having trouble with your typewriter? Let me see.' He seized the typewriter and shook it. Then he did something to the reels. Then he said, 'It is done. Nothing like a little mechanical ingenuity, hah?'

'Is it all right, do you think?'

'Certainly, certainly. But we have not been introduced, hah?' He shook my hand. 'I am Ajit K. Das, of the United Press of America. Here is my card. I am also a professor of economics in Calcutta University, and finally, I work for your father's newspaper. It was he who asked me to look you up.'

'I think Marilyn Silverstone mentioned you,' I said.*

'Hah. Marilyn! I was with her in Tezpur when the Dalai Lama came. Fine, fine! Now let us sit down. Movement is essential sometimes, stillness is essential sometimes. Tell me your plans.'

I launched into a long mournful tale. He listened, unaffectedly tucking his feet under himself and tapping his knee with his fingers. His gold-rimmed spectacles caught the light. I watched him as I talked. I have a little game I play with people, which in my nastier moments I am proud of: I take notes of their mannerisms, chuckling to myself. I was just starting the first invisible chuckle when I noticed Das chuckling too. His eyes rested on me, intelligent, sardonic, and seeing. I stopped taking notes hastily.

'All is solved,' Das said. 'Ajit K. Das has solved your problem. Come with me to Sikkim.'

'Sikkim?'

'What is education coming to? You have not heard of Sikkim?'

'Yes, of course,' I said stiffly, 'but it's inaccessible, isn't it?'

'Inaccessible? Hah! You leave that to Ajit K. Das. He knows.

---

* Marilyn Silverstone was a photojournalist, author and an ordained Buddhist nun. Her work in photography ranged from the coronation of the Shah of Iran during the Second World War to chronicling the arrival of the Dalai Lama into exile in India in 1959. Her books include *Ocean of Life: Visions of India and the Himalayan Kingdoms* and *Gurkhas and Ghosts: The Story of a Boy in Nepal.*

See, the Chinese are on the Sikkim border. The rumour is that Indian troops are moving in. It is a wild place, with beautiful scenery. We can go up to the Tibetan border. Even if you go to Assam now, it will be raining like hell, and you will not be allowed to go into N.E.F.A. for security reasons. In Sikkim you have everything that you have in Assam, and better weather. Also more poetic. Will you come?'

'Yes,' I said.

'Hah! Good. You are a real good boy. Leave everything to me, I will arrange. Only meet me tomorrow morning at seven o'clock at the air terminal. I will fix it up.'

'Tomorrow?' I said weakly.

'Tomorrow. How long you want to stick in this damn place?'

'Oh, all right,' I said.

'Very good. We go to Sikkim tomorrow. Cable your relatives and dependents saying that you are in the care of Ajit K. Das. That will stop them worrying.'

He bounced out again. I fingered my typewriter. It worked. I got a little of my breath back. I decided I liked Ajit K. Das very much indeed.

I write this in Gangtok. A thin small rain is falling in streets drifted over with mist. Almost my journey has come full-circle, since the day I flew away from London… If I stopped thinking, this could be London, except instead of buses tasselled mules jingle past under the window, prodded into speed by Tibetan muleteers in felt boots and slouch hats, like Western cowboys.

Inauspicious days…they began when we left Calcutta yesterday. I woke at four and drifted through the motions of bathing and dressing before fully waking up: then to the terminal, far too early, and unjustifiably irritable at Das for being late. He arrived exactly on time, bearing in his arms and about his person two movie cameras, a typewriter, a briefcase and an air-bag. His man followed carrying a trunk and some rolled-up bedding.

I looked at all this, then at my own small case and typewriter. Perhaps I seemed surprised. Das obviously felt he should explain.

'I always provide,' he said, 'for the basic necessities. Among other things I have brought some rugs in case we feel cold on the Tibetan border, a raincoat in case of rain, and a small brass pot for washing.'

I was a little ashamed.

There was the usual long wait. Presently our flight was announced over the loud-speakers. We bundled out, staggering a bit under the weight of Das's basic necessities, to the aircraft. At this point we were intercepted by an embarrassed airline official.

'Sorry, sir. Announcement was not for you, sir.'

'Who was it for, for God's sake?' I said irritably.

'For the crew, sir.'

'The crew?'

'Yes sir. We have lost our crew, sir. We do not know where they have gone.'

We did not argue. We carried our cargo back to the lobby. An hour later a delighted official rushed up.

'We have found the crew, sir. We have put them in the plane.'

So the delinquent crew flew us off, and two hours later landed us at Bagdogra under a glaring sky. The airport sat in the middle of flat plains: green, spotted with buffaloes and a few men: but off to the north a rim of mountains stood, helmeted in cloud. Das indicated them. 'Sikkim is there,' he said laconically, 'and Tibet.' I was as amazed as a child.

It was very hot. We took a rickety bus to Siliguri, where Marilyn had been arrested. Before we left the airport Das pointed out a room on the first floor.

'That,' he said impressively, 'is the room where she was questioned.'

'Dear Marilyn,' I thought, and felt rather like a pilgrim.

We passed the green fields, the buffaloes squelching up from mud-wallows, the groves of bamboo, the pools full of children and on every side the cool white speargrass wagging a thousand beards in the windless heat. Presently we crossed a wide rough brown river; a few peasants stood waist-deep in the water, manipulating fishing-lines with idle flutters of the wrist.

'The Teesta,' Das said. 'We follow this river a long way, it comes with us into Sikkim.'

Siliguri was tiny and ramshackle. We got off at the railway station and loaded our things into the bus for Gangtok. This bus takes the mail from Gangtok to Siliguri and back every day, a journey of twelve hours altogether; the remarkable thing about it is that the same driver operates it always. He was bronzed and wiry, a Sikkimese, chain-smoking and a little sulky. He wore a vest and blue Chinese trousers, but when he got into the bus he took his trousers off and hung them neatly on a nail. I asked him why. He replied that the only reason he could see for wearing trousers was that they had convenient pockets in which money could be kept. While actually driving, he said, he had no need of money, therefore no need of trousers. This seemed logical.

The bus itself was a peculiar one. It was long and low-slung, and physically divided into three parts. The front seat, by the driver, where Das and I sat, was first-class; then came a section cut off on either side by yellow-painted iron bars, like prison bars, second-class; and finally a section shared by mail-bags and third-class passengers. The doors were fastened by a kind of peg on the inside. The luggage went on the roof.

'How long does it take to Gangtok?' I asked Das.

'Six hours.'

'And how far is it?'

'Seventy miles.'

'Seventy miles! Are the roads that bad?'

'It is not only the roads.'

'What then?'

'You will see,' Das said darkly.

We began our journey. After we had reached the outskirts of Siliguri the bus stopped, the driver got out, and we waited. The driver's assistant sat among the mail-bags, singing, I chain-smoked, and Das read the papers. Half an hour passed. 'Where is the driver?' I asked. Das asked the assistant. 'The driver has gone for his lunch.'

The driver returned some time later and the journey went on. The mountains rose taller toward us, dappled with cloud-shadow, hairy giants, clouds like wet linen clinging to their shoulders. An hour's driving found us high up, the bus like a mad beetle skidding along a road that wound tightly round the flanks of the mountains. The driver drooped a cigarette from the corner of his mouth and one hand constantly played with the horn. The horn was rather unique: it was apparently operated through the steering-bar, in which there were a number of little punctures, like the holes in a flute, and the driver ran his fingers over these, producing a kind of horrible melody. On one side the road dropped six thousand feet into a narrow valley, where the Teesta, stronger and clearer than in the plains, roared in foam over huge upended boulders and narrow sandbanks. On the other the mountainside rose vertically, bleeding a thick green vegetation out of its clay, great trees crowding for room, exploding ferns, and jammed among them enormous insecure rocks. Every twenty yards a midget waterfall spilled down the mountainside through a pebbled and mossy crevice, slipping at last over the road to drip toward the valley. Also there were constant little wooden bridges slung over chasms where branches of the Teesta whispered to their stones. Most of the road-signs said, *Danger, Bridge Unsafe for Heavy Traffic*: but the driver's foot was firm on the accelerator, and the bridges shook and creaked beneath us as if the bus itself was a great weight of rushing water. Sometimes also the road-signs said, *Beware of Falling Boulders*, and indeed the great boulders balanced so precariously overhead seemed likely to fall out of sheer boredom, and bring the uprooted trees and porous clay down in a slow spin upon us. It was two hours of this, the Teesta always ploughing plainward away from us on one hand, and the untrembling mountains rising above us on the other, before we made our next stop, at a village sprawled across the mountainside, where a concrete suspension bridge went over the Teesta. Here the road split: one branch went on through the Himalayas to civilized Darjeeling, with its promenade and missionary schools, the other crossed the Teesta into Sikkim.

The village only had one goat-infested street. The half farther up the mountain was where people stayed, two-storeyed tin-roofed shacks with little slotted windows; the lower half was mostly composed of stalls selling fruit and condiments. This was still the Indian side of the border, but the people were all high-cheekboned and slant-eyed; the women selling fruit in the stalls were often young and very beautiful, with rosy cheeks and a shy downturned look of the face.

Two wandering Tibetans came slowly over the bridge, in their felt boots and cowboy hats, their robes kilted to the waist, and pouches tied to their hips in which each carried his private Buddha. All along the bridge down which they came, Tibetan prayer-flags flapped lazily in the wind to warn off the spirits of the dead. The Tibetans came slowly into the village and slouched down the street, bought fruit and sat down on the grass to eat it, coughing and hawking up the pink pulp like consumptives. When they kilted their robes higher one saw the beautiful embroidered linen belts of Tibet, and when they took off their hats pigtails spilled over their shoulders and turned them in a minute from cowboys to Red Indians.

I was beginning to feel a little nervous; it was clearly wild country into which we were coming, and the mountains on the far side of the Teesta huddled impassably together, forbidding in their community.

We left the littered village after an hour or so, the Tibetans sleeping on the grass, the women crying their wares, children weeping, and at the far end of the street a goat trying to make love to a girl.

Then again the mountains, the slow climbing, the descents, the bends, and always on one side the following and wandering Teesta, and on the other the hairy mountains.

Occasionally we passed people on the road breaking stones, squatting women, beautiful and wild-looking, men with slant sharp features, dying waterfalls and the growing, sprawling vegetation everywhere, forcing itself sometimes through the cracks of the road. Sometimes the road ceased to be road for a mile or so and became a bridle-path, so narrow that the off-wheel was always trembling on the edge of a terrible decision. It was all very muddy too.

We stopped in a town high up in the mountains. It was market-day, and traders had come in from Kalimpong, spreading their wares in the street, cotton and a little grain and food, and, largest of all, there was a sort of sidewalk department store: combs, sand-shoes, cheap fountain-pens, plastic teacups and glasses, charm bracelets, shirts, caps, and, strangely, pink silk knickers. 'Is there much of a market for those?' I asked the trader.

He said yes.

'I shouldn't have thought so.'

'Well, they wear them as fancy hats, you see.'

We spent quite a long while here, because it was time for the driver's tea. When we took off again I went to sleep. When I awoke we were passing a Tibetan mule-train: the mules tasselled and decorated, laced lightly together, with the lead mule free, a mirror on his breast, a bell round his neck, the muleteers loping behind. Then again the Teesta, and a bridge: Rongpo, the Sikkimese frontier.

At the far end were the Customs, a modern police station (the only modern building in Sikkim) and a faded blue-and-gold border sign. We drove on, and now we were always climbing.

As we climbed, I saw cultivation in the narrow valleys for the first time since leaving Siliguri. The fat green earth was cut into wedges, parcelled, forced to bear: the wedges turned to terraces, climbing the foothills. In the mountains themselves an astonishing thing was the number of butterflies, thousands of unhealthily vivid scraps of paper struggling in wind, and birds dressed in red velvet and blue velvet preening like courtiers among the leaves. Also the branches of every tree were wired together by cobwebs, enormous cobwebs, billowing in wind, festooned with corpses, and one gross spider sensuously fingering the threads. Even the rocks had cobwebs on them, the butterflies hesitated above them, and the birds looked down and squawked. 'Beautiful, eh?' Das said.

The bus drew up at a village called Sinthan, the driver needed more tea. This was again market-day, vegetables and fruit spread over the pavement on horse-blankets steaming with flies: red-spiked lychees, guavas with their chalky flesh, ginger and peppers. Among the traders the Sikkimese women moved, the young pretty ones with their virgin's gait, like clockwork mice, the old ones like trees floating. A few Tibetans paced about, robes flapping laxly, and everyone looked happy and anxious. When we left, the ones I had talked to stood and waved from the unpavemented street.

More climbing; spiders and butterflies; and at last as we came round the bend of a mountain Das pointed ahead. High up on the next mountainside a few houses were strung out, tin-roofed or thatched. Gangtok. As we climbed nearer we passed caravans loaded with wads of yellowish, smelly wool. 'Yak-wool,' Das said. 'They have come through Tibet, through the Chumbi Valley and the Nathu La pass to Gangtok.' It was dusk, and the caravan bells chinked rhythmically behind us for a long time before they died away.

As we entered Gangtok, the Last Post sounded from the Indian police station.

~

In the first light of day the mist that drifted over Gangtok all night would thin away into cold and brilliant sunlight, and across the far valleys Kanchenjunga come suddenly clear, like a white nail driven into the sky. It presided over the wakings of Gangtok. In the one straight street which forms the town proper the Indian traders peeled the canvas out of their windows ready for the Sikkimese women who minced in to buy vegetables. The Tibetans uncoiled their long bodies from the alleys where they slept, and the proprietor of the puppet-theatre at the top of the street came coughing and blinking out from under the stage and did a few Yoga postures to start the day. There was also a mad beggar whose sex was indeterminate under grey rags, who shuffled and blubbered from shop to shop, holding his brass bowl out in the hope of a little breakfast. He could not speak, only weep, and the shopkeepers did not understand that language and would throw buckets of water over him. This happened every morning. Once I gave him eight annas; but he gave it to a little child.

I awoke more or less with the rest of Gangtok. The hotel we were in was the better of the two in the town; but it was more dosshouse than hotel. There were only three rooms, and six people slept in each. Das's bedding turned out to be of the essence, for the hotel provided none; only low pallets set head to head. The other occupants of the room were mostly Tibetans. They slept with all their clothes on and put their knives under the pillow. This alarmed me somewhat. I took my problem to Das, who was rapidly turning into a sort of father-figure.

'A lot of these fellows may be Chinese spies,' Das said. 'They are all certainly thieves. Keep your money in your sock.'

It was very strange to me. The room smelt of yak-butter from many Tibetan pigtails. The ceiling was entirely covered with cobwebs, swarmed through by black spiders which descended on silk threads at night and bit one. Once I took a glass of brandy to bed with me: when I awoke I found the surface of the liquid covered with a small woollen blanket of dead insects. There were also a great many rats who ran over one after dark. In the end I developed a technique. I bought a lot of matchboxes and kept them by me, and when the scurry of a rat came in the dark hurled matchboxes at the noise till it went away. In the morning the floor would be littered with these matchboxes, which I could never bear to pick up. In the morning, too, the single bathroom was full of people strenuously hawking up the accumulated phlegm of the night. The floor was always covered, as a result, with a slippery liver-coloured jelly, and I could never quite face going in.

Instead I would go out and blink at Kanchenjunga and the narrow street, where the mail-bus coughed slightly, waiting to start for Siliguri. Chiranjilal, the man who ran the shop under the hotel, would come out and offer me a cigarette. Our breath clouded in the bright air. 'What news from Tibet?' 'Arre, sahib, the Chinia are moving troops to the border, a friend came last night from Yatung.' And he would shake his head at Kanchenjunga. 'What will happen to us if the Chinia come?' But then a pretty Tibetan girl would come in to have iodine dabbed on a cut finger and Chiranjilal would brighten. Massaging her hand, while she giggled and covered her mouth coyly, stroking her forearm a little, he would peer back at me, suddenly small and wicked: 'Arre, there are compensations in life after all.'

Our first visitor in Gangtok came on the evening of our arrival. The hotel had a kind of restaurant, a room with four tables and a curtained-off section for illegal coupling. It looked over the street, where after dark the puppet theatre got going. Drifts of people moved toward it, looked and went away. It was always the same show, the same puppets mincing and cackling on the same wooden trestle-stage against the same backcloth peeling a little more each day. Tonje came up from watching it. 'I watch it every night,' he said. 'It is restful to see the same thing every night.'

He was Tibetan by birth, but a naturalized Indian, and he was the only resident correspondent in Sikkim. He was stocky and walked with the swagger that all Indian hill-people seem to have: arms swung back like wings, chest out and hips paddling. He wore always an open-necked shirt, a pale blue jacket and corduroys, and on his head, with that slight touch of absurdity which I think a graceful thing in a person, a cloth cap exactly like that cloth cap with which the poet George Barker used to intimidate barmen in Chelsea. Also he laughed magnificently and very often, all white and gold.

Das had put his dhoti on to be comfortable and sat cross-legged in a chair by the window, gold-rimmed spectacles flashing, laughing his high laugh and drinking much tea. I had ordered a bottle of Sikkimese brandy, which was sweetish and rather awful, so I was drinking very fast, trying to become hazy enough to forget where I was going to sleep. Tonje who did not drink nibbled a Sikkimese cake. He did not smoke either. 'No vices I have,' he said, laughing explosively.

'Hey Tonje,' Das said in that hectoring tone which was too obviously assumed to be less than lovable, 'what about these Chinese?'

'What about them, Ajit sahib?' 'You have filed any stories?'

'I say, Ajit sahib, I will tell you,' Tonje said. 'This place is full of their spies.'

'That I know,' Das said.

'These Tibetan muleteers. Many of them are spies. Many, many. I have discovered,' said Tonje, growing excited, 'they are paid three dollars a word for every message they send back to the Chinese.'

'That is very clever,' said Das. 'Did you get these statistics straight from Chou En-lai? Or do you discuss salary-rates with the muleteers?'

'Ha, you only laugh at me,' Tonje said, laughing. 'But,' he said, 'they come to the frontier every day now. Chinese pickets come. Also by night the frontier guards see their searchlights in the Chumbi Valley. And flashlights near the frontier. Thirty thousand Chinese are in the Chumbi Valley; that is what the traders say.' They talked on, while the valley-mist dripped through the windows and a religious procession passed in the street, the chanting drowning out the squawks of the puppets below. The mountain people were happy, but where the two journalists talked, a kind of sobriety, a kind of international apprehension, was created. As Tonje spoke of the Chinese manoeuvres on the border, a small ghost came into the room and squinted at us. Preludes, preludes: to what? for what? As the mist thickened in the valleys and the singers went home, and the brandy began to work, I decided I could go to bed. I left them still talking over frigid cups of tea.

Next morning Das said briskly, 'We must get moving. Movement, movement, that is the thing, to keep moving, hah?' 'Yes,' I said meekly. Das bounced out to find a taxi. There are three taxis in Sikkim. Das returned with one of them, a Landrover with a blasé Sikkimese driver and a boy, his assistant. 'Now,' he said, 'we go to the Police Commissioner. He is my good friend.' We went bumping out of the main street and climbed for a while. Above the main town the houses of the Indian officials in Sikkim are strung out across the mountain. The Police Commissioner lived in one of these. We drove down a dirt track to reach his house. It was guarded by Nepalese policemen, and a huge blowsy Tibetan stood on the veranda, spitting lazily into the rose-trellises. 'An Indian spy,' Das said. 'Good that we also have spies, hah?'

The Police Commissioner came out to greet us, a large Sikh, handsome as all Sikhs are handsome, and a little drowsy, a little far away. He took us into his drawing-room, a large airy room with swords hanging on the wall and athletic trophies on the shelves. Das introduced me, and the Commissioner smiled at me sleepily, twirling his moustaches in his fingers with a gentle contented motion. He was very nice.

'You don't mind,' he said, 'if I see one of my men?'

The Tibetan came in, shuffling and holding his slouch-hat in his hands. He smelt, inevitably, of yak-butter.

'When did you come back?' the Commissioner said.

'This morning, sahib.'

The Commissioner had a map in front of him. He drew it toward him and fidgeted gently with a pencil. As they talked he marked the map with tiny delicate lines. They talked in Tibetan which neither Das nor I could follow, but every now and then Hindi words came in and we understood snatches.

'Chinia ko dekha, kya? You saw the Chinese?'

'Sir, yes, sir. Thirty men. One officer.'

'Kya karthe the? What were they doing?'

'I didn't follow them, sir. They were going towards Khambadzong.'

'Why didn't you follow them?'

'Sir, I was afraid.'

The Commissioner gave his gentle tired sigh. Then he said, 'Go to the bazaar. See if you can find anyone who has come in today from Khambadzong. If you find him, send him to me.'

'Sir, yes, sir.'

'Come for your money this evening.'

When the Tibetan had gone the Commissioner sighed again: 'You cannot trust any of them. They are all liars.'

Das showed him some photographs taken on his last trip to Sikkim. He was gently pleased with them, stroking his beard, and giving a peculiar courtesy-laugh which consisted of murmuring softly 'Ha ha.' Then he clapped his hands, and a servant brought tea, cake, toast, Punjabi rice pastries, bits of omelette, cheese, etc. Plate followed plate. My stomach, in a strange disorder already, received this somewhat coldly, so I did not catch much of the subsequent conversation.

'These Chinese on the border, Commissioner sahib. What about them?'

'There are no Chinese on the border.'

'But we are told....'

'Sala, that is all bazar-gup. I tell you, sometimes they come there, five or ten, but all they do is fraternize with the border-guards.'

'Fraternize in what way?'

They talk.'

'About what?'

'Arre, they ask our boys how many they are, where they are placed, what they are armed with, and like that. It is only fraternization.'

'And these lights in the Chumbi Valley?'

'I will tell you, that is simply these muleteers; when they lose some mules they take flashlights and look for them in the night.'

'But the searchlights?'

'Arre, these muleteers may be carrying portable searchlights also.'

'What about Indian Army troops moving in as reinforcements?'

'There are none.'

'But we hear....'

'There are *no* Indian troops in Sikkim.'

'Oh, well,' I thought, controlling my rebel digestion, 'hadn't we better go?' The same thought had clearly occurred to Das.

'Well, Commissioner sahib, we must not waste your valuable time. We shall take our leave of you. One thing, can you give us a pass to Nathu La?'

'Ha, yes, that can be done.' 'Thank you.'

Next morning we had to have breakfast with the Commissioner, and Das insisted on my wearing a jacket and tie. We arrived to find a wiry shrewd-eyed Sikkimese in plain clothes also in the drawing-room. He was introduced as one of the border guards. He had just been made an Inspector, and we congratulated him. The Commissioner smiled benevolently in the background, accepting his share of it all. He had just got up, and still had on the oil-soaked bandages which the Sikhs wear at night to keep their beards in place.

'We are having, you see, some trouble with the refugees,' he said. 'All the able-bodied Tibetans are offered jobs by the Sikkim Government, working on the North Sikkim road. Recently there has been some discontent, they are fighting, really giving much trouble.' He sighed more gently than ever and turned to the Inspector. 'I have ordered two constables to help you,' he said. 'If you need more take them. Go today to the road-workers' camp. If you find any trouble there, chalan* two or three of them. Nothing stops trouble quicker than a few chalans. And tell the others that those we have arrested will be sent back to Tibet. That will stop all the fuss.'

'Is that not a big decision to take,' Das said, 'to send them back?'

'Arre, the police are always justified,' smiled the Commissioner.

Das changed the subject. He turned to the Inspector with his most professional, most dentist-about-to-extract-a-tooth-ish smile.

'So you come from the border?'

'Ji ha.'†

'Do the Chinese come to Nathu La?'

The Inspector hesitated and looked at the Commissioner who was busy unbandaging his beard. He found no help in those calm eyes. 'Ji ha,' he said.

'How many at a time?'

'Sir, most days five, never more than ten. They are only patrols.'

'How often?'

'Every day, sir, sometimes in the morning, sometimes in the evening.'

'Ha!' said Das. 'How are they armed?'

---

* Arrest.

† Yes, sir.

'Sir, with sten-guns. But,' said the Inspector, getting into his professional stride, 'they have old-type sten-guns, with wooden butts like this.'

'And our boys have what?'

'Sir, rifles only.'

'This is a fine state of affairs, hah?' Das said excitedly to the Commissioner. 'They have automatic weapons and we have only rifles. What will happen if they decide to attack one fine morning, hah?'

'We have applied,' said the Commissioner placidly. 'We have applied for automatic weapons. But the Government does not send.'

'Krishna Menon again,' Das said bitterly. 'Defence Ministry. All our sten-guns are rotting in the plains and here we have nothing.'

'Sir,' said the Inspector with dignity, 'we are policemen, it is not our business to carry sten-guns.'

'But you're doing Army work,' I said, 'at least at the moment.'

'That is true,' the Inspector admitted. 'But,' he qualified, 'their sten-guns have a range of 150 or 200 yards. Our rifles have a minimum range of 300 but they go up to 400. Even to 500,' he said rather recklessly.

'Still,' said Das, 'a sten-gun is a sten-gun, and a rifle is a rifle.'

'True,' said the Commissioner profoundly. He wagged his head.

'But,' said the Inspector, 'our boys are good shots, and they know how to fight in the mountains. These Chinia do not even know how to hold their sten-guns properly. Some are boys of fourteen and fifteen. They don't even have proper uniforms,' in a tone of contempt. 'Some are coolies straight out from China and they go in rags, like coolies. These Chinia can give sten-guns to anybody, but they cannot make anybody a good soldier.'

He wrinkled his mouth with disgust, remembering.

'They are cowards as well. When a picket of five come to the border, three advance, an officer and two men; the other two stay behind covering our boys with their sten-guns. And we go up to them unarmed, we are not afraid. They are women, sahib.'

'What do they talk about?'

The Inspector suddenly revealed unsuspected histrionic ability. He imitated a soldier clutching a sten-gun and said in a falsetto voice: 'What are you doing here?'

Then in his own deep voice, holding out empty hands: 'What are you doing here?'

'We are defending our border against aggression.'

'So are we.'

'How often do you come here? How many are you?'

'We come here every day.'

'Don't you have automatic weapons? Who is your general?'

'And like that, sahib,' said the Inspector, with a gesture. 'Also, to prove that they are cowards, I will tell you that one reason they have not yet come into Sikkim is that they are afraid of wild animals.'

'What?'

'It is true, sahib. All the border guards know this. On their side, in the Chumbi Valley, they have few wild animals. On our side we have tigers and panthers and bears. They are very frightened of them. They always ask us have we seen any, are they very fierce, and like that. They are *very* frightened.'

'What do you say when they ask you?' I inquired.

'Sahib, we say that the tigers of Sikkim are the fiercest in the world, and that around the border they eat three men every night.'

He laughed charmingly.

'Each one of us border guards will eat three hundred in one night, when the Chinia come.'

After breakfast we rushed to the post office in the Landrover: Das wanted to file some dispatches, and I wanted to send you a telegram. 'We must move quickly,' Das said. 'We must get to the seventh mile ahead of the Dewan's party, so that I can take photographs. Come, come, come,' he said, whirling me into the post office. 'No gossip, Babuji,' he said to the postmaster. 'We are in a hurry.'

The driver and his assistant entered into the spirit of the thing with terrifying whole-heartedness. The North Sikkim road is a dirt track, clambering through gorges and ravines, and occasionally fording waterfalls, high over rock-strewn valleys. The driver chain-smoked his way along this dubious route at forty miles an hour, and in the back of the Landrover the assistant, clutching Das's movie and still cameras to his bosom, giggled joyfully and shrieked him on. Das and I, sharing the front seat with the driver, attached ourselves to the struts and bounced for dear life. At last, where many little landslips had littered the track with fragments of rock, clay-heaps and uprooted plants, and each new bounce took us tilting to the edge, the driver took his foot off the accelerator. The Landrover shuffled through the debris, bumping still, but less hazardously. Occasionally it had to stop to make room for mule-files. It was during this part of the journey that Das suddenly grabbed my arm. 'Look!' he cried, like Saint Paul.

When I looked farther up the track, shrouded in mist where it climbed the mountain, I saw what I took to be another mule-caravan. But Das had already leapt out of the jeep, and, followed by the boy with the cameras, was sprinting to a rock at the edge of the road. Then as the lead-mules came towards us out of the mist, I saw that their packs did not contain yak-wool, borax or herbs, but mountain-guns; and their drivers weren't Tibetans, but Sikh soldiers with rifles, their faces tired and fixed. More and more mules came down the mountain past the Landrover, some carrying mountain-guns and ammunition, some camouflage-nets, others stores and clothing. And after and among them came the Sikhs, all carrying rifles and ammunition, cocking an eye at Das, who precarious on his rock was furiously working the movie camera. After the Sikhs came Gurkhas, their steel helmets swathed in netting, festooned with leaves and twigs, like many ungraceful Daphnes. There must have been five hundred troops and fifty mules. All through their slow passage Das stylited it on his rock, handing one camera down to the boy while he used the other, and occasionally bestowing delighted winks and salutes upon the passing troops. When they had finally passed, he leapt off the rock and came cantering back, reloading his cameras as he came. 'Quickly, driver,' he shouted. The boy tumbled in at the back as the Landrover bumped away. Das dexterously reloading his cameras between bumps, yelled in my ear: 'We have beaten the world!'

'Why?'

'Indian troops in Sikkim! They may deny and deny, but we have seen them with our own eyes,' smacking his spectacles. 'We are the first civilians to have seen them!'

He yelled to the boy: 'Look behind, bahadur sahib, great general, and see if the Dewan sahib's jeep is coming.'*

We arrived at where a waterfall struck the road, bounced, and fell steeply into the rocky valley. As the Landrover wheezed among boulders and water the boy shouted. We turned. Behind us the track followed the deep inward curve of the mountain, and at the far end of the curve a small train of jeeps was crawling jerkily toward us.

'Shabash, O beloved of the world!' said Das, and precipitated himself into the torrent.

I followed him. The waterfall on our right rushed smoothly down, like a white wall, exploding as it hit the track, and spray rained on us, while the swift water, freezingly cold, tugged at our

---

* The Dewan was the Chief Minister of Sikkim and a liaison between the Indian Government and the Chogyal of Sikkim. At that time the Dewan was on a tour of the borders, after having denied to Dom and Das that his real aim was to inspect the border defences.

knees. My position was a little worse than Das's, who, mounted on a rock above the torrent, was madly working the movie camera as the jeeps inched round into the curveway. Then he leapt off the rock and we both squelched back into the Landrover.

'Chalo, chalo,' I said, catching Das's mood. 'Drive on!'

'Sahib, injin bundh hua,' said the driver gloomily. 'The engine is dead.'

'Then we must push,' Das said invincibly, and out we tumbled again.

Pushing a Landrover through a waterfall is not easy. For one thing, we had to keep lifting boulders out of the way. For another, when we got into the middle the current was so strong that it flattened us against the car and shifted that a little farther toward the edge. We managed somehow. As we dripped up on to reasonably dry land behind the Landrover the engine coughed a little and began working. Das, the boy, and I fell into the back and we pulled away as the Dewan reached the waterfall.

Das's camera was busy again. He knelt wetly and bucketingly in the back shooting away as the Dewan's jeep started fording the waterfall. It was much quicker about this than ours had been. Soon we found ourselves the leader of the cavalcade by about twenty yards.

'Scoop, scoop scoop,' Das kept saying gleefully. I was so wet I didn't care.

Finally we reached a little village of thatched and tin-roofed huts spread down the mountain toward a valley now cross-hatched with cultivated fields. The villagers were lining the road with scarves and garlands, the prayer-flags fluttering in the thin mist overhead. Under the impression that we were the Dewan, everybody began to salute and advance with the garlands. Das promptly rose and bowed. As we pulled up, however, the real Dewan arrived. Tonje tumbled out of one of the jeeps behind him and came rushing through the mud, also with a movie camera.

Das hopped out too and they both levelled their lenses at the emergent Dewan, like the nozzles of sten-guns. The Dewan wore his State clothes: a brown jacket buttoned at the neck, and jodhpurs, in his hand a sandalwood stick. He accepted the garlands and scarf-offerings and returned them with a gracious gesture. Then he walked with dignity to the edge of the road, accompanied by his entourage, and they all peed into the valley. Tonje and Das stopped their cameras hastily, and we joined ranks on the edge. Finally the Dewan buttoned his trousers, and stood gazing seignorially at the village, as if in thought, gently tapping his leg with his stick. Then he climbed back into his jeep. We all scrambled for our respective jeeps, doing ourselves up as we went, and the cavalcade began afresh. The road was worse here. The landslip ahead had precipitated other minor landslips, and the track was flooded in many places and sputtered over by newly created waterfalls. When we reached the big landslip I felt inured, but even so was startled by what I saw. The entire mountain seemed to have caved in, leaving raw fissures in the slopes, and a kind of dwarf mountain had been created on the track: earth, rocks, and uprooted trees upside-down in the debris, while water flooded through.

The entire cavalcade drew up, and everybody got out and stood peering at the landslip. 'Is it safe to cross?' the Dewan said.

'On foot, yes, sir,' said the private secretary, who wore leather shorts and a peaked cap. The porters with the Dewan's baggage appeared labouring along in the Sikkimese manner, with their packs fastened by a strap round their foreheads. They began to negotiate the landslip, while the Dewan poked it experimentally with his stick. Then we all climbed over. It was all right, save for one horrible moment, when, balanced on the slippery clay at the top, I looked down at the rocks of the valley three feet across from my right shoulder and several thousand feet beneath my right toe. Now we straggled through forest mud. Tonje, huffing and puffing under his camera, was my companion. Das galloped about the mountainside ahead, unbelievable in his energy, taking photographs. It took about two hours to get to Dikchu, a small high village, mist-wrapped and cold, and by that time even Tonje was speechless. Das still limped beside the Dewan, taking notes. The villagers came out, did obeisance, and showed us to a collection of pallets outside the headman's hut. Here we sat down and were brought Sikkimese tea, which is mostly hot milk, and buckwheat cakes. It came on to rain. Presently Das rose. 'Good luck, Dewan sahib,' he said. 'We go now back.' Tonje saw us to the edge of the village with effusive goodbyes. 'Perhaps I may never see you again, my dear friends.' 'One can always hope,' Das said ambiguously. He was a little embittered by exertion. The villagers sent a boy with us as guide.

Das and I squelched back for two hours through ever-increasing rain. It was nearly dark by the time we reached the Landrover, dumbly faithful at the far side of the landslip. The driver and his assistant were both asleep. We woke them and began our journey back in silence and very nearly in tears. I kept discovering leeches in my clothes. Das was too tired to worry about leeches.

We were knee-deep striving when a mule-caravan jingled up. The muleteers stood akimbo on dry land urging us to hurry. At length they were tired of waiting, and decided to try to take the mules across on the far edge. Four mules went over safely. The fifth stumbled in the stream and abruptly disappeared. There was a shriek like a woman's, and a heavy crash far below. The muleteers peered over the edge of the cliff, clicking their tongues. The mule had fallen about a hundred feet; and been brought up short by a boulder. It lay now straddling the boulder and heaving as if trying to bring something to birth. The mirror on its breast had splintered, and the tassels been torn away. It looked curiously nude without them, and blind, struggling against what it could not see. Thick mud-coloured blood dripped from its side.

Two of the muleteers took their knives out of their silver scabbards and began very cautiously to climb down to the mule. It was like a sacrifice, the animal on the mountain, mute and struggling to be comfortable, and the knife-carriers descending to it. But the Landrover was now across, and we drove away.

We did not reach Gangtok till midnight. Das had fallen asleep and it was an effort to wake him. I was very tired, and aching and itching all over from bumps and leeches.

Next morning Das said proudly, 'We may have over-exerted, but still we have scooped the world, hah? We have films of the first Indian troops in Sikkim.'

'Good show,' I said idiotically.

'Now we shall go and see the P.O.,' Das said. 'He may be having some hot story.'

As we went down to the Landrover Chiranjilal came out of his shop. 'Hey, Ajit sahib,' he said, 'the Press Attaché has been telephoning for you.'

'Now what does that raper of his mother want?' Das wondered agreeably. He went into Chiranjilal's shop to telephone. I talked to the driver and his boy.

The driver lolled back across the seat, a cigarette in his fingers, speaking in small blue puffs.

'You go to Nathu La soon?'

'Tomorrow or the day after.'

'I see no reason for it. It is a wild place. Yaks and savages live there, not civilized people like we have in Gangtok.'

The boy said: 'Also the Chinia are on the pass with guns.'

'Silence, boy,' said the driver. 'However,' he said, 'your friend the journalist may be interested in going tomorrow. Chhibar sahib is coming.'

'Who is Chhibar?'

The driver looked shocked. 'The Indian Consul in Lhasa. He comes out tomorrow.'

'How do you know?'

'A friend of mine came from Yatung today. He passed Chhibar sahib's mule caravan. Chhibar sahib was in Yatung last night. He is spending today in Yatung and tomorrow morning he comes to Nathu La.'

At this point Das returned. His face was as sorrowful and angry as Saint Sebastian's.

'Imagine what those sons-of-bitches have done!' he moaned, climbing into the Landrover. 'A Government order to confiscate my films of the troops!'

'Surely they can't enforce it?'

'Arre, if I do not give in, they will never let me into Sikkim again. Those sons-of-bitches! Why are they frightened that the world should know? Two hundred feet of film,' he mourned, 'at sixteen rupees a hundred feet,' and another arrow seemed to whiffle home.

I tried to think of healing ointments. 'The driver says the Indian Consul in Lhasa is coming out through Nathu La tomorrow.'

'Hah?' exclaimed Das. 'What is that?' He leant forward and began to cross-examine the driver. Finally he leant back with a small complacent smile. 'On this then,' he said, 'we shall beat the world.'

~

We left Gangtok at about nine.

'Bahadur sahib,' Das said flatteringly, 'if you get us to Nathu La by eleven, we will call you Rajkumar, a prince.'

I offered him a cigarette, and said guilefully, 'If you get there by eleven, we will pay three hundred rupees.'

'Sahib,' said the driver, suddenly tractable, 'if you say half past eleven, I can do it.'

He sucked tentatively at my cigarette as we climbed out of Gangtok into the Himalayan track.

'It will be raining. There is fog ahead. I will try. Sahib,' he said, looking at the cigarette in his fingers, 'do you make these yourself?'

'These are made by a great sahib in Bilayat,' I said, 'called Du Maurier.'

'Do you know this sahib?' asked the driver.

'Of course,' I said.

'If he comes to Sikkim,' said the driver, 'recommend me to him. He must be rich. I will take him to Nathu La for a thousand rupees.'

Then we passed into the mist.

Out of the mist, every so often, mules blundered like moths against the headlights. Behind them the tall shivering muleteers raised their arms in salute as we passed. As we climbed that spiral funnel toward the sky, the air thinned and rain began to whip tinily in with a knife-cold wind. I pulled the waterproof across the doorway, cutting off the view and saving myself from vertigo, for the track had narrowed to a strip of mud disintegrating in rain. We passed a huddle of shacks outside which cold policemen stood. 'Karponang,' Das said. 'Twenty-three miles still.' I looked at my watch again. It was ten to ten. 'Good going.'

Cigarettes gave one a strange ill feeling so I stopped smoking and squinted ahead through the mist-frosted windscreen. Only one of the wipers was working; it hissed and snicked to and fro; as a child I used to call them 'Vipers.' Presently we passed a gutted building.

'The old fifteen-mile checkpost,' Das said. 'It burnt down last year. Soon comes the new one.'

Ahead the mountainside widened and accommodated a kind of village with a worn wooden gate and a barbed-wire palisade across the road. A policeman came dripping out in a waterproof to inspect our pass. He took down the particulars, and nodded, unspeaking. We drove on. 'Nine miles to Chhangu.'

For the next half-hour we leant slowly, noiselessly, through a cotton-thick mist. Rain fell. It was bitterly cold, and I draped my knees with one of Das's blankets. Then we moved out of the mist, to a cold burning of sunlight, and the unwinding road brought us down to a great lake. The mountains lay, wobbling gently, under the water; the water was powdery and blue, like an eye, like a pearl, and shivered all over by the risings offish.

'Chhangu Lake.'

We climbed again, till we had left the mountain hollow of the lake behind us. Mule caravans were now very frequent. The landscape was changing noticeably. All the way from Gangtok, the mountains had been humped and rough with trees. Now they seemed to have broken off in the air, jagged and pointed, and furred over with thick grey-green lichen, on which broken fragments of limestone lay. Among this lichen browsed enormous antediluvian animals, hung round with black hair, like woollen blankets walking, with horns splaying massively across their low brows. 'Yaks.' The driver pointed out a reddish flower coquetting in the wind. 'Poison-flowers, sahib. You only find them here. Touch, and you die.'

The sunlight burnt on, an icy fever, and wind tacked across the shelved valleys, altering the clouds. We reached another hamlet, another worn gate, more barbed wire. Yaks were browsing between the huts. One raised his great matted head with a deep sleepy bellow.

'Sherathan,' Das said. 'The last checkpost. Two miles to Nathu La. What's the time?'

'Ten past eleven.'

'Not bad. Good. Shabash, driver. Three hundred rupees for you. Chhibar also may be late,' he explained to me.

Now we were climbing all the way, above the blue sockets of two more lakes, anthology of the tears of all the rocks. The landscape had an undated quality, prelapsarian perhaps, and the yaks, shaggy and gentle because their eyes were hidden under hair, might have floundered to Adam's hand in Eden. Ahead the road became well trained, covered with small slaty flagstones like fish-scales. Then coming round a bend we saw it lift, under walls, to where a jeep was parked and three uniformed midgets stood. Das gave a deep sigh of achievement. I looked at my watch. Eleven-thirty. 'That is Nathu La.'

We pulled in at a small shelf cut into the mountain-top, a lichen-rusted hummock rising beyond. The shelf had for ornament a small stone boundary-post, inscribed 'Sikkim-Tibet Border.' Pools of water lay about, memorials of the morning's weather. A police officer and two constables greeted us with a request for our passes.

Then Das and I climbed the hummock, to look into Tibet. The sun had come out brilliantly and coldly, and the sky over Tibet was an icy blue. From where we stood the mountain slipped steeply down, dry and boulder-strewn, into the Chumbi Valley, a succession of folds in the ground, thickly forested, rippling to a narrow V. At the point of the V, across the valley, rose a range of forested hills. Beyond them the horizon was like a picture postcard, two scarred snowpeaks vivid in the frosty sky, and a glimpse of plains between and beyond. The police officer came silently up behind us, pointing out the higher of the snowpeaks.

'That is Chumbiladi.'

'Where does Tibet start?' I asked.

'My dear gentleman,' said Das, 'we are in Tibet. It starts from the boundary-post down there.'

'Where are the Chinese?' I inquired naively.

The policeman handed me his field-glasses. I followed his finger as it swept the Chumbi Valley. Where the valley turned into hills, at the point of the V, I made out a small concrete building among the trees.

'That is their checkpost, at Chumbithan. But who can tell where those rapers of their sisters are? They hide here and there in the jungle and watch us through field-glasses. But I can tell you, sahib, there must be a hundred or two between here and Chumbithan, and that is two miles.'

'Chinia aye the aj, kya?' Das asked. 'Have they come here today?'

'Ji nahin. No, sir. They will not come till Chhibar sahib has passed. This is their diplomacy'.

I turned and looked about. Huge cairns of stones littered the hummock, ominous and druidical. Above them hundreds of improvised prayer-flags, made of tattered garments, tautened in the whipping wind out of Tibet.

'What is all that?'

'When these Tibeti folk come back from Kalimpong or Gangtok they throw a stone at the border, to drive away the evil spirits from abroad. Also they put up those flags for good luck.'

Clouds swept over the sky, and suddenly mist rose everywhere, and Tibet was blotted out of sight as completely as if it had never been there. I could understand, suddenly, why the Tibetans believe that evil spirits live in these high passes. The cairns loomed gloomily; the prayer-flags hung limp, then whiffled in the wind. I found myself strangely exhilarated. 'It's the air,' I thought; then, as the wind sang over the pass, shivered, helpless with cold.

Das, drinking the wind like a tonic, rushed sharply about, posing the policemen, the drivers and myself in various places, against the cairns and flags, drooping over the boundary-post, etc. He had given me his movie-camera to hold, and that hand had turned completely numb. I tried to talk to the police officer, but it was difficult to move my lips.

However, 'What do you think?' I said. 'Will the Chinese attack?'

'Sahib, that is what their officers tell everybody. The yak-drivers and the muleteers say that the Chinese promise to be in Sikkim before next summer.'

'What will you do then?'

'Fight, sahib. What else? Only the Sarkar* must give us material for us to fight with. Our radio transmitter here works only three hours a day. If the Chinia should come while it is not working, how can we let them know at Sherathan, so that our boys can be ready there?'

'Well, they can see Nathu La,' I said, 'through field-glasses.'

The police officer laughed.

'Sahib,' he said, 'the garrison at Sherathan has no field-glasses. They have asked for some, but the Sarkar does not send. If there is fighting at Nathu La, our men at Sherathan will not see it till the Chinia are on their heads.'

The mist was thinning. He swept the Chumbi Valley with his field-glasses. Then he said, 'Someone is coming.'

I shouted to Das, who returned from his photography at a trot. He peered through the field-glasses, then passed them to me. Four or five men on mule-back were snailing up one side of the valley.

'It doesn't look like a diplomatic party,' I said.

'It may be some traders,' said the policeman. 'Let us wait.' I remembered the brandy. We squatted, all of us, under a cairn, which afforded some protection from the wind, and passed the bottle from hand to hand. Mist went over in little puffs. The brandy had a strange, fiery effect, fifteen thousand feet up: my ears sang and I felt sick.

As the mist lifted again for a minute, we saw the mule-riders plodding up from the foot of the hummock towards us. Das jumped up and shouted for his movie-camera. He began to work it as the first rider reached us. Three others drifted after him. They were definitely Indian traders: small heavily muffled men, with nervous rolling eyes, like apprehensive ponies. The first one dismounted, and Das was at him like a terrier.

'Welcome. Where are you from? Yatung, hah? Kya hal chal hai Yatung me?'

---

* Government.

'Bahuth mushkil he Yatung me, sahib. Much trouble. Yesterday the Chinia killed an Indian trader there. Their people stabbed him and looted his shop. Therefore this morning we left there, closing our shops. There are only three Indian shops open in Yatung today, where once there were fifteen.'

The police officer interrupted. 'Have you seen Chhibar sahib?'

'He was leaving Yatung an hour after we left, Inspector sahib. We thought, if we came before, we would be safe; if we came after, the Chinia would eat our lives.'

'So,' said Das thoughtfully. 'He will still be one hour.' He glanced into the misted valley. 'Are there any Chinia down there?'

'Many, many Chinia,' one of the other traders said. 'They are in the forest, three furlongs down the valley.'

'Why don't we go down and look at them?' I suggested.

'That is what I also was thinking,' Das said.

Brandy and the thin air had brought on euphoria. I heard myself laughing and saying rather stagily, 'Two minds with but a single thought.'

'Arre, don't try these mad tricks,' said the Inspector in alarm. 'If the Chinia see you they will shoot you first and then ask who you are.'

'Sahib,' said one of the traders. 'On my mother's life, it is a mad thing to do.'

'Driver,' shouted Das, 'bring my movie-camera.' He cast the kind of glance a professional spy might have cast into the valley. 'While the mist gives us cover, we shall start. Lend us your field-glasses, Inspector sahib.'

'Sir,' said the policeman, 'on my mother's and grandmother's lives, I should forbid you. What will come to me if you are killed or taken prisoner? I will lose my job!'

'Come on, Dom,' Das said to me.

So I took a final drink from the bottle, borrowed the Inspector's field-glasses, turned my coat-collar up against the wind, and followed Das into the valley.

The slope was strewn with rocks, which afforded precarious handholds. We had to let ourselves down backward, like mountaineers, and I felt acutely conscious of the wind flapping my jacket, the field-glasses dangling round my neck, and the unseen Chinese probably even now gloating over us through their field-glasses, like uniformed Fu Manchus.

I reached the bottom of the slope a minute after Das. He did not hesitate, but set off at a brisk walk down the Valley. The ground was rough and tussocky, the mist had thickened and it was impossibly cold. My limbs were like stalactites: lifting one became a creaking, breathless effort. Conversation was out of the question. I simply followed Das, and we were suddenly among trees.

Here there was a clean acid stench of wet earth and herbs. A bird or two shrieked upward through the leaves, but otherwise everything was grave-silent. Our feet scuffing through the undergrowth sounded like a forest fire.

We walked for about twenty minutes, twice passing clearings where ashes remained in ersatz fireplaces made of heaped stones. Then Das stopped. We were both breathless. We sat down and I lit a cigarette. We talked in whispers.

'There don't seem to be any Chinese hereabouts.'

'Certainly we are not seeing any. But we must have come the best part of a mile. If we push on, we will be near the checkpost. If I can get a film of some troops without their seeing me, we shall have scooped the world.'

I no longer felt any apprehension. It seemed to me reasonable that Das should want to scoop the world. Apart from the difficulty of breathing properly in this rarefied air, I felt quite willing to go on.

'Those fireplaces, do you think they were made by the Chinese?' I was beginning to feel toward the Chinese now as I might toward the inhabitants of Troizen or Zimbabwe.

'Perhaps by the Chinese, perhaps by some muleteers. Let us get on.'

We stumbled through the trees. In the forest the mist seemed to be filtered away by the leaves, but overhead the sky was still clogged with grey. This unrewarding sky was our only window to the rest of the world for another twenty minutes, till we stumbled out of the forest on to a bare ridge, littered with chalky rock fragments, between two hillocks. Here we sat down again. I looked round through the field-glasses. We were a good way into the valley: the two great snowpeaks looked closer and the barren hummock of Nathu La surprisingly far. I put down the glasses and lit another cigarette. Das drummed his fingers on his knee.

'If we pushed on a little farther, we would get close enough to Chumbithan to take a film of the checkpost. Do you think that is a foolhardy plan?'

The clouds rifted: suddenly and fugitively the sun glared from a waste of blue. Idly I picked up the glasses and looked round. The sun caught them, and reflected light flashed on one of the neighbouring hillocks.

A moment later, there was an answering flash on the ridge where we sat. Das looked up in surprise. The flash was repeated. I looked through the glasses in the direction from which it came.

On the neighbouring hillock, clustered together, was a group of Chinese.

There were about twenty, stocky and tough-looking. Two were in a drab grey-green military uniform with peaked caps. These two were looking at us through field-glasses. The rest stood behind, sten-guns and ammunition belts hung over their shoulders. They pointed at us, and were apparently discussing us among themselves.

I told Das. He said very coolly, 'Let us get back into the trees in case they open fire. I will take a film.' We moved back to the fringe of the forest. Das fitted the tele-lens on his camera. He knelt down, swivelling it for focus. I was unnerved, but not unpleasantly. I tried to analyse what I was feeling. I hoped to God that they wouldn't think Das's camera was a sten-gun and open fire. I could feel my own heart beating very fast, and I kept on swallowing. But after the initial shock had worn off, I was able to calculate a few things. First, they could not be less than half a mile away. If our information about their weapons had been right, we were out of range. Second, we were going to have to hurry back, for they would certainly send men after us. Das's camera had begun to hum by my side. I put the glasses back on the Chinese. Half a dozen men and one of the officers were already moving downhill. The remaining officer continued to study us through his glasses.

Das's camera ceased to hum. He stood up and turned to me.

'A scoop. You noticed those men coming down the hill, hah? They are coming to get us. Therefore I think we will have to run.'

He nodded toward Nathu La.

'Run straight back. We must not stop for anything. Mind the field-glasses, they belong to the Inspector. Come on.'

Of the next half-hour I remember very little. I am not a good runner anyway and in the thin clear air of the plateau I was worse than usual. The initial stumbling gallop through the forest rendered me breathless; then my ears filled with a buzzing that shut out all other sound; finally I developed a burning stitch in my left side. That is the physical memory, and there is one visual image: when we came to a small pebbled brook in the forest, I collapsed beside it and lay on my stomach watching the weeds waver slowly in the flow of the current, two long-legged water-flies, and a minnow; the moss was cool against my cheek. When I looked up Nathu La seemed far and unreachable. I was willing to stay where I was. Das's voice, breathless but imperative, brought me to a kind of reality.

'Come on. We are nearly there. Quickly!'

So flight began again. I reached Nathu La in a daze, a small iron needle in my side. We scrambled back up the slope and sat down heavily amongst a solicitous group of policeman, traders, and drivers.

'We were beginning to worry,' said the Inspector.

'We also,' said Das, and managed a smile.

The mist had come on again, and there was no sign of the Chinese.

We lay on foam-rubber-textured lichen, getting our breath, and in my case helping it along with the remains of the brandy. One of the traders came and squatted beside us.

Das, sighing, heaved himself indefatigably up and reached for his notebook. 'This Indian who was killed. Tell me about him.'

'It was done by the Tibetans,' the trader said. 'They came to his shop in the afternoon, and stabbed him five times. Then they looted the shop, took the money from the cash-box, and left.'

'Tibetans?' Das said with professional disappointment. 'I thought you said Chinese.'

'The Chinese say they themselves are Tibetans who have come from Peking. But these real Tibetans were hired by the Chinia, sahib,' said the trader. 'They did it in the daytime and the bazaar was full of Chinia policemen, but they did not interfere, though he shouted for help.'

'Ha!' said Das, and scribbled enthusiastically. 'How do they treat you, these Chinese?'

'Sahib, in the daytime we cannot move more than two hundred yards from our houses without a permit. After nine o'clock we cannot leave our houses also. It is gaol-life. Also they have taken the custom from our shops, and anything they buy they buy on credit, and never pay.'

'Why don't you complain to the Indian Trade Agent at Yatung? He is there to help you?'

'Sahib, what can he do? They pay no attention. And if we leave Tibet, they confiscate all our goods. Now we, today, were only allowed to bring our clothes and ten rupees from Yatung. They only have contempt for us Indians. Every Saturday in Yatung they have a clown show with four clowns, and one is Nehru.'

'Good, good!' said Das, scribbling a little more. 'Who are the other three?'

'Eisenhower sahib, Churchill sahib and Khrushchev sahib.'

'Why Khrushchev?'

'They are very angry that Russia has not supported them over the border dispute.'

'What do they say about the border?'

'Sahib, the officers say one day soon they will be coming. At the checkpost at Chumbithan they told us to say that in Sikkim.'

'It may not be as easy as they think,' said the police officer dourly.

'The Chinia are strong,' the trader said.

'How do they treat the Tibetans?'I asked.

'Sahib, all the rich men they have put to building a military road from Shigatse. Also in Yatung two weeks ago they took all the young girls away. They do this to keep the men from running away; also the girls are useful in North Tibet, because they are settling many Chinia civilians there, and they have no women.'

'What about the rebels, the Khambas? Is there still any fighting?'

'With them also, they took their families and put them in gaol, until the husbands surrendered. Them they shot or put to work on the Shigatse road.'

He sat by us, sighing, gathering a little dust in his hand and sifting it away with the slow movements of a tired man. I noticed how jumpy all the traders were. They had lines under their eyes, and all of them had nervous twitchy gestures of the hand.

We sat there, thinking, drinking, and then the Inspector said: 'Chhibar sahib is coming.'

Through the field-glasses a file of mules appeared ambling up the valley towards Nathu La. It was a relief. We squatted on the hummock watching them all the way up the valley till they had reached us.

Chhibar came first. He was a large man, rosy and powerful, wearing a fur hat and leather jacket. As his mule crested the ridge, we all shouted, rather raggedly, 'Welcome!' He smiled and waved a hand. After him came his wife, a most beautiful woman in a ballooning quilted jacket that made her look like a little tent, and three Tibetan nurses, each with one of the Chhibar offspring in her arms. They were followed by a baggage-train, the muleteers prodding the mules with goads and shouting the Tibetan version of Gittup: 'To to to to to to to,' on a rising scale. 'Very picturesque,' said Das, going happily to work with his movie-camera. When he had finished, the Chhibar family dismounted, and Das handed his camera to the driver and fished for his notebook.

'How was your trip, Major Chhibar?'

'Fine, fine,' said Chhibar, smiling gently.

'What are these reports of your being hindered by Chinese troops on your journey?'

'Untrue,' Chhibar sighed.

'The Chinese were helpful?'

'To me, yes,' emphasizing the *me*.

'And to other Indians? Say, the traders?'

'Less helpful.'

'Would it be true to say that the traders are in fear of their lives?'

'Perhaps.' So large, so gentle, so like a wall blocking off undiplomatic questions.

'How many troops would you say there were in Tibet?'

'I can't say. It is a difficult question.'

'In Lhasa, then?'

'It is a difficult question. Ten thousand—fifteen thousand.'

'And between Lhasa and Nathu La?'

'It is a difficult question. Perhaps the same number again.'

'So there are between twenty and thirty thousand Chinese in the area between Lhasa and Nathu La?'

'I would say so, yes.'

'Hah!' said Das, but at this point Mrs Chhibar came up to introduce the children, and I became occupied in teaching one of the little girls how to whistle, and missed the rest.

Then the Chhibars left in the waiting jeep, and Nathu La was desolate again.

I went up to the hummock to get a last look at Tibet. All I saw was mist.

Death by Water (1970)

Geography as well as history has been unkind to East Pakistan. The Bay of Bengal is shaped like a funnel, at the apex of which the country squats amid its swamps. The disturbances that take place in the Indian Ocean, particularly in May and October, when the rise and shift northward of hot air from the equator occur, tend to be forced into the mouth of the funnel. As the landwalls on either side close in, these disturbances are squeezed into a narrower and narrower compass, till eventually they explode at the apex of the funnel, on the offshore islands and coasts of East Pakistan. For centuries now, as overland invaders tramped into Bengal from the north and west, cyclones have walked up on heavy feet across the sea from the south, smashing into the coastal areas, taking people, houses, and animals in their iron hands, shredding them, and throwing them away. In 1876, one such invader from the sea killed 300,000 people. This is recorded, but it is very likely that there were worse cyclones before that, which went unrecorded, or of which the records have been lost. There was no protection, no means to chart or ward off cyclones, and for centuries the East Bengalis accepted and suffered their frequent unwanted visits.

Over the last eighty years, forty-two cyclones have hit the area. The fact that it is prone to these phenomena is no secret, but nobody seems to have thought of doing very much about it. Since 1945, however, it has become possible to chart the course of cyclones, at first with scout planes, but more recently with radar and through satellites. In 1965, when East Pakistan was swept by a really serious cyclone, the Government promised to build embankments and dykes and implement an efficient flood-control system. It set up a radar station at Cox's Bazar, near Chittagong, to spot and chart the cyclones as they came, and issue warnings to the population affected, but it forgot, conveniently, about the flood-control system. The local peasants, of their own volition, constructed low embankments of packed mud, none more than twenty feet high, to protect themselves. These embankments were fairly effective so far as minor disturbances were concerned, but nothing large hit East Pakistan between 1965 and late 1970.

The historic cyclone of 12 November 1970 was the second to hit the coast within three weeks. On 23 October, its precursor, a noisy but smallish John the Baptist, had swept across the offshore islands to the mainland. The radar station at Cox's Bazar had spotted it some hours before its arrival, had clanged its alarm bell, and sent out reports and warnings, and though the damage to property and life was not fully assessed, it was relatively inconsiderable. But as the hubbub of the first cyclone died away, hundreds of miles away in the Malay Sea, unknown to any radar, its huge and fatal successor was slowly starting to build up.

Much about cyclones, as about cancer, is still unknown. But the genesis of a cyclone is now explicable. It starts over a low pressure area in tropical seas. The low pressure area, which initially forms and always remains the centre of the storm, is known as the eye. The main cause of all the trouble, it is a peaceful area of calm seas and clear sky, like some beautiful woman who has incited her lovers to brawl around her. As the beauty's interest in all the brouhaha decreases, the lovers quarrel more desperately: as the pressure in the eye falls, it is encircled by fighting winds, which whirl round and round it at a speed which can reach 200 m.p.h. This area of the cyclone, which is called the eye-wall, is the real killer. It may measure fifty miles across. It pushes up before it, as it comes, a jagged wall of water, twenty or thirty feet high.

The November cyclone heaved itself up, like some black monster, from the sea off the Andaman Islands. It lumbered ponderously up the funnel of the Bay of Bengal, at a speed of roughly 10 mph. On 9 November, the American satellite Essa, floating high overhead, focused on the huge dark spiral as it moved over the waves, and sent instant warning flashes to Cox's Bazar. Meanwhile Indian cyclone experts were trying to keep track of the cyclone, afraid that it could veer, unpredictably as a missile out of control, southwest to Madras or north-west to Calcutta. It did not do so. Heavy and inevitable, it moved up the Bay of Bengal, and appeared on the radar screens of Cox's Bazar. Radio Pakistan immediately started to broadcast warnings to the areas likely to be hit.

The broad rivers of East Pakistan, once so essential to trade, pour into the Bay of Bengal. The Ganges and the Brahmaputra deposit immense quantities of silt in the sea, and this masses up into islands. The silt soil is highly arable, and the islands are therefore densely populated. Few of them, however, rise more than twenty feet above the sea. On the mainland shore facing them are other low lying, riparian districts, also densely populated. The cyclone would hit the offshore islands and then the coastal districts. It was all mapped out, by Essa and by the Pakistani radar. Radio Pakistan said so. What it failed to say, curiously enough, was that the cyclone coming was an immense one, and that the areas in question were in terrible danger.

The population of the islands and the coast heard the warnings, on new transistors or rickety old crystal sets. Unprotected as they were by any organized flood control system, their choices of salvation were limited: to climb to the tops of high houses and trees, and there try and ride the tempest out, or to flee for their lives. Most did neither. There were two reasons for this. Firstly, Radio Pakistan had cried Wolf three weeks before, when the cyclone of 23 October had struck. Not much damage had been done at that time. The radio had not emphasized the force of this new cyclone, so many people did not take the warning seriously. Secondly, even if the people were to flee, where were they to flee to? The population of the islands could only hope to reach the mainland coast, which was to be hit anyway. The coastal areas in many parts had no road or rail communication with the interior. An evacuation of the coast would have to take place along the rivers and waterways, and to be caught on a river in the midst of a cyclone of whatever size was obvious madness. The livestock of the peasants, anyway, could only be moved slowly, and were far too precious to be abandoned to wind and wave.

So the people stayed where they were. On the night of 12 November, most of them were asleep, under coarse blankets, in thatched straw huts on the islands and the coast. It was high tide, with a rough, breaking sea, and rain falling. Over the sounds of rain and sea came a distant roar, swelling slowly to titanic dimensions, drowning all other sound. Then an immense and deafening wall of water towered across the waves. Nobody, obviously, took a tape and measured it, but some peasants have said it was fifty feet high. It thundered down on the offshore islands. Houses, people, animals, trees, vanished under it. As the wave roared on coastward, a blinding, driving, killing wind followed it over the wrecked islands.

Wave and wind now exploded on the mainland shore. They rushed onward, unchecked and uncheckable, cutting a swathe fifty miles across which all villages and living creatures were ploughed irresistibly under. At last the wave halted, and then came the new terror. All waves, once they have broken on land, recede into the sea. The titanic mass of water that had broken on the East Pakistan coast was in fact a wave, and it obeyed this principle. It swept back seaward the way it had come. The survivors of the villages in its forward path now found themselves enveloped in choking, muddy water as it returned. Thousands of people, together with dead cattle, the wreckage of houses and boats, and uprooted trees, were swept helplessly out into the open sea.

Communications in the coastal areas are limited at the best of times. The cyclone destroyed what there was of them completely. It was two days before Dacca discovered the extent of the catastrophe on the coast. Helicopters, humming and flickering above the disaster area, saw thousands of bodies, human and animal, afloat in creeks, waterways, and the sea. The damp and oppressive heat had already commenced its work of decomposition. There were survivors, however, even on the islands, though the extent of the destruction was such that all that remained on one heavily populated island was a dog. These survivors, enveloped by the stench of corpses, and foodless, through the still hot days, and frozen and sleepless through the chilly nights, were also in danger of death. Hunger and cold apart, the likelihood of an epidemic caused by the unburied dead was terrible and real.

The Pakistani Army was despatched to the flood zones to bury the dead and help those who still lived. Within hours, however, as the news was flashed around the world, assistance started to pour into the country. The U.S.A. and Britain flew in troops to help with the relief work, and lent helicopters and launches to implement it. Medicines, food, clothes, and money were donated by other countries. India offered her condolences and a crore of rupees, which were accepted. She also offered supplies, which were accepted too, on condition that the Indian relief lorries stopped at the East Pakistan border, and handed over their loads to local officials. Other countries which provided supplies sent their own men into Pakistan to see that they were properly distributed, and it was alleged that the local officials who received the Indian supplies were selling them on the black market.

Pakistan had twenty-odd helicopters available for relief lifts. The U.S.A., rather stingily, only lent them eight. India, however, offered fifty helicopters to Pakistan, complete with crews. The Pakistanis refused to accept them. The presence of so many Indian Air Force personnel, they said, would be a security hazard to the country. It seemed a curious time to think of security, but strangely enough most Pakistanis I met in Dacca approved of the Government decision, on the *ut dona ferentes* principle. Even more strangely, most of the flood-affected peasants approved of it too. They usually hadn't heard that the Government had refused an offer of Indian helicopters, but when they were told this, they said the Government was right. 'We should not,' said the headman of a village off the coast of Bhola, 'accept help from the Hindus.'

But Pakistan gladly accepted help from everyone else. The Red Cross sent relief workers: so did A.I.D.; F.A.O. sent experts and observers. Even quicker than the aid came the foreign correspondents, who swooped down on Dacca in rapid succession, with a loud flutter of typewriter keys, a whirr of Arriflexes and Eclairs. They made sure that the world knew all about the disaster, and the world responded. There is nothing like a natural calamity to fill people with an undemanding pity (partly caused by relief that it did not happen to them) and a comfortably temporary sense of the brotherhood of nations. East Pakistan, for a short space of time, made daily headlines in every paper in the world.

Yahya Khan flew over from the western sector, spruce, military, and full of the correct responses to the situation; that is, up to a point. Beyond that point he betrayed himself. 'We are in the hands of Allah,' he remarked when pestered with questions as to why the Government had not attempted to provide a flood control system in the East, 'Who can stop a cyclone?' He may have been speaking as a good Muslim, but he was certainly not speaking as a good leader. Another distinguished visitor was the Pope, who stopped over in Dacca on his way to Manila (where he was nearly assassinated). He donated a substantial sum towards flood relief—which the Vatican could certainly afford—posed for the cameras of the press, and wafted a papal blessing to the people of the flood areas, who probably did not know who he was, would have disapproved if they had known, and, preoccupied as they were with the problem of survival, did not care anyway. It was good publicity, however, for the Pope and for the Pakistani officials who welcomed him at the airport.

Meanwhile, the death statistics fluctuated from day to day, as in some eerie stock market. The Pakistani press, for example, by and large, estimated that there had been more deaths than the foreign press did. The foreign press figures, in turn, were far in excess of those produced by the Government. The night before I left for Bhola, I strolled over to the Cyclone Information desk in the hotel lobby for the latest press release. It said that 191,000 people had so far been ascertained to be dead. Five minutes later, in the bar, a Dacca pressman said, very seriously, that he was. sure a million were dead. 'That,' he said with an air of pride, 'makes our cyclone,' his air was positively proprietary, 'the worst natural calamity in history. When the Yangtse Kiang flooded in the 19th century, 900,000 Chinese died, but we have beaten that! Pakistan!,' he announced, 'holds the record,' and I could detect no trace of irony in his large mild eyes. It was curious how little these statistics meant to anybody. The press men and relief workers who had visited the flood areas were visibly moved when they talked of individuals they had met, who had lost families and livelihoods; but they could accept the idea of several hundred thousand individuals dying without emotion, for it was impossible to think of so many as more than a statistic. The magnitude of the death figures surprised them: it did not move them.

'Such a disaster,' said the Dacca pressman, smacking his lips over his beer, 'has also a purifying effect on young people. All over the world, young people of all nationalities are thinking of the disaster and feeling pity. This will give them a more serious attitude towards life.' He wiped the froth off his mouth with a crumpled handkerchief. At the table behind us, two skimpily skirted American blondes, neither of whom was much more than sixteen, sipped Cokes and talked to a couple of Phillipino youths. They were all, I gathered from their conversation, which was not muted, the children of relief workers, 'It would be fun to have a picnic tomorrow,' one of the girls said. The older of the two boys clicked a contradictory tongue. 'All the pretty places around here,' he reminded her, 'are crapped up with floods and dead bodies and stuff like that.' The young blonde shook her pretty head. 'Hell, I forgot,' she said. 'What a nuisance. But, I guess, no picnic.'

The village had been utterly shattered. Of its fifty huts, none remained. There were no cattle in the fields, and no children in the muddy street. In the bamboo shelters which the Americans had put up sat the survivors of the population, nearly all men. The trees around the village lay like corpses in the damp earth. Square cardboard boxes of food, clothes, and medicine had been piled up in one of the shelters, preparatory to being opened and distributed. The survivors did not look towards them.

The American chopper, in the distance, moved like a dragonfly, darting up through the still air, then hanging there as though transfixed by astonishment before it darted up a little further. It was off to drop supplies in another village. 'They will need supplies,' said Captain Tariq of the Pakistani Army, nodding towards the survivors, 'for a long while yet. The crops were ready to be harvested, and now they are ruined.' As the sound of the chopper receded a deep silence lay down in the bedraggled fields around us.

Bhola is a large district on the southern tip of East Pakistan, and statistically the worst hit part of the disaster area. 119,000 people are estimated to have been killed here, either during the cyclone or by its aftermaths of starvation and cold. Flying over the district, one has the impression of utter devastation. The green landscape is blurred and smeary with ochre water, there are hardly any trees left standing, and the small relief encampments can be seen amidst the wreckage of large villages.

In one of the shelters a man squatted alone. He was thickset and short, his tufty beard dyed patchily red. His clothes were torn and stained, but a new blanket was draped around his shoulders.

He grasped its corners, mechanically, with both hands, as though for support. His face and eyes contained absolutely no expression, and even his body was listless. When, with the Captain as translator, I spoke to him, he answered dully and automatically, as though a ventriloquist were speaking through him. 'I had eight children and a wife,' he said. 'Four of my children were boys, four were girls. The eldest, my daughter, was eleven, and the smallest, my son, six months old. When we heard the water and the wind, I tried to think what to do. But there was no time. It seemed only a moment before we were in the water. My wife was carrying the baby. I caught hold of one of her hands. I caught hold of one of the children's hands. I told the children to hold on to each other. In this way, whether we lived or died, I thought we would not be separated.

'The force of the wave was terrible. I tried to brace my feet and stand fast, but it lifted me as I would lift one of my children. It was so dark I could not see, and because of the noise of the wind I could not hear. But I still had hold of my wife's hand and one of my children's hands. Then I was lifted and thrown hard against something solid. For a moment I was stunned. When I recovered I had my arms around a tree. But my hands were empty. God forgive me, I did not try to look for my family, but clung to the tree till daybreak. I have not seen my wife or my children since.'

This man, Hussein, I was told, had wandered around for three days after the cyclone, in a state of madness, looking for his family. Then, when the Pakistani Army and the Americans arrived, he had briefly returned to his normal self. He thought that they would be able to find his wife and children, since he could not believe they were dead. After some days he abandoned hope, and lapsed into the kind of stupor in which I found him. But it struck me that most of the survivors of the village were in the same state of shock. One could hardly expect them to smile, but they did not even look sad. They simply looked numb, expressionless. It was the same in all the villages I visited. The quiet survivors answered questions in dull and uninflected voices. Some had lost husbands, some wives: nearly all had lost children. When the Pakistani Army buried the corpses in Bhola, they were considerably hampered by the fact that the survivors kept digging the graves up, looking for their dead. They had given that up now, and subsided into shock, though in one village a young man wept terrible dry tears, his head in his hands. 'They do that sometimes,' I was told.

The airport at Dacca became my operational headquarters. Behind the normal traffic area, a large sector devoted to relief operations had been cordoned off. A complex of tin sheds housed the offices of the Pakistanis and foreign relief workers.

Truckfuls of the square cardboard cartons of supplies were unloaded here: relief planes landed with more. The relief workers, too, had their martyrs: a Swedish plane had recently been lost. Tough Pakistani soldiers watched as the supply cartons were unloaded and stacked. It was rumoured that some local officials were plundering the cartons and selling supplies on the black market, but it was not a very reliable rumour.

Certainly everything looked efficient and ran smoothly, except for a gloomy man who sat over a perpetually dead telephone in a billowy khaki tent near the helipad. He was in charge of putting the press on choppers or planes for the flood areas, but his task was not easy, as one could tell from his face. I did not rely on him, but with Rahman as interpreter prowled the offices in the tin sheds, trying to find someone who would put me on a plane to Patuakhali. This was a very difficult place to reach, but one crisp pale dawn Rahman succeeded in fixing a ride for me. An amphibian was on its way there to pick up a Pakistani Minister who had been on an inspection tour of the flood areas. It was ready for take-off when my ride was confirmed, and already contained Captain Rehman, a cheerful moustached man with a pipe, who was the pilot. Captain Rizvi, a bright youngster with sideburns, and Colonel Shaukat, who was young for his rank and had helped fix the ride. There was room for one more, and I squeezed into the back with Shaukat.

As we roared down the runway, he lit a cigarette, smiled, and said, 'Never been to Patuakhali yet. Always flown the other way so far. That's why I'm coming along. Always interesting to see new places, isn't it?' Rehman talked into a stuttery intercom as we tilted up steeply over the sprawl of Dacca, then switched it off, and looked back at me. 'You realize, of course,' he said, 'you'll have to find your own way back from Patuakhali. There won't be room for the Minister and you.' Since I already knew this, I was not as horrified as I might have been. Grinning, Shaukat said, 'I hope there *is* another way to travel from Patuakhali. Godforsaken damp, from all I hear.'

We flew at a low altitude over the emerald landscape, streaked with broad yellow waterways, to which I had now become accustomed. Small boats floated down the waterways, triangular sails raised to the wind: the flow of life had restarted after all the deaths. After roughly an hour, Rehman turned back to yell, 'Fasten your belts. We're going in now.' Below us lay a wide river, with a scatter of huts and houses on its left bank. The water was cluttered with fishing boats and launches. Rehman clicked his tongue in irritation, so loudly I could hear it above the roar of the engine. Then he flew in low on a trial run. We thundered in over a huddled village of boats, the fishermen ducking and shielding their heads with their arms, and pulled out and round on the wide sweep back, trees and huts twirling beneath the slewed belly of the plane. 'O.K.' said Rehman.

We curved round, and came back in over the boats. As we zoomed down over for the landing, Shaukat yelled a warning. Coming rapidly towards us, directly in our path, was a large launch. Our engine roared, Rehman threw himself on the stick, and we shot up, feet above the launch, and pulled round in a screaming vertical turn, back over the huts and trees and round once more to the river. Rehman is a fine pilot, who during the extreme crisis period had brought his amphibian down in places where nobody else had ever landed, but all this had obviously shaken him considerably. As we shot downward over the boats towards the now launchless river, Shaukat shouted, 'Too high! You're coming in too high.' He plunged forward for the stick, with which Rehman and Rizvi were now wrestling in obvious panic. The creased sunshot surface of the river hurtled up at us. Then we hit.

There was a sound like an explosion. Yellow water rose round us like a wall. Shaukat bellowed in my ear, 'Can you swim?' I was about to say that I couldn't, when the water subsided slowly into spray. Shaukat slumped back in his seat, fumbled for his cigarettes and said, 'No need, after all.' We had come down nosefirst, but had righted ourselves somehow. As the spray settled, the world came back into place. The amphibian drifted idly on the surface of the water. There were green banks on either side of us, dotted with trees, some tilted at crazy angles, huts, and startled, craning people. Each of us in the amphibian felt languorous, inclined to lie still and relax, as though after a satisfactory act of love. Rehman lit a stubby pipe, pointed down at the river, and remarked, 'It's full of sharks and crocodiles, you know. The sharks come up from the sea for the corpses.'

A rowboat came towards us from the left bank. 'That'll be the Minister's luggage,' Rehman said. 'We'll load it on, and the boat will ferry you back.' The boat came alongside, sunk to the gunwales. It contained three large suitcases, two airbags, a holdall, an impressive briefcase, and a roll of bedding. 'How long has this chap been here?' I asked. Rizvi smiled a cryptic smile. 'Two days,' he said, 'but he's a Minister, you know.'

The boat, divested of its burden, sped me back to shore. The Minister stood in a very ministerial pose on the deck of the cabin launch where he had apparently spent the night. He was attended by a valet, the local District Commissioner, and a number of police officers. I had been told to ask for the District Commissioner, so on clambering into the launch I approached him and told him my business. The Minister overheard me. He swung round, smiling affably, and extended his hand and climbed into the rowboat. It paddled him slowly out to the amphibian, which he entered, pausing unsteadily on the step to wave a hand shoreward. The amphibian belched into life, threw up an angry wake of water, and flew off to Dacca. The District Commissioner watched its departure without comment. There was an ambiguous look in his eye.

Cattle and people disputed the narrow, dusty alleys of the little town. Beyond it, up an unmade road, stood a squat concrete structure which housed the Commissioner's office. He sat down at his desk, a dapper young man, his eyes shielded by tinted spectacles, and offered me an American cigarette. Then he lit it for me, took off his spectacles, and blinked his large liquid eyes, which unlike the Minister's were rather tired, several times in rapid succession.

He was something of a poet. He lifted his long fingers, a cigarette smouldering down to white ash between them. 'Who has counted the dead? Some, the earth has swallowed them up, some, they are floating in the sea, some, they are in the bellies of the sharks. Their trouble is over, but for those who remain the real trouble has only begun now. They have lost everything except their lives. Many of them may feel that they are better dead. But basically they are courageous people. When a little of the shock has died, I think they will fight for life once more. The Government will subsidize them with small amounts of money, new seeds and fertilizer, and materials to build their houses. It is the mental shock they have received which will be the most difficult thing to fight.'

At this point a fat, elderly man in khaki entered the office. He was introduced to me as an important police officer of the district. 'No,' he said in answer to my question. 'The police have not had much to do, so far as the disaster is concerned. In the first days before outside help arrived, my men helped with the distribution of food. But now there is nothing for us to do. We are not doctors or nurses, our purpose is simply to keep people in order, and now there is no necessity for us to work, because nobody is disorderly.' 'For the police force,' he added, warming to his topic, 'the cyclone has been very lucky. This is normally the time of the year, as the harvest is reaped, when most crimes take place. Murders are mostly committed over crops or land, and of course women too, because this is winter and the people are more active. But this year the people are too preoccupied with how to survive to think of murdering others. Yes, I tell you, this cyclone has been very lucky for the police, and we are all on holiday.' He rubbed his hands together, with a noise like two scraped biscuits, and said, 'It is the Commissioner who has to worry.'

The Commissioner smiled, a wry twist of the lips. He started to describe his own difficulties at the time of the cyclone. 'This,' he said, 'is the largest town of Patuakhali district. Eighteen thousand people live here. I am not of this place myself, I come from Dacca. The town was too far inland for the cyclone to hit it with much impact. Still, it hit quite hard, though only fourteen people were killed here. But the morning after the cyclone I knew that the havoc down the river must be terrible. I could not reach this office, because of the floods and the wind, until the afternoon. A few other officers also managed to reach the office. We found that we could establish no radio or telephone communication with anyone anywhere. The town is not connected by road to any other place, and we had no boats, either to send to Dacca for help or to proceed to the coastal areas and the offshore islands to see what had happened. All we could do was sit and wait. We sat in this very office, without food or drink, for twenty-four hours. Then an Army helicopter came. I flew in it over the coast and the islands. I could not believe my eyes. So many dead. They were floating in the water like drowned flies. And where the villages had been, there was nothing. I had not dreamt it would be like that. Bad, yes, I knew that it would be, but not a catastrophe of that kind. When I returned to town, I opened the emergency rice stores. I bought rice from every merchant in town to add to the Government supply. Next day there was some transport, and we were able to take rice to some of the nearer areas. Afterwards proper help started to arrive: doctors came, and the Army, and after that the British Marines.'

'They have been wonderful here,' the policeman said. 'They have done wonderful work. That is something which the Western people, the British, the Americans, have: they have this kindness, they are ready to help. But our own people, they are not kind. They do not care.' The Commissioner chimed in at this point. 'He means, the British and Americans are sensitive, they have heart. They value life. You know, I read a lot, as much as I can in this place—I have a complete file of the *Readers Digest* for last year—and from reading Western books I have found out how much Westerners value life. It seems to me that in Asia we are not sensitive in that way, we do not value life, because there are so many people who are born and die every day in Asia.' He nodded, pleased with his assessment. I said, 'But the Indians are helping too. They gave you money, and supplies, and they offered you helicopters which Yahya Khan refused.' The Commissioner's thin, handsome face puckered a little, as though at an unpleasant smell. 'That is different,' he said slowly. The police officer slapped his hand on the tabletop. 'The Indians help us for their own reasons,' he told me. 'If we had allowed their helicopters in, they would have set up a Fifth Column here. Who can trust a Hindu? My grandfather told me what the Hindu zamindars did here in Patuakhali. Perhaps we may trade with them if Sheikh Mujib wins the election, but that does not mean that we should accept charity from the Hindus.'

~

'The only way for you to return to Dacca,' the Commissioner said to me. 'Is by the river steamer. It is about to leave but I have reserved a seat for you. It will take, I am afraid, sixteen hours, but there is no other way.' His jeep bumped me hastily down to the river, where, unsteady on its hawsers, an extremely battered steamer, coated in rust, awaited departure. It had two passenger decks, which were packed solid with peasants, sitting or lying on the floor: a passage through them had to be accomplished by main force. On the upper deck were two small cabins, each of which contained about ten people wedged together on wooden seats. I was wedged by the policeman the Commissioner had sent with me into one of these cabins. The boat, which I had noticed was called 'High Speed', snorted, cleared its throat, and began to shuffle very slowly upriver towards Dacca.

The landscape which we passed was one of the most beautiful, I think, I have ever seen. It was very green and very flat, but trees nodded slowly over the river as it coiled idly by, dropping their long shadows over the turf and the crops. The few people on the banks shouted and waved cheerfully as the steamer passed. At evening, in the scented dusk, one could see their small fires on the shore, and the tall tilted silhouettes of the trees that followed us up the river. It was a pastoral landscape, and a pastoral way of life, that had endured for centuries, and it seemed absurd that a countryside that so obviously mirrored the flow of human life should have been hit by so inhuman and uncontrollable a force as a cyclone.

At Barisol, the port of Bhola, eight of the ten people in the cabin left. The remaining passenger beamed at me, shook my hand, told me that he was an Army doctor from Patuakhali, and inquired who I was. When he had learnt all he could possibly learn about me he shook my hand once more. 'So you are British,' he said, 'but you come here from India. How do they treat the Muslims in that dirty Hindu country?' I said I thought the Muslims were treated reasonably well. 'What about Ahmedabad?' he retorted. 'Last year those dirty Hindus killed five million Muslims there.' I told him that this was not true, that I had been to Ahmedabad myself, and that though the whole incident had been deplorable, not more than two thousand Muslims at most had been killed. 'Of course, the Hindus would not tell you the truth,' he said. 'But I heard it on the radio. Let us not talk of these dirty Hindus. You are my guest. You have come from a long way to my country. Now the accommodations on this boat are very bad. There is no food here, and no water, and no bedding. But *I* have all three. You will share my food and water, and I will lend you a pillow and a blanket.' He overruled my feeble and rather false protests, and we dined off fish curry, spiced potatoes and rice. The doctor then opened the cabin door to visit the lavatory. This was something I had resolutely decided not to do, since one lavatory served the whole ship. Outside the door lay a young, and perhaps once beautiful, woman, clutching a very small and fragile baby to her breast like a child with a doll. Her eyes were shut, and she was moaning spasmodically. The doctor bent over and looked at her for a while. Then he straightened up quickly, and stirred her with his toe. He addressed her angrily in Bengali. Very slowly, without a word, she rose, clutching her child, and moved towards the passenger deck.

When the doctor returned, beaming once more, I asked him who the woman had been. 'I do not know,' he said. 'But I think she was suffering from cholera. It was not healthful for us that she should sleep outside the door.' I protested that if she really was suffering from cholera, it was up to us to do something. 'No, no,' said the doctor, 'in this large ship we will not be able to find her anyway. Besides, though I have the greatest sympathy for the cyclone victims, the peasants live like dogs, and they die like dogs. Her case is nothing unusual.' He occupied the rest of the evening, until we went to bed, in showing me photographs of his wife and four small children.

~

A heavy hand on my shoulder roused me from an unquiet sleep. I peered blearily up into the broad placid face of the doctor. 'We have reached,' he said. 'But we are very early.' A glance through the porthole showed me what he meant. It was pitch dark outside, except where the uneven flare of kerosene lamps revealed the interior of a quayside shed. A sepulchral mist shrouded the river. I shook the doctor's hand, said goodbye, and plunged through the cabin door. The narrow corridor outside was packed solid with people. They were fighting their way towards land with an intensity which suggested that they feared that the ship was about to sink. Children wailed, adults shrieked, and a powerful rancid smell of bodies filled the air. I battled my way slowly through to the ramp that led down to the quay.

The alleys beyond the harbour exit were providentially cool and still. Two or three cookshops, illumined by kerosene lamps, exuded steam and odours of food. The passengers off the steamer poured avidly into them. I went on to where, in the throat of the alley, a solitary cycle rickshaw stood, climbed into it, and told the driver where to take me. We set off, in a slow and meandering style, through a sequence of narrow, unlit, totally deserted streets. I started to feel nervous. The driver, however, showed no tendencies towards murder or theft: he wheezed asthmatically over the pedals, and I eventually felt rather sorry for him.

We came out of the old city at last, and proceeded at a smart clip down the wide boulevards towards the massive bulk of the Intercontinental, lit like an ocean liner on the dark sky. The streets were deserted, even here, except for a few quiet defecators in the shadows. I remembered that today Pakistan went to the polls. Nobody seemed very excited about it, this early in the day. The chalked symbols and occasional posters on the walls looked spectral under the horned moon. At the Intercontinental, I climbed out of the rickshaw, paid, and limped upstairs, hoping to be able to sleep, bathe, and have breakfast in bed.

My hopes were shattered when Wahid* telephoned at seven.

---

* A poet whom Dom had met, and been befriended by, soon after his arrival in Dacca to report on the cyclone.

'This is all very exciting,' he said. 'You must see the people at the polls. It will give you a good story. Perhaps there will be riots, murders, arson. I do not think so, but who knows?' I dragged myself out of bed, had a rapid and unsatisfactory bath, dressed, and limped back downstairs to find Wahid awaiting me. He insisted that we should return to his flat for breakfast. A number of the other young men were already there.

We drank tea flavoured with cardamoms, and ate sticky sweets. This was not exactly what I had in mind for breakfast. As we ate, however, everyone suddenly ceased to speak. They all looked delightedly at the kitchen door, and expectantly at me. When I looked towards the kitchen, a young woman stood in the doorway, clutching a baby to her hip with one hand and a small boy to her side with the other. An odhni covered her face. 'My wife,' said Wahid with considerable pride. 'She made these sweets.' Before I could think of a word to say, the young woman slipped back into the kitchen. 'Now,' said Rahman sententiously, 'Wahid has proved that he is your friend.'

We sat on, talking. Nobody made any move to leave. This was not, my conscience told me, the way a foreign correspondent should behave. Ideally, at this moment, I should be racing round the polling stations trying to spot trouble. But I had no desire to do so. I listened to the young men instead. They talked of their relatives abroad—most of them had some remote kindred in England or America—and of how they would like to visit a foreign country. 'China, I suppose,' I teased, but they did not smile. 'No, a rich country, England, America,' Wahid said. 'We could make money there. Perhaps that would be bad. If we made very much money, perhaps we would not wish to return to Pakistan.' But they continued to speculate on which country would offer the most opportunity. 'Because,' one said, 'if we remain in Pakistan, we will remain poor. Even though we are Government servants.' Everyone laughed. 'Because we are Government servants,' Rahman said. 'The Government does not pay properly to anyone. Look at the peasants in Bhola and Patuakhali. They should pray to Allah to send a cyclone like this every year. It is the first time the Government has ever fed and clothed them free, or taken any interest in them at all.'

Wahid said, 'This is the only political cyclone in history. Look how it has changed our politics. We are a Muslim country but we should adopt the Christian calendar. BC and AC. Before the cyclone, and after.' Downstairs a radio belched out news bulletins, and the noise in the street slowly built up. I suggested that we should visit the polling stations. 'Yes,' Wahid said. 'We must remember our duty as citizens and cast our votes.' I asked if his wife intended to vote, 'No, no,' he said. 'How could she know whom to vote for?' We climbed down the resonant stairs into the full day. By this time, though the shops were all shut, steel eyelids sealing off the windows, the roads were full of people, on foot or in cycle rickshaws. The pedestrians floated along in talkative clumps. They were all headed the same way, but had a rather aimless look about them. Those in the cycle rickshaws were often burkhaed women, with children in their arms. 'Will they vote?' 'Yes,' said Wahid, 'Their husbands will have told them who to vote for. But I, I have too much respect for the freedom of my wife to dictate to her like that.'

The sun was very hot, and I had started to feel very tired. So when Wahid and his friends went off to vote I returned to the hotel. The huge lobby was empty for once, except for a local newspaperman sipping beer. He informed me that all my colleagues were out, keeping an eye on developments. I said it was probably very unprofessional of me not to be doing exactly that. 'Why?' he asked, his eyebrows quizzically lifted. 'There are no developments to keep an eye on.' Comforted, I went up to my room, switched on the air conditioner, and fell asleep.

It was afternoon when I awoke. I hired a taxi and went for a ride round the city. The heat of the day had faded, and there were more crowds than there had been earlier, hurrying on foot or by cycle rickshaw to cast their votes before the polling stations closed. On the pavements, groups of those who had already voted listened to forecasts and early results on transistors. Radios blared in restaurants, which were packed like concert halls with attentive auditors. As the cool, scented dusk came down, and the lights of the city flicked to life, I went back to the hotel. Most of the other correspondents, hot and tired, were in the bar. A deeply depressed American, who had heard the previous day that there would be a bloody riot, and had spent precious and now wasted hours polishing a pile of phrases to describe it, kept asking people if they had seen any trouble at the polling stations. A Japanese photographer said yes, he had. The American came abruptly to life. His hand flew to his notebook. 'What did you see?' he demanded. The Japanese replied, 'I saw a man arrested because he tried to vote twice.' Neither he nor the American understood why everybody laughed so much about it.

Dispatches from Indonesia (1972)

Writers in Captivity

When we landed at Jakarta, I was horrified to discover that it was Ramazan, the period when all Muslims fast. It would not be possible to interview President Suharto, or indeed anyone, until it was over. I hired a young man who had a connection with a local paper, to get us small stories. I particularly remember one of these, which had to do with the oldest taxi in Asia. It was a 1902 Lincoln, and its driver was much older than his vehicle, which he had acquired in 1907. He still plied for hire in it. The morning we visited him and the taxi, both had been polished and spruced up for the camera, but the vehicle bore the unmistakable marks of extreme decrepitude. All the seats in the car had been removed, and cane chairs substituted for them. A burst and stained mattress served as the roof. The driver pointed to it and said with difficulty (for he had no teeth) that we would never guess how many babies had been born on the mattress as he drove their mothers to the hospital. *Dozens,* he told us. Bits of the machine were tied on to the body with string, and the tyres were worn smooth. Fischbeck dealt the bonnet a sharp rap with his fist, and, in slow and synchronized movement, all the four mudguards fell off.

When we left, Fischbeck said ruminatively, 'D'you think, if I'd given the driver a tap, his arms and legs would have fallen off?' He specialized in black humour. He was South African, an athletic Aryan with golden hair and pale blue eyes. He had gone from South Africa to England, and finally wound up in Hong Kong. Apart from his photography, he had an import-export business, and a shop high up on the Peak. As a photographer he was excellent, if not imaginative, and he was absolutely fearless, as I was later to find out.

We had both become rather frustrated with the days of inanition, but there was a large press corps in Jakarta, and they were very helpful. Frank Hawkins, of the Associated Press, one day said, 'Instead of farting around here, why don't you try and get to Buru?' Then he explained what Buru was; I had at first thought he was talking of some influential politician.

In 1965, seven years before our visit, General Suharto came to power following a military coup. Sukarno, whom my father had interviewed (and I had met briefly in 1949) was ousted. A roundup was made of all those suspected of Communist affinities and sympathies. They had been docketed as A, B and C-class prisoners. The A-class had usually been incarcerated in Java, and the Cs executed. The Bs, however, had been despatched to prison camps hastily set up on remote islands, where they had been kept ever since without trial or any hope of it. 'Pramudja Ananta Toer, who's supposed to be the greatest living Indonesian writer,' Hawkins said, 'is supposed to be there, and so are a lot of other intellectuals. Suprapto, who used to be the Attorney-General, is supposed to be there too. But nobody really knows. There's been nothing heard from them.'

Buru, like the other prison camps, was under a commandant. The commandant changed every so often, since this was a post of extreme hardship, and a new one would be on his way to Buru in the next few days. The Indonesians, who had previously refused to allow any members of the press on the island, had now agreed that six correspondents could travel with the new commandant. They had flatly refused the *Tass* man, and made the price for the round trip so high that most newspapers and agencies, including

AP, would not consider it. 'It's not only the prices,' Hawkins explained, 'but the amount of bribery involved.'

It was a very big story. The cost would be immense, but there were two arguments which would predispose Pandit* towards paying it. One was that so many other people had said it was too expensive for them. He might very well accept the cost, because the *Asia Magazine* would then prove it could spend more on a story than its Western counterparts. The other argument was that I had been awarded the Citation for Excellence by the Overseas Press Club of America for my *New York Times* pieces on India. Pandit had been much impressed by this, and the suggestion that I—and therefore the magazine—might win some further award for this kind of story would weigh heavily with him.

But something else Hawkins had said was on my mind, and, before telephoning Pandit, I took Fischbeck into my confidence and we sat down together with a map of Indonesia.

In my childhood I had possessed a book in which there were coloured sketches of primitive tribes. The picture which had most impressed me was one of a New Guinea aboriginal, with his face painted for war in red, white and yellow stripes, and the brilliant feathers of murdered birds of paradise sprouting from his kinky hair. He had an axe in one hand, and a long spear in the other. Not much was known about him, the book said. I looked at the picture often, and intensely wanted to know more about him.

Hawkins had told me, 'Most people don't know that half of New Guinea is Indonesian. They took West Irian from the Dutch a while after the rest of the country. West Irian's not that far from Ambon. You have to fly to Ambon to reach Buru. You'll come back to Ambon from Buru, and then from Ambon to Port Biak, which is towards Australia. From there, pal, you fly to Djayapura,

---

* R.V. Pandit, journalist, restaurateur, publisher and film producer, was then the editor of *Asia Magazine*.

which is the only town in West Irian. After that, it's up to you. It's only a trip of about 15,000 miles altogether. Maybe 300 miles inland from Djayapura, you'll find the cannibals. The Yali and Dani tribes are still in the Grand Valley of the Baliem.' He laughed. He had been there.

Hence the poring over maps in the Hotel Indonesia. I was very close to the coloured picture of my childhood, I could almost recall how the page that contained it smelt, and I was determined to reach New Guinea. Ambon, I saw, lay on the Banda Sea, with Buru, or Boroe, as the map had it, slightly to the west. South-east from Ambon was New Guinea, and a little beyond it Australia. No established airline flew to these parts of the world from anywhere; my information about precise distances, modes of transport and prices, would have to depend on the Indonesian authorities. Ramazan was now almost over, and I was able to get hold of the proper people for information.

Next day I called Pandit. When I told him, rather nervously, what the distances involved, the time factor, and, last of all what the costs were, his scream down the line was audible to Fischbeck, who was lolling in a chair cleaning his cameras. 'These are the biggest stories the magazine has ever handled,' I said. 'I'll bet my life on them.' Pandit didn't seem as convinced as I was. 'It's a huge sum,' he said, and, then, to my immense surprise, added, 'Pledge your faith as a journalist that these stories are worth it, and I will consent.' To require such pledges in this way seemed preposterous. However, I said, 'Yes, yes, I pledge my faith.' Pandit replied, 'And Fischbeck, does he too pledge his faith?' Frank put down his cameras. He ambled over to the phone and said, 'Yeah, Pandit, I heard all that. You talk loudly, don't you? Well, anyway, I'll do my best, and I think Dom will too.' This seemed to satisfy Pandit. 'You are good men,' he said, not meaning our moral characters, 'and I will trust you.' Shortly after this, alone in my room, I received a call from him, saying, 'Control Fishbeck's spending. He is extravagant. But I trust you.' An hour later, Frank called me to say, 'I've had a call from the great panjandrum, telling me to control your spending. He says you're very extravagant, but he trusts me.' I said that was splendid.

Next day the money arrived, and, by means of bribery, in part, and also by paying the vast sums the Indonesian Government required, we arranged our trip. A couple of days later we met our travelling companions at the military airport. Errol Holmes of Australian broadcasting, and Pieter Schumaker, a Dutch freelancer, were coming to Buru too. Errol was a quiet, clean-shaven man; Schumaker was tall, gaunt and bearded, but also calm in manner, with a dry sense of humour. We made ourselves known to each other on a grim, warm dawn. Then the commandant and his henchmen arrived, and we all got into a tiny transport and flew off to the southwest, the rising sun behind us. It was a long flight. I decided to acquaint myself with the commandant, who was squat and porcine, and Schumaker acted as a kind of interpreter. His Dutch, obviously, was fluent, but his Indonesian wasn't. The commandant's Indonesian was fine, but his Dutch flawed.

However, we accomplished a small coup of our own. Schumaker had some gin, we had some whisky. Each of us made the commandant an offering, which he accepted. He drank a mixture of the two, and, towards the middle of the flight, fell fast asleep while vowing that we would have a free hand on Buru. 'He von't say that vhen he vakes up,' Schumaker said wryly. 'He vill have vun hell of a hangover.' Still, it was a start.

The other officers had been drinking, playing dice or cards, or snoring. Beneath us lay a turquoise sea, the water so clear that one could see the coral reefs and rocks below, and even the lazy flicker of large fish as they moved through their element. We were flying low, but suddenly came out of cloud over Ambon. The whale-backed hills under us were thickly forested, and mist seemed to steam up from them, as from some prehistoric swamp. This proved to be cloud, and we landed at a primitive airstrip, where jeeps waited. Ambon, Schumaker said, was famous for a fort left by the Dutch, but we saw only trees, flowering vines, and streams, till the jeeps reached a camp.

There were some barracks, in which we all slept. It rained heavily. Schumaker, Fischbeck and I sat in the balcony, drinking whisky. Errol had wisely retired. The officers were further up the balcony still playing their endless card game, and also drinking. Presently, one of them staggered up to us, carrying a quarter-full bottle of schnapps, with a small discoloured object bobbing about in the remnants of the liquor. Without saying a word, he seized our bottle of whisky, filled his bottle from it, and staggered off. Schumaker held Frank back: he had wanted to remonstrate.

'Remember, ve must live vith these fellows,' he said. 'They are mad, bad men. Buru is very near, also.' He laughed heartily. 'Ve don't vant to find ourselves locked up in it. Vot vould happen to our stories?' I was curious about the officer's bottle.

'There was something in it,' I told Schumaker.

'Ah, yes, I saw,' Schumaker said. 'It is a human baby foetus. They mix it into the liquor they drink, to give them virility.'

Early next day, the jeeps took us to the harbour, where a kind of landing craft was anchored. The whole of Ambon was drenched, the trees and vines dripped, the muddy streams were in spate. But a huge sun came up, and the earth started to steam. The landing craft set off under a cloudless sky, over smooth seas. Presently we saw a great hump of land, with hairy forests on its flanks, ahead of us. 'They say Buru is larger than Bali,' Errol said. The landing craft put in at a pier where there was a reception committee, waiting for the new commandant. We left the sea behind us and walked some distance through the forest to an assembly of small buildings: the main command post on Buru. Soldiers stood simply to attention in a central square. A tattered Indonesian flag hung, slack in its tethers, overhead. While the commandant inspected the guard of honour, we were taken to a room for coffee, rice, and a briefing in English.

The English, as spoken by the officer who briefed us, left great gaps of information open, but we understood that there were fourteen camps on the island, and some 10,000 B-class prisoners distributed among them. 'Some may be dead now,' the officer said. 'Check up later. Dese men no escape. In sea, many big fish. How to escape?' He answered himself, 'Is better be dead.' We could extricate no further concrete information from him, except in regard to our programme. There were no roads inland. But the commandant would be walking round the island, inspecting some of the camps. We were to accompany him. I asked about the writer Pramudja. 'He here,' said the briefing officer. 'He in Camp 14, on top of mountain.' He pointed to the hump in the distant centre of the island. I realized that it was an extinct volcano. 'Camp 14 for very bad men. Very dangerous men. Very hard camp.' The officer picked up a cane and struck the desk in front of him several times. This was what happened to the prisoners in Camp 14. 'Leave soon,' he said. 'You want wash face, you want shit?'

The officials in Jakarta had gone to great pains to tell us how beautiful Buru was, how happy the prisoners were, and, how soon, after they had been cured of communism, they would be released. The camp officers didn't seem to know exactly who we were. But, since we had come with the commandant, they felt that we needed to be told what he was being told: that is, how firm, even brutal, they were in their treatment of their prisoners, and how sternly they enforced discipline. Later someone asked all of us who had been on Buru about this. Did we not think, they asked, that the soldiers we met had exaggerated their own brutality, because they thought that that was what we wanted to hear, and thought we would commend them to the commandant for it? That may be so, but, from all that I saw or heard on the island, they can only have exaggerated their brutality a little.

We started from the main camp on foot, the commandant in front with the officers. We trailed along behind him and a number of soldiers followed us. Gravelled footpaths had been laid down between the fields where prisoners were at labour. They wore grimy vests and trousers, and some the big conical straw hats of Indonesian peasants. The guards had received no clear orders about us; we were able to go over to some of the men and try and talk to them. Most couldn't speak English, but we struck lucky with a thin person called Barzuki Effendi. He not only spoke English but was a film director. One of his films, he said, had won an award at Cannes. 'You are only able to eat what you grow yourself,' he said. 'That is very hard on the older men.' He was digging up potatoes. 'It is hard on everyone,' he said. 'Hardest on the small boys.' We had not heard of any small boys on Buru, and we asked for further information.

Barzuki said, 'They arrested many people when there were protest rallies in Jakarta and other towns. Small boys used to run after the marchers, and they were arrested with the rest. Some were sent here. They must have been five or six years old then. Now they will be seven years older. Many prisoners and guards use them for sex. They are mostly illiterate. Their parents must think they are dead, since they cannot write letters. But even we, who can write, we don't know if the letters are delivered. We receive no replies. It is, you know…agony. After a while you get resigned. At first they used to beat us. Not so much now. Yes, Pramudja is here. But he is up on the mountain, far from this place.'

We began to see the boys of whom Barzuki had spoken. They were now in early adolescence, pitifully thin, and, like everyone else, sun-stained and sad. We could not talk to them. Pieter tried out his Indonesian without much success. Several of the prisoners we met had eye diseases, and sores, both the result of inadequate diets.

A thatched construction stood off the road. It was an infirmary. Inside there were camp cots, on one of which a patient lay. He had malaria, the attendant said, when we asked through our briefing officer. There was no doctor, but he was being given quinine. That seemed to be all that was available. 'Malaria very bad,' the officer said. 'Very much malaria.' It struck me that the patient looked rather plump for a prisoner. When I asked, the attendant's reply was translated. The man was not a prisoner, but a camp guard. This place was not for prisoners. They were treated in their own camps.

'Some prisoners is doctors,' said the officer helpfully. '*Real* doctors.'

The sun was high. Sweat flowed down our faces and bodies. Clouds of midges and flies collected round our heads, and when brushed away returned within seconds. The prisoners in the fields were similarly affected, but one assumed, as Errol said, they were used to it. I talked to the commandant about Pramudja. Were we going to Camp 14? The briefing officer translated. We weren't going to Camp 14. It was a very hard climb to the camp. But the commandant would send orders ahead, for Pramudja to be brought down from the mountain, and with him Dr Suprapto, the former Attorney-General.

A runner set off ahead of us, and we laboured on. Overhead the sky filmed over with clouds, which shortly melted into cascades of rain. The prisoners continued to work and we to walk. Late in the afternoon the rain stopped, and we were shrouded in wet heat. At roughly the same moment Schumaker and I said to each other, 'I am going to fall down and die,' we reached a thatched hut with a glutinous brown river oozing past it. There was dense tropical forest all around, exuding strange scents and the cries of monkeys and parakeets. Inside the hut there was a field kitchen, which dispensed rice, curried chicken and fish, and fresh coconut water. The decapitated coconut shells, thrown from the hut by the officers, heaped themselves up outside.

At about the time we finished this bizarre meal, a clanking of chains announced that Pramudja and Suprapto had arrived. They were fettered and escorted by armed guards. It seemed a bit excessive; both were slightly built and small; both were dressed in good clothes that did not fit them, and Pramudja also wore spectacles and a black cap without a peak. They were taken into an adjacent tent. 'Dey come down mountain,' said the briefing officer happily, 'specially you to see.' We entered the tent, which was immediately surrounded by guards and soldiers. The commandant came in with us, and sat down on a chair, squinting at his prize prisoners.

He then said a number of things in Indonesian, which were meant to be orders. When he had finished, I said to the briefing officer, 'Mr Fischbeck wants to take pictures of all of you.' Meanwhile Errol set up the tape recorders all of us carried, and Pieter said urgently to the prisoners, 'Do you speak English?' They nodded. This was a prearranged plan. The commandant, after a long period in which he got his muddied boots cleaned and polished, went off with all the other officers to be photographed. The guards followed them, hoping to be included in the picture. We said to Pramudja and Suprapto, 'If you have any messages for your family, or anyone else in Jakarta, speak now.' They began to speak, in Javanese, after giving me the addresses of the people they were speaking to.

They were, by then, a little relaxed. Frank was prolonging the photographic session outside as much as was humanly possible. Pramudja said, 'We are not well treated here. We cannot eat anything, except rice, which we do not grow with our own labour. Dr Suprapto and I…are not used to this, but we have managed. The other prisoners have been kind.' Suprapto said, in punctilious, slow English, which for seven years he had had no occasion to use, 'It is the lack of knowledge of our families… We write letters, we receive no answers…. We do not know if the letters have ever been sent. If I could speak to my wife, I would say remarry…. I have said this on your tape. We shall never leave this island alive.' Pramudja said, 'They used to beat us, now they don't. It is that we are dehumanized. I no longer feel like a man.

And I am a writer. My whole life is writing. And here I have no materials to write. I want to write my memoirs.'

Frank could not continue his delaying operation indefinitely. The commandant came back into the tent, followed by the briefing officer and a variety of lieutenants and captains. 'You no miss something,' asked the briefing officer, 'because I not here?' We said we hadn't. But, I added, to the commandant, 'Why don't you allow Mr Pramudja writing materials?' The commandant quizzed the briefing officer, who said to us, 'He can have enough paper, many paper.' He then guffawed heartily, and translated to the commandant, who slapped his thigh and roared with mirth. 'As many paper he wants, he can have, but pens is dangerous weapon! Paper he can have, but no pens!' All the officers and soldiers in the tent were falling about. Frank suggested to the commandant that the sun was coming back. The officers and he should pose for more photographs.

They all went out. Errol, Pieter and I thrust our spare notebooks and ballpoints into Pramudja's hands. His pockets weren't large enough to hold them. He clutched them to his breast. The briefing officer came back and issued orders. The soldiers began to fasten the chains back on the prisoners. The briefing officer said, 'You come now.' We followed him to the riverside. Looking back, I saw Pramudja and Suprapto being led away in chains. A number of guards surrounded them. Pramudja's long fingers were spread as though he was trying to protect a bird. The guards were busy breaking ballpoints in their hands and stamping notebooks into the mud. 'We know,' said the briefing officer, 'we *know.* Tonight you give me tapes. *All* tapes. Good, OK; is OK.'

We evaded that by supplying the commandant with a good deal of liquor instead. Then we returned to Ambon. We were now coming, for some reason, from the other side of Buru, which involved a long trip by night, during which a great storm exploded over us. The vessel was a troop transport, carrying the former garrison of Buru by slow stages to Jakarta. The soldiers lay on the unprotected deck, lashed by rain from above, while tall waves burst on the poop and washed back over them. Since we were amongst them, we didn't waste our pity. The storm subsided before dawn, and I stood damply by the rail, looking down across the clear turquoise water to heavily forested islands. Flying fish raced the ship across the water.

Schumaker and Holmes went back from Ambon. Frank and I waited for the flight that would take us to Port Biak; from there another flight would take us to Djayapura, the only town in West Irian. Both of us had the tense satisfaction that follows the completion of a good story. It was not the same as that pleasure that follows the completion of a good poem, but I told myself firmly, that was part of my past. Behind my new mask, my new identity as an adventurous press correspondent, I was content to hide.

The Cannibals of Djayapura

As we waited at the airstrip for the plane that would take us to Djayapura, a thunderstorm broke. The plane, nevertheless, bucketed down through the deluge, and to our surprise was far from empty. It disgorged a large number of elderly white men, who came dripping into the concrete shack which constituted the terminal. They were Americans who had been stationed on Biak during the Second World War. 'I see the weather hasn't changed since 1944,' said the group leader. 'This is the first time we've been back and we're gonna make a party of it. You boys live here?' The question seemed, from what we had seen of Biak, almost an aspersion on one's character. We denied that we were residents of the place. 'Anyway,' said our new friend, 'have a drink with us.'

Cases of beer and hard liquor were carried in from the plane. We were the only passengers now, and the pilot seemed unwilling to forego the proposed party. One of the veterans complained that there was no ice. 'Shit,' said the leader, 'did we have any ice back in 1944?' They launched into separate stories about what Biak had been like: the flies and mosquitoes, the heat and unpredictable rain, the fighting, the cave in which the Japanese made their last stand. They inquired anxiously if the bones were still there. We said yes, and a lot of burnt-out US Army vehicles as well. They emitted whoops of delight. They were like characters from Norman Mailer's *The Naked and the Dead,* only thirty years older. The party went on till well past dark.

Nobody was expecting us in Djayapura, and after midnight it came on to rain. So we were agreeable when the pilot proposed that we fly at dawn. We had slight headaches when we landed at our destination on a muggy morning. Djayapura had a dishevelled look, as though some gigantic god had flicked a finger at a few white houses and they had landed in a small, random cluster by the sullen sea. There was a neat square populated by flowering trees (Djayapura had been founded by the Dutch, under the name of Hollandia), and a church. The church, Frank Hawkins had said in Jakarta, would be very important to us, since the priests knew all about the territory and ran mission stations where we could stay in the interior.

We checked in at the only resthouse there was, primitive but with nets over the beds, to keep out insects and rats. Then we went to register with the army commander. I showed him the permits we had for the interior. He was fat and sweaty, like the commandant of Buru, and he shook his head over them. 'If you can get into the Baliem valley, you can go there,' he said. 'We cannot help you, eh?' Also, he said, we would need a military escort. 'But I cannot spare mens, and my mens are too afraid of the natives there. Very bad mens, those natives. They are eating other mens. So....' With some difficulty he found two forms, which stated in Indonesian and Dutch that neither the Indonesian Government nor the army were responsible for our safety, that we indemnified them from all claims of relatives or friends in case any harm came to us, and that we were undertaking our trip on our own responsibility and of our own free will. The commander stamped the passes with a flourish, and then asked for a fee. This was rather large, and was not mentioned in the documents we had signed. 'If you meet soldiers, you show these,' the commander said, 'and soldiers will help if they can.' But, he added, sucking his moustache, 'I think you not meet soldiers, and, if you meet, I think they not help.' We went to the church.

Here we received a different welcome. The church and the community house beyond were neat and scrupulously whitewashed. The Dutch priests offered us coffee and cake. The librarian brought out books on West Irian, and offered to lend them to us. One of them was *Gardens of War* by Michael Rockefeller. 'He went,' said the librarian, 'to the Baliem valley, but it was not there he was killed. He was killed on the Sepik river in the south.' The tone in which he said this was far from heartening.

The other priests were less gloomy in their outlook. They said that the Dani tribe in the Baliem were cannibals. As we would learn from Rockefeller's book, they practised a ritual form of warfare, conducted between the clans, and afterwards ate each other's dead. 'The valley was only discovered in 1938,' said the head of the community. 'It is not yet thirty-five years that the first outsiders went there. So they are still wild. They have killed a few outsiders, but not many. Normally they are very gentle people.

'But,' he added, 'they like not the Indonesians. The Indonesian soldiers are afraid of them, and, because they are afraid, they treat the Dani people badly. So the Dani, they like not the Indonesians.' He seemed pleased at this thought; he chuckled, and offered us cigars. Outside the window of the refectory where we sat were trim vegetable plots and civilized flower-beds. It was different from our resthouse, to which we returned after having done our work. Frank went off to the airstrip, where the priests had a Cessna four-seater plane which they hired out. It could take us into the Baliem valley, at least as far as Wamena, an Indonesian military outpost in the mouth of it. From then on we would have to walk to Giwika, the nearest mission station. A Father Jules Camps was *in situ* there: he spoke the tribal dialect, and would be able to help us.

While Frank was away, I read about the place we were due to visit. The Grand Valley of the Baliem, to give it its proper name, had, for many years, been unknown to the Dutch settlers. It was locked in by a high mountain range, which no colonist had ventured to cross. In 1938, an American flyer, Richard Archbold, had spotted it from his plane, but had not landed. Towards the middle of the war, a US Army plane had crashed there. The survivors were fetched out across the mountains by the Dutch. That had been the first time outsiders had entered the valley. After the war, missionaries had been sent in. Some of them had been killed and eaten by the Dani. 'Particularly,' one of the Catholic community at Djayapura told me, 'the Protestants.' But Father Camps had endured fourteen years at Giwika, uneaten.

Frank returned to say that the Cessna would fly us to Wamena in two days' time. Later the pilot, a young American called Chris, turned up for a drink. He was trying to log up flying time to become a master pilot. West Irian seemed a peculiar place to choose for this exercise. It was certainly a long way from Denver, Colorado, where Chris had been born. 'But it's fun,' he said. 'I fly to Wamena once a week, taking supplies and mail. It's a fun trip.' He was *very* young. 'The mountains are pretty big out there,' Chris said, 'and I have to fly through them blind. There's no radar on the bird, you see.'

At dawn, in the distance, we saw the mountains ahead. Chris was at the controls, Frank beside him; I was in the back, beside a monumental black lady in a printed cotton frock. All the Irianese in Djayapura wore the European clothes, which sat badly on their bodies; they seemed a different shape from Europeans. Very black, they looked more like Australian aborigines than Africans, but, unlike the aborigines, seemed cheerful people.

At the spectacle of the mountains, the large lady began to tremble gelatinously. Chris started to whistle. Mist enveloped the flanks of the mountains, and low cloud covered the summits. 'There've been a coupla crashes in the last year,' Chris said. 'Strap yourselves well in.'

We plunged into the clouds and mist. The Cessna shook violently, but Chris seemed perfectly confident. Perhaps he wasn't entirely so; he kept on whistling. At one point the mist rifted, and through the window I saw a piece of mountainside, wet trees and black rocks, perhaps twenty feet beyond our starboard wing-tip. Then the mist resealed itself, and we rattled onward through it, and suddenly burst out into sunshine, with a great valley beneath us. At the mouth of it we could see a few tents and buildings, their corrugated iron roofs flashing under the sun. 'Wamena,' Chris said.

Wamena looked pathetic. The valley behind it sprawled out to the horizon, speckled here and there by trees. Low hills, rocky and enveloped in grass, rippled together a little way beyond Wamena, then turned into open grassland. There was no sign of human habitation beyond the military camp, nor any token of life whatsoever. We landed.

All round us were Indonesian officers. A priest had come from the Wamena mission, looking incongruous in his white cassock; particularly so because, beyond him and the officers, were a large number of aborigines. The bodies of the men were bedaubed with a greyish mixture of earth and ash, and some had feathers in their hair. They were naked except for long penis sheaths held on by twine tied round their waists. There were not many women, but those present were hideous, their bodies smeared with the same substance as the men's, their breasts pendulous and black-nippled... They wore minute loincloths. Long carrying nets hung from their heads, swathing them like a kind of cape. 'These are the wild guys from the bush,' Chris said. 'All Dani. The Indonesians make them leave their weapons outside the settlement. Otherwise they'd be carrying spears and axes.'

They had come simply to watch the plane land. Until very recently, Chris said, they had followed the cargo cult; they had thought that the winged things from the sky were gods of a sort, and endeavoured to please them with offerings of grass, fruit and water. The officials and the priest had come to collect their supplies of mail. The priest, who was Dutch, came up to us, and said, 'I a radio had from the fathers in Djayapura. They me have told to bring two mission boys for guide and porter. Please with me come.' We followed him to a small house. Tribespeople followed us, staring. Our mountainous fellow-passenger came too; she was apparently a housekeeper for the Wamena mission.

At the house, the priest offered us coffee and fruit and told us a little about the Dani. 'You have their peculiar colour seen? On themselves they put the fat of pigs, yes, the cold to keep out; and above they put the ash of fire, and some yellow mud.' They had come to the weekly market, and the priest took us to it. It was situated inside a low structure with a tin roof and no walls. The Dani brought in produce, which the women carried in their nets. This consisted mostly of yams and some fruit. Two piglets, trussed with twine, squealed on the earth underfoot. They were covered in long, coarse black hair. The Dani traded these comestibles for iron and steel implements, needles, cooking utensils in clay. Their language was guttural and slow, and they seemed at ease.

The nearest thing to an insurrection to take place in the valley had occurred recently, the priest told us. The government had been shocked to its Islamic core by the nakedness of the Dani, and revolted by their odour, largely due to pig fat, though, admittedly, they never bathed. It had launched Operasi Koteka, which meant 'Operation Penis Sheath'. The garrison at Wamena had been ordered to seize every male Dani who came to market and forcibly bathe him, then burn his penis sheath and recompense him with a pair of shorts and a cake of soap. Unfortunately, the Dani had not taken well to this. They had disappeared into the hinterland, so that the small population of Wamena was bereft of fresh food for weeks. Eventually, the camp commander had sent two very reluctant soldiers out to tell the Dani that Operasi Koteka had been abandoned. After this, things had proceeded as before. The soldiers in Wamena looked much more nervous than the Dani. Government officers in Djayapura were remunerated at a high rate because it was supposed to be a post of extreme hardship, like Buru. If that were so, I wondered how much the government officers and troops at Wamena got as compensation money.

While we sat in the veranda of the priest's house, two black mission boys appeared, in shirts and shorts. 'They are good boys,' the friendly priest said. 'From Ambon. The big one, English he speak. The other, not so.' The big one reminded me vaguely of a blacker version of someone I had seen. Frank felt this too and pinpointed the feeling. 'He looks like Cassius Clay,' he said. 'I'm going to call him Cassius.' Perhaps logically, I called his companion Brutus. They piled themselves high with our baggage, and we set out for Giwika. A sort of footpath took us through grass that rose above our heads, dripping with recent rain. The trail was very muddy, but the sun beat down with a dry rasping heat. At first we met a few Dani, coming in to Wamena to market. They were mostly men, carrying fifteen-foot bamboo spears and axes with heads of black stone. We had been advised to shout 'Ey, narak,' whenever we encountered a tribesman. That meant, 'I see you, man,' and, if he responded in the same fashion, friendly relations were established. One wasn't usually supposed to speak to women, but, if one deigned to do so, the correct address was 'Ey, nara!' She was to nod in answer.

I shouted, 'Ey, narak!' to the tribesmen we passed, and established friendly relations so much so that one of them turned back to accompany us for about three hours in the mosquito-ridden heat, finally pointing towards a distant mountain and saying something which Cassius translated as being, 'It is three days' walk to Kurulu.'

Sometimes I have nightmares about this walk. We went, at times, through dripping forest; at times, through the high grasslands, like ants in a tunnel. Sometimes we climbed shaly hills, sometimes we came to rivers. The bridges of the rivers usually consisted of a single bamboo pole. This solitary support connected two banks of the river; each end was wedged between unsteady rocks. Cassius and Brutus ran surefootedly across these terrifying bridges, though they carried heavy loads. I had seen similar bridges in the Philippines and in remote parts of Malaysia and Thailand, but had not been required to cross them. Those, I remembered, had had hand ropes to assist one's traverse. But the Baliem bridges were slippery with the rain that fell at a prescribed hour every day. They had no hand ropes. Even Frank went over with difficulty, straddling the pole and pulling himself along with his hands. I couldn't do this.

My vertigo forbade it. There were, sometimes, short drops under the single pole which was the bridge, and the turbulent river below, rushing scummily over rocks. But usually the drop was in the nature of three or four hundred feet, and, if I looked down, I was lost. So I straddled the pole with Cassius holding me from behind and Brutus pulling from the front, until we had negotiated the abyss; once I remember the flutter in my heart, as, having come over one such bridge, Cassius said, 'Thirty minutes, more river.'

But at length we trudged up a hill, my boots bursting, and beneath us was a white mission house with a white church and a schoolhouse beside it. The Dani came up to us when they saw us. They helped us downhill, or at least they helped me. Cassius and Brutus seemed in rude health, but even Frank was tired. The solicitude of the Dani made me feel grateful; but there were other aspects of them which we had met in the grasslands.

At mid-afternoon one day, we heard the sound of drumming and chanting through the total, underwater silence. Loud whistles shrieked in between the noise of the drums and chants. Cassius and Brutus dropped their considerable loads and rolled their eyes. 'Bad men, sir!' Cassius said. 'Very bad men, sir! They kill us, sir!' And he and his companion departed into the high grass. Frank and I now found ourselves in the classic, if stereotyped, and somewhat ridiculous, situation of explorers whose porters have deserted them.

Frank picked up his equipment from the black earth and said, 'We might as well go and see what's happening.' This, again, was a classic and ridiculous situation. But there was nothing left to do but that. We didn't know when, and if, Cassius and Brutus would come back, and, alone amidst miles of grass higher than our heads, there seemed no option but to seek the nearest source of human activity, such as that from which the drumming and chanting, and the prolonged and eerie whistles, came. We walked towards it.

A clearing opened before us. It contained about a dozen Dani warriors, with feathers in their hair, their faces painted in red, white and black stripes. They flourished long spears and stone axes as they danced. It was not exactly a dance: each holding the hips of the man in front, they shuffled in a circle round and round a primitive fire-pit, covered in leaves, from which blue smoke idly rose. On a little stump beyond this slowly turning wheel of black bodies sat the drummers and a man with a whistle, and also a small, wizened, nearly naked woman, her toothless mouth open in pleasure.

We were concealed by the high grass. Frank got a camera out and began to take pictures. He moved further forward, and suddenly the dancing and sound all stopped. The empty plains spread out around us for miles, wholly silent. Into the great silence the click of the camera exploded like a gunshot. The warriors turned towards the source of the sound, and saw us. They emitted loud yells and ran towards us, long spears poised.

About two yards away, they suddenly pulled up, snorting and panting like hard-ridden horses. The gleaming drops of sweat on their bodies, and the sharp points of their spears, seemed magnified by my eyes. The warriors loped back to their starting point, then turned and charged us again. This time they stopped a few yards away.

We said, 'Ey, narak.' Nobody had told us the plural of the phrase, but it seemed to serve. They gathered round us, laughing and talking. We could not follow what they were saying; but then Cassius and Brutus crawled out of the grass on the far side of the clearing. They came up, rather fearfully. Whether they were afraid of our wrath or the warriors', it was hard to say. Cassius, however, began to interpret for us.

The Dani were apparently inviting us to lunch with them off whatever was baking in the fire-pit. Speculation as to what it might be was futile. We took the safest course of action and told them, through Cassius, that our religion forbade us to eat anything that was not tinned. We fished some tinned ham out of a case. Frank also took out some of the steel knives we had bought. These went down very well. So, indeed, did the ham, for on being offered some, they wolfed it all down with little cries of appreciation. We attempted to explain, through Cassius, what we were doing. Frank took some pictures of them, while they talked excitedly. Pointing west, they said, 'Kurulu!'

This was not the first time we had heard the word, but Cassius did not know what it meant. It might be a place, he suggested. Frank said, 'Perhaps it's a god.'

After our encounter in the bush, it was a relief to find the Danis at the mission so friendly, though they were as scantily clad as the wild ones. Cassius told us what they were saying. Father Camps had gone to some nearby village on his motorcycle, but would be back by nightfall. Meanwhile, they gave us water, and showed us into the small house where the priest lived. The front-room was full of books; a Cona coffee-maker stood on a table, with a tin of coffee beside it, and several cups. We slumped down in Father Camps's chairs and sipped coffee made by someone who said he was the cook. We equipped ourselves with old magazines from a pile on the floor. Cassius and Brutus disappeared with the mission boys to the rear of the house.

A rustle at the door, and an old man came in. One supposed that he was old because his frizzy hair was streaked with white, and his features bore the sour lines of experience. He wore the penis sheath, and a white bib made of minute seashells. He carried a stone axe. He looked at us and said, 'Ey, narak,' and we replied as required. Then, seating himself on a chair, his stone axe across his knees like a parson's umbrella, he leant forward and began to study us intently with yellow, feral eyes. This inspection was unnerving, but presently he stopped, and with a sophisticated smile, poured himself a cup of coffee. Picking up a magazine on the way, he went back to his chair. Whenever one of us took a sip of coffee, he did the same. Whenever we turned a page, he followed suit. We had the opportunity to observe that he had lost several fingertips on either hand, also that he was holding the magazine upside down.

At last he broke a silence which had become oppressive. He said something, rose, and went to one of the bookshelves. He selected a blue volume, slowly turned the pages, and finally emitted a satisfied grunt. A tipless finger on the page he wanted, he showed us a picture of himself, younger, but little different from what he looked like now. The caption said, 'The great Dani chief: "The Wise White Heron", Kurulu.'

Father Camps returned on his motorcycle. It must have been a very strong one to traverse the Baliem valley, as it apparently often did. Father Camps was a strong man: short, bespectacled and squat, with a Roman head. His English was not perfect, but he was a great deal more comprehensible than our other interpreters so far. Kurulu was still there when he arrived. It was getting dark and very cold outside. Though in a valley, we were high above several others. The chief was now with several warriors, who had come not only to satisfy their curiosity about us, but to get out of the cold. Father Camps eyed them without favour, and said, 'That man, with feathers in his hair, is a big thief. You must not leave your possessions about when he is here.' He shouted orders to the cook. 'Chicken for supper,' he said. 'I breed them. It makes a change to eat chicken.'

What he usually ate, like the Dani, was yams, varied by tinned food. He got eggs (sometimes) from the chickens. The Dani delicacy was pork from the huge, hairy pigs, rather like wild boar, which we had seen all the way down the valley. 'But I don't like pork,' said Father Camps sadly. A Dani's wealth was counted by the number of his pigs. They were only killed on special occasions. 'Murders over pig thefts are common,' said Camps. 'Less so for wife thefts. Pigs are more valuable. If a man runs away with your wife, it is a good thing, because the compensation is paid in pigs. It's only if the man won't pay you that you kill him.' He shooed the Dani out into the rain that had started. We gave him two bottles of whisky, which were rapturously received, and each of us had a very small drink before the cook brought in the chicken, stewed with yams.

Next day we crossed the mission compound to the tiny schoolhouse, which was also a chapel. The students were few, and female, and they were clad in white or pink frocks, supplied by Father Camps. None of them was more than about eight years old. 'In a few months,' said Father Camps ruefully, 'they will stop coming to school and go to work in the fields.' He taught them catechism, though they were not converts. 'I have been fourteen years here,' Camps said. 'In all that time I have only made one convert. He died.' He shook his head over the children, and said, 'If they do not go to the fields, they will be—how you say—affianced. Not in terms of the church, but affianced.'

What seemed to me admirable about Camps was that he was resigned to the fact that he would never achieve what he had been sent here for. He would never convert the Danis, and was more intelligent than to try and do so. But he had done something more valuable. He had acted as a liaison officer, a bridge, between the Dani and the total impact of civilization. He also acted as a block to the Indonesian idea of an enforced culture. An unknown man in a hardly known valley, he was playing the role history had assigned to him. It didn't matter to Father Camps if he was forgotten in the future. He had a flock, even though it wasn't the kind of flock his church would have hoped for. With his one convert dead, his mission boys still animists, the girl children at the school ready at any moment to shed their frocks and bed some ardent young warrior under a convenient tree, he was undismayed. He probably understood the Dani better than they understood themselves. And, the Dani probably understood him.

Staying with Camps was an experience to be remembered. Before dawn the air was bitterly cold and laden with mist. The Dani were out, however, in the compound of the mission station. They wrapped their arms round themselves, to keep warm. White plumes rose from their mouths. The ground, then, was silver with dew; by a slight exercise of the imagination, it could be turned in the mind's eye to a snowscape in which the naked black figures with their penis sheaths seemed surrealist. The Dani traded with the Yali tribe in the next valley; they swapped salt for feathers and seashells. The source of the salt was a brine pool on top of a stony hill.

We climbed this hill early one day, in the wake of a number of old women with banana tree-trunks in their carrying nets. The women were witch-like, grotesques from medieval art: some were almost hairless, their faces deeply wrinkled and seamed, and few of them had many teeth. Their pendulous udders flapped like empty bladders as they moved up the slope to the brine pool. My feet should have hardened through all the walking I had done in the recent past, but they had suddenly started to bleed. Halfway up the hill I found my boots were full of blood. Frank went on and a young Dani warrior stayed with me. I took my boots off, and my sticky socks.

The blisters oozed pus and blood. The Dani clicked his tongue in real sympathy, and shook his head slowly in commiseration. Camps had given me some antiseptic cream from his small dispensary, and I anointed the blisters. The young warrior, in the meantime, scrambled off down the hillside and returned with a long tubular piece of grass. He squatted down some distance away and began to blow into it; a soothing music, like that of a flute, floated out into the cool and sunlit air. I put my socks and boots on, and continued the climb. He ran ahead of me, his large feet sure of themselves on the slippery stones; with trills of the grass flute he encouraged me to climb. When we reached the top, we found Frank busy. He had plenty of material.

The brine pool was not very large, but it was very dirty, and insects hovered over its scummed surface. The witch-faced women crouched around it, chewing on the banana trunks which they held to their mouths with claw-like hands. Once a section of trunk had been thoroughly chewed in mainly toothless mouths, it was immersed in the pool. It had been made porous, so as to absorb the salt water. When the trunks had soaked up as much moisture as they could contain, they were fished out and spread to dry in the sun. The salt crystals that were left after this were scraped off and carried in pots down to Kurulu's village beside the mission station; they were damp and yellowish, and, like no other salt I have ever encountered, exuded a definite and unpleasant smell.

One day a messenger brought Camps the news that a chief had died of malaria in a village some distance away, and his funeral was scheduled for the afternoon. Camps seemed unmoved by this, but he gave us guides and we set off for the village. To my horror, it lay across more of the one-bamboo bridges. Frank had accustomed himself to them, but I never did: I always had to be manoeuvred across by two men, feeling very undignified. Dignity, in these circumstances, was dispensable with. Eventually, we reached the village.

It lay in a cup between hills, and was surrounded by a high bamboo palisade with spyholes hacked into it. Smoke rose from the village centre, and also ululations of grief and the throb of drums. We scrambled down a slope and took up positions outside the palisade, by the spyholes. Camps had told us not to disturb the mourners. But we had a good view from where we were. Beehive huts stood behind a front courtyard in which two fire-pits had been dug. It was from these that the smoke came. The dead man had been strapped to a chair made of banana trunks, and sat facing them. Facing him, across the pits, were the women of the village, wailing and crying out incoherently. Behind the corpse stood the warriors. From time to time, without any apparent order, one or the other of them would gash his arm with a stone knife. Across the country, long files of people were approaching the village from different directions, some carrying young pigs trussed for slaughter. One of our guides nudged me, and pointed up the slope we had descended. About a dozen warriors were coming down it, carrying axes and long spears. In Dani country, one was never really frightened. But I felt that each new situation was delicate, and should be handled with care: that it would take very little to ignite whatever sullen fire lurked in the blood of the Dani.

The newcomers arrived and encircled us, looking very unfriendly. We shouted, 'Ey, narak,' and presented them with the last of the steel knives. The oldest of them, grinning, flung his arms around me, leaving indelible stains of soot and pig fat on my clothes, and led his companions away to the entrance. One of them turned and made gestures that seemed to mean that we should stay where we were and not follow. After this, though I think everyone in the village was aware of us, we were left alone.

The ceremony proceeded in slow stages. The wails of the women were prevented from becoming monotonous by the accompanying screams of the piglets, who seemed to have a foreknowledge of their fate. Presently, it fell upon them. The warriors drew stone knives, advanced upon the screaming, kicking animals, and sawed their throats open. The New Guinea pigs are hairy, with a tough outer integument. The killing process therefore took a long while, and the noise made by the dying beasts was fantastic. When each one had been bloodily slaughtered and eviscerated, the carcass was dumped in a fire-pit. The pits consisted, so far as we could see, of layers of flat stones, earth, and banana leaves, between which the dead pigs were packed. The smell of smoke in the air changed to a smell of baking pork.

Darkness had nearly fallen. The guides insisted that we go back. Later, Camps said, 'The boys were correct. It was good that you left. Some things they do not even allow me to see, though, for fourteen years, I have been their friend. For instance, I know that when all the pigs are cooked, they will have a feast. But as to the disposal of the dead man....' He shrugged his shoulders, and continued with his dinner.

Camps was constantly in touch, by radio, with Wamena and even Djayapura. For some time the weather had been cloudy and wet. Continual thunder sounded in the mountains, and rain fell in occasional fierce squalls. We had planned an expedition into the next valley, where the Yali were, but one morning Camps returned from the radio set to say, 'A typhoon is coming. I thought so, because of the thunder and rain, but now the radio confirms. We will not be much affected, but it will rain very much. We should tell Chris to fly here and take you out.'

After some discussion, we did this. The Dani smoothed out a rough airstrip from the remnants of an old one. At dawn one day the Cessna dropped out of the sky, with rain and wind behind it, and pulled up a few feet from the end of the improvised runway. Chris turned it round and took us back to Djayapura. Rain and wind shook the Cessna all the way, but he seemed calm, though he whistled as we flew through the misted mountains. Before we left, Kurulu presented me with his stone axe. Its fierce black head was wedged into a bamboo handle, fastened safely with twine. 'He says to tell you,' Camps said with disapproval, 'that he has killed 150 men, some with this axe, and afterwards eaten them. This I hesitate to believe.' Kurulu only grinned.

Many things remained to be seen: not only the valley of the Yali, but caves which Kurulu had told us of, high up in the mountains. These held ancestral bones, and the spirits of tribal ancestors. Father Camps averred that the bones were of canine origin, but dogs were rare in the Baliem, and we wondered. I had also wanted to talk to some women. 'No use,' Camps told me. 'They are not intelligent women, and very loose in their habits. Seven wives have already run away from Kurulu. Of course, he has others.'

We returned to Jakarta. Our exposure to the Dani had been brief, but our entry into their world, and our exit, seemed to enclose a part of life I had never before experienced. This feeling, as well as my extreme exhaustion, and my damaged feet, made me look at civilization as though from a great distance. It took time to readjust; Frank decided to have a holiday, but my desk in Hong Kong called me. From Jakarta I was able to phone...Pandit, and tell him I was on my way home. Pieter Schumaker was in Jakarta; he helped us in our final task before Frank flew to Bali and I back to Hong Kong. On the tapes we had brought out of Buru there were messages from Pramudja and Suprapto to their families. We felt we must deliver them.

Schumaker said, 'Look, it is seven years since these men disappeared. All kinds of things may have happened since then. Suppose the wives have remarried? Their old lives have already been destroyed. If you go and tell them that their first husbands are not dead, you will personally destroy their new lives.' Frank was inclined to agree; but I felt that the wives should know. If, at any time, their husbands were to be released, unlikely though it now seemed, it would come as less of a shock. As it turned out, Mrs Suprapto had left Jakarta, and nobody seemed to know where Pramudja's wife was.

The government would not have helped us, and in any case I didn't ask. I was afraid that Mrs Pramudja would suffer. But there was a café in Jakarta much patronized by young poets, and I went there for assistance. One of them had heard of me and read my poetry, and because of this they were willing to help. Pramudja's wife had not remarried. She had several children, the last of whom had been born three months after her husband's arrest. Having no money, she now worked in a bakery to support them. The young poets gave me her address, but, as a payment in kind, asked to be allowed to listen to the tapes. All had read Pramudja, some had been influenced by his work, and a few had actually met him. I played them the tapes in my hotel room, and some of them wept as they listened.

Mrs Pramudja did not weep. She was a lady of great dignity. We could not forewarn her, and our sudden visit with her husband's voice must have come as a shock. She gathered her children round her, and they all listened to the tapes. We gave her a copy of them. Apart from the two eldest children, who were adolescent, none of her brood remembered their father.

My two big articles from this trip, 'The Prisoners of Buru,' and 'The People Time Forgot,' about the Dani, each filled an entire issue of the magazine. The Buru piece brought an immense and violent response from the Indonesians. Both Frank Fischbeck and I were placed on the official blacklist, and told we would never again be allowed to enter Indonesia. The article was syndicated in the *Sunday Telegraph* in London, and in other magazines outside Hong Kong. Amnesty International then approached us for affidavits about the camp's conditions. I would have thought that the article and the photographs would have been sufficient proof, but we signed and sent the affidavits, and copies of the photographs and tapes. Some time later, 7,000 of the 10,000 people on Buru were released. This wasn't entirely due to the article, but it had been the first report out of Buru, and played its part. It was the most effective piece I have ever written as a journalist. But I was unable to find out if Pramudja and Suprapto were among the people released, and I still do not know if they were.

'The People Time Forgot' was published as a small book, with Fischbeck's pictures. Often, when I glanced at the text and photographs, it seemed to record the experiences of someone I did not know. I could hardly believe that I had been to West Irian at all. Even now that part of my life is a kind of dream to me. Father Camps was sent a copy of the article, which he mildly criticized for certain commissions and omissions. His letter was some proof to me that my visit had in fact taken place. The more I travelled around Asia after the Indonesian trip, the more anticlimactic my travels became.

The Unknown Plateau (1981)

The Maria youth lolls picturesquely against a flowering tree in the courtyard of the Narayanpur* rest house. It is early afternoon, but already in the town behind us, where hundreds of tribals have collected for the annual fair, the drummers busily warm up in preparation for nightfall and the dancers. The dull thud of the drums comes from the tribal camps, through the dehydrated trees, over the powdery yellow dust, into the courtyard. The youth, who wears a flamboyant red dhoti and a purple turban, listens to the drums. An indolent smile on his lips, he idly watches the verandah, where I am attempting to interview a number of tribal elders through an interpreter from the town.

These are all Marias from the hills, 'wild tribals' who come from several different villages, close to one another but ninety kilometres from Narayanpur. It has taken them only two days to walk across this harsh country to the town. The Maria dialect they speak has a slow cadenced sound to it, like forest drums, a sound completely different from that of Hindi. It does not entirely suit the appearance of the elders, who are clad in distinctly dirty white vests and checked cotton dhotis, obviously their town clothes. They accept the bidis, cheap midget cheroots, which the General†

---

* A district now in the state of Chhattisgarh, part of Madhya Pradesh at the time of writing.

† A government official, P.S. Dhagat, nicknamed the General by Dom.

offers them, sucking in the smoke through cupped hands, their puckered eyes bloodshot and a little wary.

There are several Government officers with me on the verandah. This causes the wariness in the eyes of the tribals, since they do not know what they are expected to say. The redness is evidently caused by liquor: the gourds in which they have borne it from the hills have been left politely stacked beneath the verandah steps. There are a number of improvements in their living conditions, they tell me: they no longer starve, and their children attend school, only the boys of course. They do not know what the children learn at school, but it must be of some value. They have got the impression that I do not approve of changes in tribal life: it hasn't changed, they assure me, not one bit.

I inquire whether there is any tribal tradition about their history. A song used to be sung in the hills, they say, when they were young, full of useful information about this, but none of them can remember it. They have come to the madai, the fair, to buy cloth and utensils. Both, they assever in chorus, hopeful eyes on me, are now very expensive. Of course, the State Government provides them with free cloth, to some extent (more hopeful looks), with salt, and with oil. Matchboxes, which they need, are provided. But the Government is very kind, and they all voted for the Prime Minister in the last elections, though unfortunately none of them can immediately recall the Prime Minister's party or name.

After a while they leave, carrying away their liquor and several packets of bidis. Once on the road outside the rest house, the gourds are lifted and tilted to thirsty lips. The youth, still lolling against his tree, takes from behind his ear a cigar made of a green leaf wound round a twist of tobacco, ignites it from a matchbox which he uses like an expensive lighter, and surrounds himself with smoke. A Forest Officer tells me: 'Certainly we provide the tribes with salt, cloth, and oil, and it helps them a lot. But in the old days, which are not so long back, they would never have accepted all this. An important part of their culture is not to take any charity from any other person.'

Some years ago, he says, he was camped in a Baiga village in the interior. Before dawn every day he was roused by the clatter of the chakkis, the wooden rice-pounders, as the women of the household started to prepare the morning meal. In the hut next to his tent, however, the chakki was always silent. After a while he asked the owner of the hut if he was short of food. 'He said no. I asked him repeatedly, but he said no. Finally I asked him why the chakki in his hut was always silent. Only then did he break down and admit that his family was starving. But when I offered him a little help, he refused to accept it.' This Forest Officer has a weathered face, and eyes which have obviously looked into distances.

Meanwhile the Maria youth in the courtyard makes leisurely preparations for departure. He assembles his appurtenances: a gourd of liquor, a furled umbrella with holes in it, a bamboo flute. An officer calls him over to the verandah. He ambles up, with a slightly amused air. His appearance is faunlike: even from a distance, he smells of woodsmoke and alcohol. The delicate, lemur-like effect of his hands is rather spoilt since one of them clutches the umbrella, a status symbol among the tribals. He doesn't know how old he is, but as yet is unmarried, a state of affairs he intends to correct shortly, for he has a young woman in mind. Courtship is the main reason for his presence at this madai.

Apparently engagements to marry are often established at madais. The couple will probably have come from the same village and known each other since childhood. When the celebrations start, they will drink and dance with their peers, 'but then,' says the interpreter rather surprisingly, 'they will elope.' What he means, the Forest Officer elucidates, is that they will 'retire to a secluded place and have private discussions.' After these are over, the parents of the pair meet, and a marriage settlement is made. The Maria youth seems anxious to leave for his private discussions, and I sympathise with him, especially when a local headmaster asks him if he has ever been to school.

He hasn't been to school, nor does he seem to regret the fact. He doesn't want to be educated, he says: he is perfectly happy in his village, he says, which he does not intend to leave. His family has some fields there. He gets up very early, long before dawn, to work in these fields. Around 9 o'clock, he returns home for his morning meal. Afterwards he rests, then takes his flute to the forest, where he meets his friends, 'doubtless of all sexes,' says the interpreter with a slight leer. Then he may fish in the streams and pools, or collect fruit and flowers, or simply sit and play on his flute until he feels inclined to sleep. Education certainly does not seem essential to this serendipitic life.

The headmaster, however, manifests horror. His school, a higher secondary school in the town, has 542 students of whom 59 per cent are tribals. 'Since their environment is not educated,' he says, 'most of them are inferior students, except in their calligraphy. Also in geography, since they like to draw maps.' The unexpected potential in tribal children is left unexplained. He glares at the youth, who plucks a flower from a bush (Government property) and unaffectedly tucks it behind his ear. 'Only if you ensure that they exercise less freedom will the tribals ever be able to live properly. The adults must be disciplined as their children are in school.' Disgustedly he concludes, 'We must change their whole society.'

But already the Maria youth is loping spryly away towards the distant sound of the drums.

At dawn the previous day, after fourteen hours in a train, we had arrived at the town of Raipur, and from there had started by car towards the Bastar borders. The countryside was dusty and flat, but a giant hand seemed to have strewn it with random rocks, some cracked and precariously balanced one upon the other, some hollowed by weather and water, some mysteriously shaped like monstrous quoits. The Gondwana formations in Madhya Pradesh are some of the oldest rocks extant. They reach back beyond human history to millennia when India, Africa and Australia all formed part of a lost continent. The geologists have called it Gondwanaland, after the tribe. The landscape around us was very ancient: from it we came into deep forest.

This shaggy, dense pelt covered the bison-like humps of the Maikal range, into which the anfractuous road now conducted us. At Keskal, 2,500 feet above sea level, we slept, the massive miles of forested hills all around. Much of this was mixed forest, but great stands of sal spread beyond it: a thin, tall tree, evergreen, and lonely by choice. It is seldom found with other trees and lives amidst its own kind for about 140 years. So far as I can ascertain, it has no English name. The springy, resilient wood makes excellent railway sleepers and household attachments, but unlike satinwood, which has the same properties, does not take kindly to varnish, and is therefore useless for furniture. There is a lot of wood in a sal tree: it grows to an optimum height of 120 feet.

The seeds are by far the most valuable part of the sal. The wood may dislike varnish, but the seeds yield an oil which can be utilized in its manufacture, and also, curiously enough, in the production of chocolate. Some Japanese firms are buying sal seeds in bulk for this purpose. But a considerable number of trees have been felled over the years, and a dead tree furnishes no seeds. Fortunately, there was so much sal to start with that a lot is left: and now that they have been proved more profitable alive than dead, the welfare of the tree is watched over. Thousands of them rustled tractably around us when at dawn next day we started out on the road to Narayanpur and its madai.

We came down the hills into more flat country. The weather had turned, and the summer announced its approach in clouds of yellow dust and increased heat. Where the sal and teak beside the road had been decimated by axe or tribal fire, attempts had been made to replant: skimpy, feathery saplings stood in disciplined lines under the sun's eye, 'Do you see that?' sighed the General. He indicated a blackened field. 'That is the effect of the shifting cultivation which the Adivasis practise. Every three years, an Adivasi cultivator will leave his former fields, and burn down all the trees in some nearby area. Those become his new fields, he sows his crop there: ash is a fertilizer.'

We reached a small village, forests beyond it. 'Charama,' the General said. 'Now we have entered Bastar.' Immediately, as though summoned as evidence, people who were unmistakably tribals started to appear, dark people with sturdy bodies. All the women wore saris in bright basic colours: perhaps not so much saris as knotted and draped cloths, for mostly they scorned petticoats or cholis. The breasts of the young women were as firm and ripe as figs. Some of the turbaned men only wore loincloths, others tunics and dhotis. The turban of one young man was adorned with black and white feathers: no ordinary villagers would have dreamt of such ornaments or have smiled like a sun as we swept by.

Both men and women carried loads. Poles were balanced on the shoulders of the men, with baskets of livestock or pots filled with forest produce suspended like weights at either end. The women carried their burdens on their heads, their splendid buttocks swaying as they walked. They came out of the forests and across the fields, or streamed down the paths by the road, which was unpopulated except for our car and a few bicycles. All of them were headed the same way as us. 'They are going to the madai,' the General told me. 'They are carrying forest produce into Narayanpur, to sell or barter for things they cannot find in the forest, things they need to have, matchboxes and salt.'

The madai is not simply a fair. It is an occasion where people meet, and a marketplace. Every tribal village has its madai, but the Narayanpur event was particularly important, because it took place only once a year, in the main town of the district. We turned down a dusty forest road into the crowded town: a rumble of sound and a diffusion of odours surrounded us. Grey piles of salt, brown and wizened stacks of medicinal bark, were spread out for sale on mats: there were garishly coloured fruits and vegetables on display: cheap ornaments: implements and utensils. Beyond the stalls were the encampments, where cook-fires smoked sullenly, watched over by chattering women, often with little children.

Gourds of liquor were constantly lifted to the lips of the men, who squatted apart. Small axes hung from their shoulders, knives rode their lean hips. 'By nightfall they will all be drunk.' the General said with some disapproval. 'They all drink and smoke: not only the women, even the small children. They will not dance until they are drunk. But once they start to dance they will not stop. They will dance all night until day.' Preparations had already commenced: a number of men, and some of the older women, were visibly approaching the stage before stupor: from the encampments came the slurred stutter of drums, and birdlike trills as young men expelled their breath through the delicate nostrils of flutes.

In the late afternoon, we returned to the madai. Many other people seemed to have arrived from the mountain during the day. More crude shelters, made of sheets propped up on poles, had been erected, and more campfires lit. Great wooden cartwheels were now strewn inexplicably around in the dust. An officer, when I asked what these were for, shook his head. 'They puzzle me too,' he said. 'Perhaps they are for the dance.' Goat-skin drums, taut within cane frameworks and painted black, stood in stacks outside the encampments, and these were obviously connected with terpsichorean activity, but I did not cease to speculate on the purpose of those cartwheels: indeed, I still do.

By this time a sizeable number of people were very drunk indeed. Belligerent, amorous, or beatifically bemused, they staggered about till they fell and were conveyed by friends to recuperate in the shade of trees. The young tribal women were not afraid of the drunks. They chaffed them as they did the youths who approached them, then swung their shapely hips away through the crowds, confident and free. Yet when they approached the stalls which sold cheap ornaments, their huge eyes filled with wonder. Tentatively, reverently almost, they turned over the shoddy artefacts which they could not afford. This unsureness with the unfamiliar made them suddenly seem the shy children they actually were.

So were the youths, however assured and muscular they appeared. Our photographer pointed his camera at a young man whose turban was ablaze with feathers. The boy uttered a terrified cry and flung up his arms defensively. 'He thinks it is witchcraft,' somebody explained, but the youth was far more sophisticated than that. He came up to the photographer, apologised for his reaction, and said, 'I thought it was a revolver.' The tribals are much addicted to Hindi feature films, which the younger ones watch whenever they happen to come to a town with a cinema. Presumably this is where they acquire the impression that nobody in the world outside the forest points anything at another person unless it is a lethal weapon.

The crowd, hitherto widely scattered, now started to formulate itself inside a kind of compound. It massed on either side of a runway, down which processions began to pass. Each came from a different tribal area, and reeled down the runway carrying white and red banners and what seemed to be totems of the tribe. Drums thundered and flutes shrilled. A bearded, painted priest walked at the head of each procession: his followers were mostly doped or drunk, and some appeared to be in the throes of epileptic fits. Skewers were driven through the cheeks of many of these men. They exhausted themselves, became limp, and were supported by their fellows as the procession went on.

The compound was now a solid mass of naked and ecstatic flesh, an indivisible fusion of bodies acrid and slick with sweat. A cacophony of sound swelled skyward: film music from a loudspeaker system contested with the drums and flutes: there was confused singing and yelling, shrieks from lost children and tribal belles fondled by unknown hands in the crowd. Nevertheless, though the whole scene resembled a riot, the audience seemed in excellent humour. Laughter periodically rippled over the faces of the crowd, stemming from some unprovoked mass impulse. Such childlike and pure happiness is rare anywhere. It illumined the doped or drunk visionaries, the dust, the noise, and the chaos.

~

The officer sat with me on the guest-house verandah and cast a doleful eye over the deserted and dusty thoroughfares of Narayanpur. It was some weeks since the madai and not a soul was to be seen. A hot breeze picked up a few dead leaves, toyed with them briefly, then threw them scornfully away. 'Hardly anything is available here,' said the officer. 'Even bread is not available. Once a month I drive to Raipur for supplies of things like onions and carrots and fruits for my children. It's terrible. And you tell me you are off to Abhujmarh. Well, at least here we can find rice, flour and dal. There you will find nothing at all. You will be very lucky if you find water.'

A male Cassandra, not content to leave well alone, he continued, 'In Abhujmarh the mosquitoes are the worst in the world. A WHO team found that the diseases you get from them are very peculiar, very unique. They are not exactly of a malarial nature but they are completely incurable. Mosquito repellent and quinine will be of no use whatever.' Having delivered himself of this disquieting information he smiled and discreetly left me, though not in peace. I questioned the General, who shrugged and said, 'I have been thrice to that area. We will manage.' I was by no means as certain of this as he was. But at dawn next day we left for Chhote Dongar, one of the four gateways into Abhujmarh.

The name Abhujmarh translates into English as 'the unknown plateau', and it is highly appropriate. The whole area covers some 4,000 square kilometres. A bulky fortress of forest, it looms up in Bastar, its western bastions occupying a small area in the Chandrapur district of Maharashtra. Its high ridges and deep valleys are cut into by the icy scalpels of many streams. About 2,800 square kilometres of it are without any kind of road at all, and the very steep, thickly forested slopes have to be negotiated by means of improbable trails. Such roads as do exist, on the northern and eastern perimeters, are impassable in the rains, and are in any case unmade, potholed, on unimaginable gradients and liable to landslides.

This rebarbative terrain precludes the maintenance of a police force or indeed of any other form of Government control. Even traders, usually as ubiquitous in tribal territory as lice in an Adivasi blanket, do not enter Abhujmarh. It is not a friendly place, not even to the Marias who are its natural inhabitants. In 1938 there were about 11,000 people inside the Marh: now there are 15,000, not a phenomenal rate of increase over forty-three years. Between 1977 and 1980 there were more deaths than births, due to various causes: malnutrition, mosquitoes, and murders. The absence of doctors in the area makes it difficult to combat the first two: the absence of police facilities the third.

The tribals eat coarse rice and millet, scoop fish from the stream, and scour the forest. They drink mahua and salfi. It is difficult to understand why they suffer from malnutrition, except that supplies are often scanty, hence theirs is a somewhat irregular regimen. The main crop is kosra or kutki, a kind of small millet. It is produced, as in other tribal areas, by the penda system of shifting cultivation. The trees in a certain area are felled and the seeds broadcast amidst the ashes, a natural fertilizer. After three or four years, when the soil is exhausted, the Maria cultivator moves on. This is done far more often and in a more concentrated manner in Abujhmarh than in other tribal areas.

On the rough, arid road to Chhote Dongar we bypassed a number of tribals, both Maria and Muria. The male tribesmen wore coloured headbands and bright abbreviated lungis. They carried axes on their shoulders hanging by their heads. Most tribal men have permanent welts and scars on one shoulder, caused by the chafing of the axehead. The women wore only cholis. It is remarkable, considering the amount of artificial suspension required by the bosoms of urban ladies, that tribal women achieve the effect their city sisters appear to desire without recourse to nylon and elastic. They swung freely down the road, red flowers in their hair, and even in their tattered saris had a queenly look.

The rest-house at Chhote Dongar was perched on top of a small hillock. The chowkidar, like a lizard, was peacefully dozing on the ragged lawns in the late afternoon sun. Obviously we were the first visitors he had seen for several weeks. Shukul Saheb, a senior officer in the Bastar administration, the General, and I took our cases into the rest-house, which was equipped with an empty water filter and a large dead clock. All around the landscape was barren and fairly open, unevenly patched with clumps of trees which in the middle distance came together and became thick forest, spreading back over a semicircle of low and menacing hills behind which the sun dropped slowly.

They were burning the forest on the hilltops. The flames had been bleached by the sun, and were so pallid as to seem invisible. Only where spires of smoke rose could anyone tell where the fires were. As dusk fell the spectacle reversed itself: sullen fire rimmed the hills and the smoke became invisible. These orange roses of flame, which seemed unmoving, painted upon the semicircle of hills before us, had the appearance of a canvas by a French primitive. Shukul Saheb drove off to look for food in the nearby villages. The General, who had purloined a papaya from a tree on the road from Narayanpur, started with infinite care to peel it. I watched the fires on the hills.

Shukul Saheb returned with a crestfallen air, half a dozen mouldy potatoes, and a promise of more substantial provender the next day. While the potatoes were being prepared we drove off on the road towards Orchha, the first village in Abhujmarh, looking for wild animals. It was nearly midnight by now, and the forest that slipped past us looked impenetrable and spectral. Below us through trees on one side the Marhi river flowed in moonlit swirls, and mist rose from the waters. If an arm had risen from the mist, with Excalibur shining dully in its hand, I would not have been surprised. We saw no wild animals but presently Shukul Saheb pointed ahead and said, 'Abhujmarh.'

Under a hunter's moon, obscured from time to time by scudding clouds, Abhujmarh loomed in the distance. A great indefinite mass, darker than the dark, it still conveyed its solitude and its wildness, its infinity of animals, blood, and secret people. It was less a place than a creature that dwelt in the dark. The mist wrapped itself like damp cotton round the crowns of its loneliness: rolled down towards us from the mountains and up from the river: wiped everything from sight. The jeep, enfiladed by this mist, bumped very slowly back down the rutted track to Chhote Dongar. Midway down the road the mist suddenly lifted off us like a magician's handkerchief, and showed us the stars.

When we returned, it was past one in the morning. Mosquitoes whined accurately towards the exposed parts of our bodies and as we ate our potatoes and papaya, they ate us. There was a birdless silence outside, unusual in Madhya Pradesh, and, even more unusual, no rustle of trees or smell of leaves and flowers. It was as though the whole landscape lay under the mortmain of the mountain. After dinner I wandered out into the verandah. It was surprisingly cold: in the distance the semicircle of orange roses remained, but with the hills beneath them obliterated by darkness it seemed that they hung suspended in the air, angels of cloud afloat overhead.

Morning came, with the discovery that there was no milk for the tea: indeed, it was fortunate that there was water. Shukul Saheb set forth once more to scour the vicinity. Meanwhile we curried the remaining potatoes for breakfast. Our emissary returned with a squawking fowl and some vegetables, but no milk. We drank milkless tea and ate potatoes, then thought we would start for Abhujmarh. At this point we discovered that the spare cans of diesel had all sprung leaks and we only had enough fuel to return to Narayanpur. Shukul Saheb and the General set out to refuel at Narayanpur, leaving the chowkidar and myself to kill, pluck, and cook the chicken.

I sat at one end of the verandah while the chowkidar murdered the chicken at the other. Finally, to escape its terrorised cries, I went out on to the road, reflecting on the tenacity to life shared by all things: even flowers, we are told, scream when they are plucked, if we could only hear them. This applies less equally to the human race, the only species which can choose to die. In a sense, this is its first freedom. In Abhujmarh, the tribals have chosen a way of life which is also a way of death. Some fifteen years back, it was proposed, despite the considerable engineering hazards, to drive a road across the plateau and open it to the world. The tribals all protested.

They believed that, with a road, officials and traders would start to come in. This, in fact, was the whole intention: but the Abhujmarhias did not like the idea. The officials would need porters and food, and would not pay much for either. As well as this, the tribe would have the responsibility of keeping the road in repair, a responsibility which it did not want. It also logically followed that once the road came and destroyed the privacy of the people, other invasions of their way of life would follow: for example schools, hitherto unknown in the area. The Abhujmarhias, however, knew what schools were: they knew that schools would divert the attention of the children, hitherto useful as field labour.

~

Sitting by the roadside on a rock, with the sullen sunfire, for it was now noon, making my body incandescent, I looked up to see a tribal youth riding past on a bicycle. He sat very erect and stiff in the saddle, holding the handles with his arms at full stretch, as though fending off some hostile animal. He wore a turban and loincloth, and his axe hung from his shoulder. However, from the handlebars dangled, on one side, a furled umbrella, and on the other a small transistor radio. He had affixed a small mirror, covered in pink plastic, to the pivot of the handlebars. Into this mirror, as he pedalled onward, lifting his knees high, he stared with a look of intense admiration.

Detach the boy from the bicycle, and he would have his own dignity. On the bicycle, with its appurtenances, he seemed both laughable and pathetic. Yet the bicycle was necessary to the boy now that he had found out that it existed: it assisted him in his life. This was the process of change now taking place amidst the tribals, crystallised into a symbol in the mirrors of my eyes. Greatly cheered for some reasons, I went back up to the rest-house. The verandah was covered in blood and feathers, and the chowkidar, his unattractive face embossed with a broad smile, held up the freckled, molluscent, and naked corpse of the chicken, and inquired politely what I intended to do with it.

I was cooking the chicken, a difficult process for one unaccustomed to charcoal stoves, when the others returned, the jeep refuelled and loaded with food and water. We lunched late, and then headed back up the Orchha road. It was a long, wild, bumpy ride to Orchha, and the scenery changed considerably as we neared it. Mountains rose around us. The road, already bad, became steadily worse: twice we stranded ourselves in rocky riverbeds and had to push. The General had not come: with Shukul Saheb and myself were two guides, both of whom, by some weird coincidence, were lame. Across the Marhi river we entered the Marh.

Orchha, once a hamlet, had become Block Headquarters, and was full of Nissen huts, officers, and tribesmen of discontented appearance. More mountains rose directly ahead, wrinkled and hairy. Mist covered their summits, and Orchha lay at their feet. Shukul Saheb inquired from an officer how we could get up. 'You cannot get up,' the officer replied. 'Not like that. It is impossible without a four-wheel drive.' The jeep was put into four-wheel drive, but the officer who had been watching closely, shook his head. 'It is very dangerous,' he said, 'without two vehicles. If you wanted to climb really far up, the arrangements should have been made a week ahead. Now you can only climb up a short way, not too far.'

Very soon, I saw what he meant. Even on four-wheel drive, the road was next to impossible. It was muddy and strewn with rocks, and veered this way and that amidst dense forest. At one point Shukul Saheb pulled up, since a tree had fallen across the road. As we climbed out to survey the situation, he placed a bundle wrapped in newspaper on the bonnet. 'We must be very careful with that,' he said. 'What's in it?' I inquired. 'Gold?' Shukul Saheb did not appreciate this weak effort at humour. 'Bidis,' he said. 'We have to take presents to them, and bidis are what they most appreciate.' Then we started, with no little effort, to move the tree. It took us approximately half an hour.

About a quarter of a mile further up the tortuous trail, Shukul Saheb suddenly said, 'Where are the bidis?' I replied that I did not know. One of the guides then volunteered the information that they had fallen off the bonnet while we were moving the fallen tree. Why he had not picked them up it was difficult to say. 'They are most important,' said Shukul Saheb, and sent the guides back to find them. Another half hour passed in this fashion, while dusk approached. Shukul Saheb honked the horn irritably. Some minutes later I saw the searchers returning at an approximation to a run up the steep path. I had forgotten they were lame. Their hirpling approach brought a touch of black comedy to the scene.

We struggled onward and upward, and presently came to a very large flattened piece of land, a plateau in itself. Patches of blackened earth and charred treestumps showed where the penda had been. Huge tracts of land were surrounded by rickety picket fences. 'Those could be called cooperatives,' Shukul Saheb said. He is a slight, intent bespectacled man, and he seemed to evoke a plangency from the pickets as he ran a long finger through the air to indicate the length of the fence. 'A number of cultivators work this area together. There should be some kind of village further on.' The quality of the land had not improved with its incursion into cooperative civilization. We bumped on.

Then, ahead of us, we saw a hamlet. It consisted of huts of straw and thatch, which seemed to be set down at random over a cleared area. Some children and women, all in an advanced state of nudity, stared curiously at us, then, gracefully as antelopes, ran or floated in the opposite direction. We climbed out of the vehicle and stood about, and presently they returned, shyly, with huge eyes. About this time a muscular young man with an axe turned up. He spoke broken Hindustani and proved to be friendly. Everyone, including some very small children, took bidis, and, having lit them, became very helpful. They showed us around the hamlet, which I gathered had a population of about eighty people.

The houses were small and dark, and unfurnished apart from the odd charpoy. Each had a kind of hearth inside, in which utensils, usually of clay but in a couple of instances of metal, were kept. At outer extension behind each house was apparently reserved for women during their menstrual periods. In front of the hamlet, with no houses beyond, was a pigsty, full of animals which resembled wild boar, in an excessively filthy state: there were also curious little patches of turned earth, which I was told were vegetable plots, though no vegetables were visible. Since the tribals have their own names for plants, it was difficult to ascertain what vegetables they cultivated.

By this time more people had started to turn up: naked women with pots on their heads, who had been down to a nearby stream for water: naked men with axes. They all took bidis and lit them, sucking the smoke down avidly through cupped hands, letting it trickle out between their fingers: it was exactly as though they were drinking water. A granary, mounted on stilts, stood between two houses, looking a little empty. There was also the ghotul. This was a small, dark hut, cluttered with charpoys, with drums and flutes hanging on the straw walls. The ghotul, in the Maria way of life, is a dormitory shared by adolescents of both sexes: part of the activity is sexual.

Among the Hill Maria, however, which these people were, the ghotul is only for boys, though girls may visit it from time to time. The youths sing and dance, or ask one another riddles. An example is: 'When I am not yet born they beat me as hard as they can. After I am born, nobody dares to touch me without respect. What am I?' The answer is an earthen utensil, pounded into shape by the potter, but thereafter treated carefully lest it break. The youths also simply talk: the idea is that they will learn from one another. It is very much a community idea. Since these boys will shape the future of the village, they should establish close ties between themselves in adolescence.

We talked on for a while. But dusk had now fallen, and the trip back would be hazardous in the dark. The tribals, puffing at the bidis we had left them, faded away into mist: as we descended the mountain the misted sky seemed lightly drenched in a pinkish colour. 'They are burning the forest,' said Shukul Saheb. What neither he nor I realized was that they were burning miles of forest, all down the road from Orchha towards Chhote Dongar. When we started down this road we seemed to plunge into the incandescent heart of all fire, its source, distilled from the earth, a burning liquid that filled the crannies of the night. All round us the flames rose till the mountains seemed made of fire.

The outline of the ridges ahead was stencilled in fire on the sky. Flames made immense arabesques down the faces of the cliffs: they formed pools on the flatlands, which flowed one into the other. The hunched shapes of the flames on one mountain created the illusion of a lighted city at its crest. There were eidola of fire above us and all around us in the darkness, and fire seemed to float from the mountaintops. No smoke could be seen, so that the flames seemed to have assumed a life of their own, without cause or effect, eddying from the slopes and valleys, forming circles on the flatland. Sometimes, when on the mountains they stayed static, they looked like solidified sunlight.

Unwieldy and ugly though it was, the jeep, bathed in this radiance, became in my mind a chariot, and Virgil rather than Shukul Saheb sat beside me on the flaming road. The shadows between the oceans of fire had that 'deep but dazzling darkness' of which [Henry] Vaughan writes: I had never been able to visualize the line clearly before. We ran on between the fires till in the lee of the burning mountains we came back to Chhote Dongar. All round the little rest-house the hills were rimmed with flame, like dormant volcanoes: but seen from the rest-house, this was not the unquiet liquid flame through which we had passed, but the orange roses I had seen before, silhouetted on the summits.

The air whirred with mosquitoes next day as we reloaded for the trip back to Raipur. The chowkidar looked very distressed, and was not cheered by a tip. At last the General asked him what the matter was. He uncaulked his bosom in a free flow of speech.

Would the sahebs not stay one more day? It was very lonely here. We understood his emotions, but couldn't help him. We had our own commitments. I reflected that perhaps the last people in the world to retain a sense of human community are the tribals, and even they are preoccupied with their own community, not with others. People act for reasons unconnected with humanity, as we now did. The chowkidar said there would soon be a madai at Orchha.

If his intention was to persuade us to return, he succeeded. The General hastily took down notes in his diary and started to peruse the schedule so he could rearrange it. The chowkidar stood in the verandah looking triumphant as we slowly moved off. As we drove towards Raipur and away from Abhujmarh I had a terrible sense of returning to civilization, to transistor radios and cinema halls, barbers and tailors, knives and forks, people with furniture and theories. It was a very long hot drive and I had plenty of time to think about all this. The General took another papaya from a tree presumably belonging to some innocent cultivator. It tasted warmly of the forest.

About a week later we were coming back down the same road, headed for Orchha once more. The weather had now suffered a dramatic translation: rainwhipped at the car, first in occasional showers, then, as we neared Chhote Dongar, in a downpour so terrific it seemed the whole sky, a sac of waters, had collapsed. The windshield bleared over like an old man's eye. The tyres swished and hissed as the wind swept the surface water up in deep ripples from the flooded road. There were explosions of thunder like stage thunder. Javelins of lightning stabbed into the clouds, and seemed to puncture them. More and more water came down, and at last we had to stop at the first rest-house we could find.

Next day the rain had stopped, and the sun was out. The mahua was in flower: waxy white petals strewed the earth around every tree: barebreasted young women with baskets were busy picking up the petals: the bright primary colours of their skimpy saris streaked the brown earth like paint. At Chhote Dongar the rest-house was full of officers who had come for the madai: there was no room for us: but the chowkidar was happy with all this company. We wound up at a very primitive rest-house at a place called Dhodai, with no indication of human habitation in the vicinity. It came on to rain once more as we started around midday towards Orchha, down the now familiar road.

There were great black patches on the mountains, memorials of the night of the fires. Charred treestumps lay about the slopes, pathetic, like toys the tribals had used and then destroyed. After the rain, the riverbeds flowed thickly with brown water, and in this we were twice becalmed, the engine whirring and roaring as it strove with the current and the rocks. Eventually we arrived at Orchha, and encountered the same officer who had warned us about the mountains on the previous trip. 'You aren't late,' he said, 'The tribals couldn't come yesterday because of the rain. They are coming now. By nightfall there will be hundreds, some of them from the deep interior of the Marh.'

They were coming in, trickles of them like brown water down the hirsute slopes. The women were often in white, and carried pots on their heads and baskets in their hands. The pots contained liquor and the baskets forest produce to barter with at the bazaar. Their firm breasts were bare, their pectorals covered in dark blue tattoo marks which were repeated on their arms and faces. They wore hibiscus in their hair. They were, nearly all young women: I supposed they would have to be for the trek over the mountains. They looked towards the dozens of stalls that had been set up in the open space at the foot of the mountain with awed but covetous eyes.

The men wore headcloths in heavy colours, and langotis: their muscular brown bodies were not usually tattooed. Axes hung from their shoulders. Often their thick raven hair was done up in a bun, and adorned with a comb. They also had small knives sheathed in their coiffures. Some had flowers in their hair, some the exotically brilliant feathers of wild birds. They wore coloured bead necklaces, shining on their dark chests, armlets and headbands. At each man's waist was a bottle-shaped yellow gourd containing liquor, quite literally a hip-flask. Most also carried, tied to their waists, a cloth pouch containing a supply of homecured tobacco, and had green leaves for cigar making rolled up and tucked behind their ears.

~

By the afternoon there were hundreds of tribals all over the area, numbers of them leaving the madai to look around Orchha. Hundreds, however, stayed at the madai: crusts of dry tamarind bark piled up as they deposited their forest produce, and quantities of dry fish of different shapes and sizes squinted up from the spread mats. Garlic and onions were on sale. Eggplants, okra and yams appeared to be popular. Middlemen bought produce from the tribals, who promptly went and spent the money in the stalls. They seemed dubious of the small notes and coins and surprised when they produced results.

Meanwhile men, women, and children alike drank mahua and salfi in prodigious quantities, sucked at leaf cigars or bidis, and ate. The cookfires spat and smoked under iron pots, which appeared principally to contain millet and salt. The tribals scooped the porridge out of the pot with broad leaves, in which they then buried their faces, lapping the mixture up from the leaves. Some also ate dry fish. They were happy: there was liquor: there was food: there were strange sights to see: things to buy, money to buy them with: they had one another. The stallkeepers were doing the roaring trade they had prophesied, the goods, cheap and flimsy, melting from the kiosks and off the tattered mats and blankets.

I saw a very drunk tribal with a bar of soap in his hands. He caressed it in wonder, pressed it to his breast, raised it to his nostrils to inhale the smell. He obviously didn't know what it was for.

Presently, tentatively, he licked it. He didn't like the taste, from his expression, and ceased his investigations in that direction. The more sophisticated visitors, tribals in lungis from Chhote Dongar area, who had arrived on bicycles, brandishing umbrellas, laughed heartily at him. The girls who had come off the mountain with hibiscus in their hair had replaced it with plastic flowers acquired from a stall. They had fastened the raven hair to the sides of their heads with red plastic hairpins.

A very old man in a langoti, wearing ornaments in his ears, told me he had bought vegetables and millet which was what he normally ate. This was not available to him in his village, though I couldn't work out why not. In the past, he said, he had supplemented his food supply by hunting, but he as now too old to hunt. He had also bought himself an embroidered waistcoat, because it was very cold in the high place where he lived. I noticed traces of ash on his upper body and legs. Noronha, who went up to Abhujmarh in 1950, notes that elderly people and children were covered in ash, as protection from the cold.* He also notes that the tribal villages communicated with one another by means of drums.

When I was in the Dani valley in West Irian in 1972, the cannibals there used to cover themselves in pigfat and ashes to keep warm. The communication between villages was by means of drums, and the cannibal's main weapon, which he always carried slung from his shoulder, was an axe: an axe with a stone head, but it is not many years since the Abhujmarh tribals started to blade their axes with steel. Like the Abhujmarhias, the Danis kept pigs, and maintained small vegetable plots: like the Abhujmarhias, they cultivated yams, and slaughtered pigs for special feasts. Noronha also describes an Abhujmarhia funeral, where the corpse 'was wrapped in bamboo matting and red cloth and lashed to a pole'.

---

* R.P. Noronha, a former Chief Secretary of Madhya Pradesh, who also wrote *A Tale Told by an Idiot* (Vikas, 1976).

I witnessed a Dani funeral. The corpse was wrapped in a net made of bamboo twine, and lashed not to a pole but to a chair made of banana trunks. It was not buried like the corpse Noronha saw, but burned. But the correspondences between the two tribes, divided by thousands of miles, are more remarkable than the divergences. Both tribes live in high forested country, the Dani much higher than the Abhujmarhias, yet the concept of clothing seems not to have evolved among either, despite the dampness and the cold of their habitats. The Dani also have the curious habit, when absorbed in thought or deep in conversation, of standing on one leg with their arms crossed. I noticed that several Abhujmarhias did the same. The Abhujmarhias are, of course, so far as is known, not cannibals.

A desultory dance with drums started up as the dusk fell. The cookfires continued to fume around the camp. The tribals were now really drunk. The stalls were empty and the summit of the mountain above us completely wrapped in clouds and mist. It was clearly about to rain. A wind approached delicately as though on stilts, then rasped the embers out of the cookfires and sent them racing round the camp like a thousand fireflies. Leaf cups and plates whirled myriad through the air, dropped to earth and skidded on out of sight, a crazy version of an English autumn: blankets and mats were blown away, their twisted shapes borne skyward and silhouetted on the moon, a coven of airborne witches on their way to an unholy tryst.

A giggling girl, who was trying to prevent a drunk boy from pulling her sari off, screamed suddenly. People ran towards the couple: an axehead flashed in the darkness. A man stooped and came up with a long writhing shape in his hand. The girl, about to surrender her sari and herself, had seen a cobra. One of the men who had run up when she screamed had decapitated it with his axe. He now, leaving the head behind, carried the body, squirming still with the unspent reflexes of life, triumphantly back to his family by their cookfire. 'They will eat it. They like to eat snakes.

Rats also. So far as food is concerned they have few taboos.' A sigh in the darkness: the sigh of civilization...

The drums and the dance restarted, and those who did not dance pushed forward to watch. I found myself standing next to the old man with the waistcoat. The dancers shuffled and stamped in the flare of the fires. The girl who saw the cobra and her clumsy courtier slipped past into the dark. 'She has gone to see another kind of snake.'

The Company of Dacoits (1981)

'Lajjaram,' said the police officer. He nudged the body, as though he and it were conspirators in its death, with the scuffed toe of his boot. 'He was the gang leader.' Each syllable he spoke dropped into the depth of silence that had fallen after the firing, and produced a small echo. Violent action is always succeeded by this silence, and by an accompanying lassitude in which the mind becomes abnormally receptive and sensitized, like a convalescent's. Every impression then assumes tremendous importance. The ears fill with echoes, the eyes drink distances, the living world is tremulously inhaled till all the shocked senses are healed, and there is a resumption of reality.

We were all, the dead man, the eleven policemen, the General and myself, together on the flat escarpment of Kalapahad, the black hill. Below us was the scrub-filled nallah in which the gang had holed up the previous night. Informers had apprised the police of their whereabouts. In the predawn darkness both ends of the nallah had been bottled up by armed constables. The only way out was to climb a dry and different water course, mailed with rusty scales of shale, to the top of the black hill, where another police party of sharp-shooters had been placed. In the chilly dawn, the dacoit leader heard his name spoken for the last time, when over a loudhailer the police demanded his surrender.

The dacoits had stirred in the nallah scrub, then scattered down the declivity. Three escaped and two were captured. Only Lajjaram himself, rifle in hand, had scrambled up the watercourse to the hilltop. He had blundered blindly into a thicket of bullets, staggered halfway across the hilltop, bleeding as he came, dropped his rifle, thrown up his arms, spun around a pivot of shock and pain, and fallen on his back. He was recumbent now on the black rock in a thick sticky pool of blood. His grimy white vest had been dyed crimson. His checked lungi had ridden up to his crotch. His puny arms and legs were flung wide in an attitude of crucifixion. His tongue protruded from his open mouth: his eyes, also open, showed no pain or fear, only the complete vacancy of the newly and violently dead.

'That's the way they die,' said the police officer. The dawn sky was cloudy and cool, and farmers were already at their work in the fields below. A glimmer of distant water showed from the Tigra reservoir. Winged things infested the rough pelt of the sky overhead, pilgrim ants were already flocking down the bloodtrail that marked the dacoit's rush towards death, and blue flies hovered like microscopic helicopters above the open eyes, assessing the possibilities of breakfast. The country rifle he had carried lay near the body, a crude weapon with a chipped wooden stock. A policeman pulled the lungi down for decency and we saw the bandolier of bullets strapped round the skinny hips.

'The gang was a small one,' the police officer told me, 'but vicious. This fellow had a high price on his head. Now that he's dead, the gang is finished. Those who escaped may try and survive on their own, but they won't last out.' He issued orders: two of the policemen took the corpse by the heels and dragged it away to a waiting halftrack on the slope. It was picked up and thrown into the back, between the seats. Some of the constables climbed in, to occupy these seats, and since the body was in the way, used it as a footrest. The lungi had rucked up once more, but this time nobody bothered to pull it down, or to close the eyes and mouth. The halftrack rumbled slowly downhill.

Later, at Tigra police station, the body was thrown in the dust of the courtyard and photographed from various angles for the official record. Tea was made, and we sipped it inside the station. The corpse was left in the courtyard. 'If no relative claims it,' said the officer, 'we shall have to dispose of it ourselves. In the circumstances, it's unlikely that any relative will.' One of the policemen outside, laughing, placed his foot on the body and suggested that he be photographed in the attitude of a successful shikari. The officer ordered him away. 'Don't think too badly of him,' he said to me. 'You haven't seen policemen killed, or any of the atrocities in the local villages.'

Thorny branches whipped back at the windshield, yellow dust swirled thickly around us, and the driver cursed steadily as we bumped over the boulders. The jeep shuddered to a stop, the dust settled, and we all climbed out and looked around. A deep series of ditches, strewn with rocks, lay ahead. The driver kindled a bidi and shrugged in a philosophical way. The policeman slung his rifle to his shoulder and announced that we would have to walk. The ridged, tawny plain sprawled out around us towards the hills on the horizon. As we plodded on, the sun heavy on our shoulders, I asked the General what the village was called. 'Pawa,' he said. 'But I am told it's not really a village.'

It was, in fact, a hamlet, and had two days previously contained about a dozen thatched mud huts. As we approached it, we saw that few of these huts still stood. The mud walls had been smashed: broken bricks, charred by fire, lay about in the dust. The byres and barns had been destroyed, fire had scarred the remnants, and the burning breeze sifted over cold piles of ash. Scrawny cattle were visible in the fields nearby, but there was no trace of any human presence. 'They must have gone away,' said my photographer and heaved his cameras from one shoulder to the other. 'Nobody is here.'

Then, ghostly, a grey figure rose from behind a burnt wall: an old woman, her sari the colour of dust, tears on her wrinkled cheeks. She raised her arms towards us as though for succour:

she seemed a revenant from death. We stood around her as she wept to the sun and the hills, and presently other people started to come out of the blackened ruins, mostly old women and very small children, but eventually two elderly men and a young woman with an infant. The border of her green sari was pulled across her face, showing only two wide, beautiful, shocked eyes. We all squatted down in the shade afforded by the remains of a wall and I asked the people what had happened.

One of the men pointed towards the hills. Apparently dacoits had always lived there, and had visited the hamlet from time to time for provisions. These the villagers had supplied because they were afraid. The next hamlet, three miles to the west, had also provided the dacoits with food, so there was no help there, and Gwalior was far away. The dacoit chief was Paan Singh, who is famous for his cruelty. Two days previously, the gang had come to the village, but not for provisions. 'They said,' the old man told us, 'that some of us were informers. They burnt down the village and forced us to watch. Then they tied four men up. Three were young men, and he was the other, this man here.'

The other old man, to whom he pointed, still shook with shock: he seemed unable to speak. 'They beat these four people,' said the speaker, 'and told them they would be killed. Then they dragged them away. All of them were crying and trying to touch the feet of the dacoits, begging to be spared.' The women had not so far spoken, and did not attempt to speak, but at this point some of them started to weep without uttering a sound. The green sari slipped from the face of the girl with the infant. She was beautiful, but something in her seemed destroyed by shock: she was like a doe which a tiger had leapt at. 'They did not touch her. But her husband was one of the men.

'He was dragged away with the others. The dacoits took them towards the next hamlet, saying there were more informers there. Our village was burning all this while. When they had gone some distance, the dacoits released this man, they said he was old, he would die soon anyway.' The person who had been spared mouthed inaudible words. Spittle ran from the corners of his mouth. 'The people in the other hamlet had realized what had happened to us. Some of them ran away, but some did not. Two of these people were seized by the dacoits. Now they had five prisoners. They dragged them all out into a nallah, and they shot them all dead. Next day the policemen came here, many policemen.'

He lifted a hand towards the hills. 'All the policemen went away. But Paan Singh and his people are still there. We know that they are watching us, we can feel their eyes upon us from the hills. Who can say when they will return?' He indicated our escort. 'Will this one stay to protect us?' The policeman said he had no orders to that effect. 'Our young men are dead. Our village is burnt down. Our crops are ruined. What shall we do?' There seemed no answer, except that the Government would provide some financial assistance. I suggested that when the villagers received this, they should move away. 'Even with money,' said the old man, 'where can we settle? All this is our land.

'This girl has lost her husband. Her child has lost its father. These women have lost their sons. What compensation can be made to them?' Clouds had sealed off the sun. 'Soon it will be dark. We will hide in what is left of our huts and pray that Paan Singh's people will not return. You ask why they should want to kill us. Why did they want to kill our young men? They were frightened of the dacoits, too frightened to report to the police, but the dacoits said they were informers and killed them. They were only poor farmers who worked for their families. We begged for their lives. We swore that they were not informers. Anyone with reason and mercy would have listened.'

As darkness fell, we left the ruined hamlet. Wind scattered the ashes and lifted dust around the people, who stood in a listless cluster to watch us leave. They said nothing more. They seemed not only to have lost all hope, but all semblance of life, as though the fires set by the dacoits had wrecked not only their walls but their wills. It was probably not true, the policemen remarked, as we trudged back down the track, that Paan Singh and his followers were still hanging about in the hills: the police had searched there and found nobody: after the atrocity the dacoits had obviously decamped. But for the villagers they would always be there, their terrible companions for a lifetime.

At Gwalior police station, Inspector Mishra said, 'A young dacoit surrendered himself today. He was with Malkhan Singh. Would you like to speak to him?' When I said I would, the Inspector issued crisp orders. 'Don't be surprised,' he said, 'when you see him in police uniform. Malkhan Singh's people usually wear these uniforms. Meanwhile, take some tea.' This was brought, and presently the prisoner was brought as well, his approach heralded by the clink of chains in the verandah outside. He was a tall, sturdy boy in khaki shirt and trousers, fettered at the ankles and wrists. He was obviously not accustomed to these appendages, the farther ends of which were held by bored constables.

'His name,' Inspector Mishra said, consulting a file, 'is Lakshman Singh Rathor. He's known as Lachhi. We are doubtful about his age, but he's about eighteen, perhaps a year or two more. He had admitted that he was with Malkhan Singh, and that he was implicated in some murder or other.' He signalled: the constables twitched the chains: Lachhi was made to squat on the floor beside my chair. He was certainly very young: he had a shy, handsome, rather simple face adorned with a small adolescent flux of moustache. The Inspector said, 'Malkhan Singh is one of the most terrible dacoits.' Children peered at Lachhi through the barred window. They whistled and waved. One threw a pebble at him.

He looked abashed, and kept his face lowered: the chains rattled on his wrists. They were obviously heavy, and must have chafed him. He squatted there in silence, and the Inspector inquired what I would like to ask. The children hooted derisively at the window, were driven off by a policeman, but returned immediately. 'Why doesn't he have some tea?' I said. 'And please won't you take the chains off so he can drink it? They must be very uncomfortable.' The Inspector laughed: he had a very kindly face. He ordered the chains to be removed. Lachhi raised his face and smiled shyly at us. At first he declined the tea: when pressed, he drank it thirstily, but was still nervous.

When I did question him, his answers were shy and incoherent. He obviously could not understand what all this was about. The attention he continued to attract from the children at the windows had started to surprise and disquiet him: in this ambience of uniforms, offices, inquisitors, and spectators, he had become nervous, like a wild creature which, newly admitted to a zoo, realizes that these circumstances are beyond its previous experience. 'He seems to be under a misconception,' said Inspector Mishra. 'He thought that when he surrendered he would be safe. I am trying to explain to him that this is not so. Having surrendered, he will be charged, and he will stand trial.'

The surroundings were not suitable for any proper interview. I asked if I could take Lachhi back to the circuit house, since he might explain himself more clearly there. Inspector Mishra said that if an armed escort came with us, I could. He added, 'I have not yet studied the case, but he seems to me an innocent boy. He needs some kind of help.' He was obviously the right kind of policeman. Lachhi was chained up once more. Then he, two armed policemen, and I drove back to the circuit house. The fetters were taken off. Lachhi, the General and I withdrew to a room. The policemen stood sentry at the door with their rifles. Lachhi refused a chair, he squatted on the floor.

The benevolent presence of the General made him unwind. It was explained to him that we had nothing to do with the police, but wanted to hear him out, and he spoke far more understandably than he had hitherto done. He had already made a statement to the police, but what he now told us was what I wanted to hear, not a statement but his own story. His father had been a poor cultivator in a small hamlet some distance from the town of Alampur. He had wanted to acquire some land, and managed to raise some of the money by himself. However, he was Rs. 500 short, and he borrowed this from a person called Panna Chamar. The terms of the loan had been shady: Panna Chamar seized all the land.

This made the family destitute, and things became worse when Lachhi's father, shattered by all this, died. About this time, Lachhi met some other youths who had thrown in their lot with the dacoits. Malkhan Singh had recruited them, and they felt they would get rich quick. Lachhi's mother was entirely dependent on him: he had no way to raise money. He also had reason to hate Panna Chamar. So he became a dacoit under Malkhan Singh. Some time later, three gang members had ambushed Panna Chamar and shot him dead. Lachhi said he had been present but only as the lookout. His functions as a dacoit had so far been purely menial: like the other recruits he had been a hewer of wood and a drawer of water.

After the murder of Panna Chamar, more was demanded of him. The dacoits pointed out that they had killed for him: now he must kill for them. Confronted by the reality of the situation, he shrank from it: he did not want to kill anyone. His mother had been appalled when he became a dacoit: she still pleaded with him, through messengers, to abandon this way of life, which would end in his imprisonment or death. But it was difficult, now, for him to do so. He had only been with the gang for three months, and his knowledge of its activities was limited. But he did possess some, and Malkhan Singh would probably have him killed if he tried to leave. So Lachhi went to the police and surrendered.

The General seemed much perturbed after he had heard all this. 'He appears to be a good boy,' he told me, 'but he may be in serious trouble. Malkhan Singh is a very active criminal. Lachhi may be charged not only with complicity in this Panna Chamar murder, but in any other crimes the gang has committed recently. I doubt if he realizes what may happen. They may sentence him to a long term in prison: and he is only a boy.' We tried to explain this to Lachhi, who bowed his head. Looking at the carpet, he murmured a few words. 'He says he knows he has acted foolishly,' the General interpreted. 'If he has done anything wrong, if he is punished, he says he has to accept it.'

It was now late, and the police escort seemed restive. Lachhi stood up and held out his hands to be chained. Then he impulsively bent and attempted to touch our feet. The policemen led him out to the vehicle, and they drove away. The General and I looked at each other. 'The situation,' he said reflectively, 'has now become very complicated,' and I knew exactly what he meant. Lachhi seemed innocent, even the police had thought so: and whether innocent or not, he was helpless, friendless and alone. All that he had told us, I felt, had been the truth. He had trusted us, and he seemed to hope that we would help him in a situation which he had not previously dreamt would be so difficult.

This had turned into a business completely different from an ordinary interview. Whether we wanted it or not, we had a certain responsibility towards the boy, even if the only reason was that he had nobody else. 'We will have to ask about this,' the General said, and next day we did. The consensus of opinion among the police officers we asked was that Lachhi would be acquitted when he was tried, he seemed not to have committed any serious offence, and he was young: but it might take months before he was tried. If we stood surety, he could be bailed out: in such a case bail was unlikely to be refused. But if we bailed him out, what, the officers asked, would we do with him?

He would simply be back where he started. Malkhan Singh would not be kindly disposed towards him, which meant he might be in some danger. Alternatively, after his experience of chains and cells, he might be in a mood to return to the dacoits. Either way, it would be a very open and difficult situation, and without any other options it would be pointless to bail him out at all. 'They are correct,' the General said. 'We must not only try to release him, but rehabilitate him.' We had to leave Gwalior, and there was no time to see Lachhi before we left, but the General plunged himself into introspection and trunk calls for the next two days, and emerged with what seemed to be an answer.

Some friends of his near a place called Saheli had offered us help. They had offered to provide Lachhi with five acres of land, materials for a hut, seed, fertilizer, and the occasional loan of a bullock. He could make a fresh start on this land: it would be his own. 'His father was a cultivator,' said the General, 'so he must know how to cultivate. With his own land, the pressures will be removed. And Saheli is not far from Bhopal. Malkhan Singh will not come after him, there will be no undesirable influence on him, and I can keep an eye on him. We must hire a lawyer to arrange bail, and when he is bailed out, we take him to the land. Then the lawyer will try for an acquittal.'

Assuming that he was acquitted, Lachhi could then return to the land, bringing his mother with him. Perhaps, I thought, he could also be taught to drive, or be trained to some technical skill. If one young dacoit could be rehabilitated, so could others. It all seemed beautifully simple, at the time. Neither the General and I foresaw the difficulties which we would soon have to face. When we were next in Gwalior, we visited the prison to inform Lachhi about this. But he had been taken to another prison, we were told. The police were rather vague about it: they thought it was Alampur prison. The General bought fruit, sweets, and books, and we drove off into the hinterland.

After many miles and misadventures, we finally located Lachhi in the prison of a small town called Lahar. He seemed delighted to see us and hear what we had to say: and childishly pleased with his presents. It was only a fortnight since his surrender, but he had become sallow, and thinner: he asked if he could have a bath, since he had not been allowed one since his arrest. We arranged this: I gave him some clothes. He authorized us to hire a lawyer for him: the General provided him with some inland letter forms, so that he could write us. Surprisingly, he could read and write, and the General's books, he said, would help him tremendously: the days were very dull.

He seemed stricken when we had to leave. He said, 'I have not thanked you.' We shook hands with him and stepped back to allow the policemen to replace the chains on his wrists. We had ascertained his mother's address and sent her a message: the village was in the interior, but she had come to meet us on the road as we drove back to Gwalior. She must have been young, under forty perhaps, but looked older: her forehead was lined and her mouth sad. She understood that we were trying to help Lachhi, but she found it difficult to understand why. 'Nobody in our village,' she said, 'has helped us.' She had sold a milch buffalo, the last family possession, to pay for her son's defence.

We sat with her on the curb of a well a little way off the road, and ate sweets. Her initial nervousness subsided, and she talked to us frankly. The Panna Chamar story came out once more. 'I was always afraid for Lachhi,' she said. 'He is a good boy, but he is simple. He believes people. Born here, where there are dacoits everywhere, he had no chance, there was nobody to help him, and he listened to the other boys. They told him what a fine life it was to be a dacoit, how Malkhan Singh would have Panna Chamar killed and how he himself would become rich. Lachhi had no thought of killing Panna Chamar till these boys talked to him. He has told me he did not kill the man. He is a very truthful boy.'

Her own life in the village seemed to be very hard. She worked in someone else's fields to maintain herself. 'Before I sold the buffalo, I made a little from the milk.' She was somewhat fatalistic, but a realist: 'Why should anybody help poor people? Nobody offers help for no return. Why should any Government help us? We are no use to them.' She didn't know who the Prime Minister was, but rather touchingly said, 'If you want to find out who he is, Lachhi can probably tell you. I made sure he went to school: you see.' When told that the Prime Minister was a lady, she seemed amazed. 'If that is true, she would understand the way I feel. All women have suffered for their sons.'

We returned to Gwalior. Here we hired a lawyer to arrange bail for Lachhi, and to undertake his defence when the case came to court. Before we left the city, we had yet another talk with the police. I had come to respect most of the policemen I had met: in this area they had a hard task, yet they remained human. One policeman on this occasion, however, seemed rather sardonic. 'I don't think it will be as simple to bail your friend out as you seem to imagine,' he said. 'I have looked into the file on the case, and this innocent boy has a price on his head in two other states. Rajasthan and Uttar Pradesh both want him for offences under Section 302.' He smiled at me. 'That means murder.'

Lachhi wrote to us from prison. He sounded fairly cheerful, and had been transferred from Lahar to Bhind, where he was to stand trial. We were fairly cheerful too, for we had talked to several lawyers since our last visit to Gwalior. 'He may be wanted in other states,' they said, 'but this is a matter of police procedure. He has admitted that he was with Malkhan Singh for some weeks. During this time, the gang must have committed murders in those states. It does not mean that the whole gang was present, only a few of its members. Unfortunately they are not in custody, but this boy is. So they have charged him with the crimes, but it is very unlikely that they have any proof.

'That is,' they added, 'if the boy is as innocent as you think he is.' It is very difficult to maintain implicit faith in another person's innocence if the only basis you have for it is your own belief in him. I tried to interest a number of important people in Lachchi's case, I pleaded that his rehabilitation, if it took place, could be the first of many. Subba Rao pledged his sympathy and offered to help if he could, but the weakness of our case was seen by others:

the General and I were asserting the innocence of someone we hardly knew. I had a nightmare, once, in which I stood a second time on top of the black hill, and looked down at the dead body of the boy.

Next time we went to Bhind, we visited the prison, only to be told that Lachchi was now in hospital. We found him there, rumpled and reduced, crouching in chains on a charpoy. Two policemen squatted watchfully nearby, their rifles propped on the wall behind them. The charpoy was in an odorous corridor filled with other patients and their visitors, and the guarded, fettered boy had obviously become a kind of public spectacle for these people. He had typhoid. He looked listless and ill, but a lady doctor assured me that he had been a model patient and would soon recover. He smiled when he saw us, but very tiredly. He was still officially in judicial custody: no charge sheet had as yet been drawn up.

A journalist from Bhind, Baburam Jain, had undertaken to visit him weekly and supply him with whatever he needed. The lawyer who was helping us also paid him a visit. The SP, Mr. Vijay Raman, and I had another beer together. I told him about Lachchi. Amongst other things, I said it seemed cruel and unreasonable to chain him up when he was ill: also to be guarded day and night by armed police would obviously affect him psychologically. Anyone not a criminal, when thus treated, might well turn into one: a very young person would suffer worse than someone of mature years. Mr. Raman heard me out with a slight quizzical smile. Then he said, 'I told you that dealing with dacoits desensitizes a man.

'All my experience in Bhind teaches me that there is no profit in pity.' He picked up the telephone which stood on the table and cradled it in his lap. 'I also told you, I have had to harden myself. However, this once, I'm going to give my human feelings a chance'. He dialled the number of the police station and issued orders that Lachchi should not be chained while he was in hospital, and that though the guards should stay on duty, they should not carry rifles. This was not only a humane, but a courageous action. 'You do realize,' he said to me when he had finished the call, 'that if this protégé of yours takes it into his head to run away, his escape is entirely my responsibility.'

Next day, when we said goodbye to Lachhi, his chains had been removed and he looked considerably more cheerful. But later we received a puzzled letter from the lawyer. The bail application had been refused owing to police opposition: Lachchi faced serious charges, they had said, too serious for bail to be advisable. Then we received a second, even more puzzled letter. The charge sheet had now been drawn up, and the trial was to be in the next few weeks. There was no reference to any Panna Chamar in the charge sheet, he wrote: Lachhi had been accused, with another person, of the murder of one Wali Mohammed. 'Who,' asked the lawyer, 'is Wali Mohammed?' We didn't know: all we could do now was wait.

During all these days, we were incessantly in movement, in jeeps, cars, trains, helicopters, from one end of the state to the other. After our trips into dacoit country, images of black hills and weeping women populated my mind. Ujjain was at least peaceful, surrounded by history and a river: the Shipra, which drapes protective blue folds around three sides of the town. It is an old river, and an old town; when in the third-century BC, Ashok, then crown prince, had been viceroy of Malwa, his headquarters were in what was then called Ujjayeni. The town had been caressed by its names, of which it has several: Amaravati, Kushasthali, Avanti, Vishala: harp music by the Shipra.

The gods and demons, Hindu scriptures say, once, when embattled, churned up the water of the sea, which regurgitated, among other things, an urn full of nectar. There was a fight for the possession of this urn, which lasted twelve days. During the tussle, drops of ambrosia fell in four rivers, one of which was the Ujjain Shipra. It thus became holy, and every twelve years the Simhastha festival takes place in the town: a giant fair which is also the occasion for mass worship and purificatory immersions in the river. At the other three places where the drops of nectar fell, he festival is called the Kumbh Mela. But pilgrims visit this city all the time; it is one of the seven holy Hindu towns.

As a result of this, there has been a proliferation of temples by the river banks and further into the crowded, noisy centre. Bright little buggies, with plumed ponies and flamboyantly whiskered and dressed drivers, flutter down the narrow lanes; the ponies are obviously sturdy, since the tiny carts are packed with pilgrims. 'The buggies,' I was told, 'are now being replaced by buses': a pity, I would think. The temples, flying their pennants, their interiors redolent of musk, music, and dead flowers, are usually crowded. Garlands and huge heaps of coloured powder, both to be used in worship, are purveyed in specialist shops, which seem to have an excellent turnover.

It is, in fact, a most vivid town, embossing the eye with colour wherever it turns. Gaudily clad village women shriek like parakeets round the shops: the flights of steps that lead down from the riverside temples to the holy Shipra are alive at dawn and before dusk with people descending for a sanctifying dip: in the afternoon saris and other brightly patterned items of attire are spread out on the steps to dry. There is a murmured submarine current of prayer under all the other noise: prayers for health and prosperity, for tractable wives and male children, for heavenly help in cases of family illness and, more frequently, family litigation, or in school examinations and sex problems.

At Bhind, on the day of the trial, the General and I sat in a little courtroom amidst lawyers dressed for a funeral. The trip from Bhopal had been eventful: circumstances had delayed our departure, and we had only started after dusk. Kamal, the driver who was as committed as we were, kept the car on the road for twelve hours in torrential rain. We had reached Gwalior at dawn, breakfasted hastily, and leaving Kamal to recuperate, went on with another driver. Halfway to Bhind, on a rough patch of road, we had an accident which fractured both axles of the car. We had had to hitch a lift into Bhind but we were here, and we were in time. We had had a discomforting discussion with our lawyers.

Lachhi and the co-accused, Puran, they had told us, faced a very strong case for the murder of Wali Mohammed. The police said they had six eye-witnesses. There was no witness for the defence. Unless something really remarkable happened, the lawyers said, the two accused faced long prison sentences. Lachhi and the other boy, Puran, whom we had not previously seen, were brought from the lockup in chains by grim policemen: they looked depressed and apprehensive, but Lachhi saw us, and smiled in surprise and pleasure, and we had a rapid word with him: everything, we said, would be all right, expressing an optimism which we did not feel. Lachhi smiled. 'Yes,' he said, 'you are both here.'

After such knowledge, what forgiveness? The two accused stood fettered in the dock: the lawyers whispered and rustled papers: the magistrate, also in black, appeared: the court orderly, in a thunderous voice, called the first witness. Karim Khan was a shrivelled old farmer, a relative of the dead Wali Mohammed. In Wali Mohammed's village, he said, there were two factions. Wali Mohammed, a muscular young man, had been the bullyboy for one faction. One morning Karim Khan's wife told him Wali Mohammed had been murdered a few minutes previously. He had gone to look at the body, which was incontrovertibly dead. He had not witnessed the murder. Of the two accused, he knew Puran by sight: not Lachhi.

When Karim Khan stepped down, the General and I suddenly felt some hope. If all the witnesses were like this, the whole situation would be different. And, miraculously almost, the witnesses who followed Karim Khan were if possible less helpful to the prosecution than he had been. They denied that they had told the police that they had seen the murder. They denied, in fact, that they had ever been anywhere near the scene of the crime. They could not understand why the police had called them.

Some of them said they knew Puran by sight: none of them knew Lachhi. The only evidence that stood was that Wali Mohammed was actually dead, murdered by two unknown men, one armed with an axe, one with a sickle.

By the end of the day, we had to return to Bhopal. The General managed to see Lachhi and to cheer him up a little more. It now seemed highly likely that he would be acquitted, and two days later, after some very inconclusive forensic evidence had been produced, we heard that he had been. He returned to his mother in the village, and some days later we had him brought to Bhopal. It was unfortunate that the only way we could contact him was through the local police. When a constable turned up at the village and ordered him to come to Gwalior, Lachhi had understandably thought he was about to be arrested once more: but everything had been clarified, and at Saheli his new land awaited him.

The Rattle of the Bones (2002)

In the first week of April 2002, when the Gujarat riots were already a month old, I landed in Ahmedabad, the state capital. The air was thick and heavy, and smelt of burnt houses. About 500 people, almost all Muslims, had already been slaughtered. The Hindu mobs had used choppers and iron rods, but had incinerated several victims in their own homes, having first looted them. The taxi driver asked, quite civilly, if I was a Muslim. For the sake of truth and safety, I said no.

The dusty streets on the way to my hotel were deserted apart from policemen and army reservists. Even at its best, Ahmedabad isn't a pretty city; though perhaps this is not a fair remark. All my trips there were connected to calamities. In 1969 I covered older, milder communal carnage that had occurred, in hindsight, for clearer reasons. In 1998 I came to the city with Sarayu. This was after Hindu fundamentalists attacked an architectural college because 'the students behaved in a Westernized way'. We were back three years later, in 2001, after an enormous earthquake exploded under Gujarat, killing hundreds of peasants, and making thousands more homeless. The Hindu fundamentalists who now ran the state had proved unable to help the people, many of whom, a year later, were still homeless and had not been paid any government compensation as they had been promised. Everyone had forgotten them, and now the riots had dwarfed their miseries and made them part of the past.

In January and February 2002, the name of Ayodhya was once more heard in the hinterland. The RSS ordered the building of a Ram temple on the site of the Muslim shrine destroyed in 1992. Many people travelled northward from Gujarat to stand by in Ayodhya. They changed trains at a junction called Godhra, near the Madhya Pradesh border.

Godhra has a population which is sixty per cent Bohri Muslim. They have the reputation of being quick to anger. (Amongst other Bohri Muslims, hot-headed and intemperate people are known as Godhris.) The food vendors, cigarette sellers, and small shopkeepers around the station are nearly all Muslims. Trainloads of RSS and VHP workers came through Godhra. They are said to have argued with the shopkeepers about prices, and insulted their religion. It remains unclear why.

On February 27, a train pulled out of Godhra, headed north. A few miles beyond the station it was stopped and surrounded by a mob of Muslims. They attacked the train with firebombs, and in one carriage, fifty-eight people, including women and children, were burned alive. What seemed curious was that the state police arrived during all this and made no effort to disperse the mob or rescue the victims.

Most of the burnt bodies were Hindu, though only a few of them had been RSS workers. But next day, the RSS ordered a state bandh. This was an invitation to violence. The chief minister, Narendra Modi, also an RSS leader, did nothing to stop the bandh or the sequence of events that followed.

All over Gujarat, Hindus fell upon the heavily outnumbered Muslims. Ahmedabad in particular became a killing field. The police apparently stood by in silence and watched. Modi declared that he had always been in control, despite the long casualty lists and the people flocking into refugee camps, and that the riots were officially over.

'Nobody disputes that he was in control,' classical dancer

Mallika Sarabhai said angrily, 'but in control of what?' I had a lunch appointment with her, in her ancestral house.

The Sarabhais are an old, famous Gujarati family. Their house is situated amidst gardens. As I walked towards it, in the trees overhead, parakeets, doubtless ancestral, disputed my right of way. It was peaceful inside with her and her family, and Yasmin Begum, her Muslim woman friend whose home had been looted and burned. She had taken refuge with the Sarabhais. 'The strangest thing,' she said, 'was that the people who looted our houses weren't poor people. They were rich people; they came in cars to carry our valuables away. Then the poor people came, took whatever was left, and burnt our houses.' She was very calm, but exceptionally tired.

Mallika said, 'The fundamentalists have used Gujarat as a laboratory to see if their concepts of life in India can work. It's been going on for years. It's as though we were watching Hitler experiment on how far he could go with the Jews before the world started to protest. It sounds silly, but it's true. I'm involved in two refugee camps. I'm going to visit one after lunch.' So were her mother, the great dancer Mrinalini, and Yasmin Begum, though the camps they were bound for were different.

All the women at the table spoke English naturally, in accents acquired at convent schools. All their reactions were those of Western liberals. They were all doing and feeling what one expected them to do and feel. They were the kind of people my parents, and Sarayu's, were like. It was comfortable to sit with them and talk. They were not at all like the killers who lived outside their gates and gardens; the killers were Indians also, but from a different India.

I was already slightly debilitated by the heat and knew I had a long afternoon ahead. My mind was soothed by all these gentle, compassionate voices, the smell and movement of women around me. But an image of India was made for me that day by the wooden wheel in the centre of the table. It was flanged, and each of the compartments created by the flanges carried a different dish. An option appeared in front of you, but if you didn't know how to operate the wheel, each one, with a slight rumbling sound, slid away. For many Indians, successive options had slid out of reach over the years. Random killing was now the most reachable.

~

I am now in the interior of an afternoon that resembles a blast furnace, with two Muslim leaders in their forties, Iqbal Tadha, a businessman, and A.A. Sayyed, a lawyer. We are in Sayyed's office. All the other offices in the building are locked. Tadha has a gaunt, distinguished and haunted face; Sayyed wears an affluent look. He is slightly rotund, the kind of person who, in better times, might tell me funny stories he has carefully culled from paperback collections, and play golf as a status symbol. They want to drive me round the city, but insist that we need press stickers for our cars. 'Otherwise we may be in danger from the police.'

After several phone calls, I discover that an old friend from Patna, Bharat Joshi, is chief reporter at the local *Times of India* office. He agrees to supply us with press stickers. He isn't supposed to. 'But,' he says thoughtfully, 'I am not convinced the trouble is over. Anyway, come to my office.' Tadha and Sayyed talk to me on the way there. For generations their families have lived in Gujarat.

'In the last ten years, as the BJP became more and more powerful, strange things started to happen. Our Hindu friends avoided us. Business contracts stopped. Once our wives used to shop with Hindu wives. That stopped. The kids started to have trouble at school. Even shopping became hard in certain localities. We started to develop a ghetto mentality. We became afraid of shadows. See, even now we have pestered you to get us press stickers before we drive.'

At the newspaper office, Bharat Joshi says, 'I've been posted in five different cities all over India in the last few years. I have never seen anything quite like the deliberate polarization of the communities that has happened here.' He eyes the Muslims with a kind of detached pity, as though they were lost astronauts from another planet, and asks where we are going. As we leave, he says, 'Take care.'

We drive through an area of Muslim shops, all of them burnt down to shells. Here it is as though the city has been eviscerated, its blackened entrails exposed. Tadha points to a gutted hotel. 'The mobs knew that the hotel business is mostly in the hands of Muslims.' Here and there amidst the charred ruins a few houses remain, like teeth left in a skull. 'Those are Hindu shops. They were left alone as you can see.'

We drive on, the burnt smell harsh in our nostrils in the afternoon heat. Presently we reach a more affluent part of town. 'This is where the richer Muslims lived,' Sayyed explains. 'Here the way the police behaved was different.'

The mobs had swept through the poorer parts of town, irresistible, like the wall of brown water a cyclone sweeps across the sea ahead of it. Thousands of people had beaten drums and screamed war cries as they came. 'They butchered the people and burnt the houses,' Tadha says. 'The police were there in great force, but they simply stood by and let it happen. Some officers now say that they were under direct orders from the chief minister not to intervene.

'But here, in the wealthier areas, the police warned the residents that the mobs were coming and they should leave. This was at very short notice. The police also warned them that if they didn't leave they couldn't expect to be protected. The options were limited; most people left very quickly.'

We trudge through some of the burnt houses. They had been solid, middle-class homes, with gardens and lawns, now destroyed and strewn with charred bricks and chunks of masonry. Inside, also, staircases had fallen down, the walls were blackened, rubble filled the otherwise empty rooms. 'The looters took everything,'

Sayyed says. 'Furniture, TVs, refrigerators, even clothes and books.' The shells of incinerated cars stand outside some of the ruined houses.

We pass on. Occasionally I glimpse groups of Muslims, some weeping over the charred ruins of their former homes. 'The looters have left nothing inside the houses,' Sayyed says, 'and these people have nothing left inside themselves.'

Flapping from a blackened wall, I see a poster for a circus. An image rises to my mind of Gujarat as a circus clown. Grotesque and tormented, staggering around a floodlit arena, it flails its arms for balance. A huge, astonished audience watches its agony. Its face is daubed with saffron, its body dyed red with blood.

In a refugee camp I encounter a bearded boy who sits propped against a pillar. His limbs are bandaged and his face is swollen. One side of it is scalded. 'All my family is dead,' he says. 'I tried to fight, but they were too many. They took all our property from our house. Then they set fire to it. There was so much noise.... They beat me with sticks, then they threw me in the fire.'

A harassed doctor tries to attend to him. He partly raises the bandages on the boy's arm so he can look underneath. All round us the room smells of unwashed bodies and human waste. This stench is now added to by a peculiar smell: like decayed fruit. I remember it from Vietnam. 'Gangrene has set in,' the doctor tells me.

He says kindly to his patient, 'I don't have the facilities to look after you here, chhota bhai. You'll have to go to hospital. I'll arrange it.' A look of terror twists the boy's scarred face, and he starts to shake convulsively all over. 'No, no,' he says in a shout. 'I can't go outside! How can you send me out? The streets are full of Hindus!' This is a war, and I hear the same atrocity myth that has circulated in every war I have ever covered. A pregnant woman has her belly ripped open. Both her unborn child and she are killed. In some versions she is raped first. At least six people in the camps tell me they saw it. But Amina, whose husband and two small children were murdered last week, says she hasn't heard of any event like this.

Her eyes, the colour of smoke, are wide and puzzled. She says, 'My neighbour had a beautiful daughter, about sixteen. When the Hindus came, she begged them not to rape her daughter. She said she had twenty thousand rupees hidden, she would give it if they spared her child. She gave it. They raped her and the child. Many men used the child.'

She starts to cry, and says in an indecisive way, as though she isn't certain I will understand, 'Many men also used me.'

In the same room, a man sits with his five-year-old daughter lying across his lap, face down, asleep. She wears what may once have been a pretty dress, yellow, but now ripped and stained. His large work-worn hand mechanically strokes her small dishevelled head. 'She does not speak,' he says. 'Since it happened, she has not said a word. She only cries. She cries and cries. I don't know what to do.'

He pulls up her dress. Her back is purple with bruises. Blood and fecal matter encrust her buttocks. From time to time, though she doesn't wake up, her body quivers and she utters plaintive, indistinct sounds. She is having a nightmare. 'Maybe she can still be married,' her father says. 'I was anxious that she should marry well. But they took all the money I saved for her dowry. And now she can't speak.'